The Penguin Book of
Bird Poetry

Edited with an Introduction by
Peggy Munsterberg

Allen Lane

ALLEN LANE
Penguin Books Ltd,
536 King's Road, London SW10 OUH
First published 1980

ISBN 0 7139 1334 7

Set in Monotype Ehrhardt

Printed in Great Britain by
Fletcher & Son Ltd,
Norwich

808.81

Birds - Poetry.

My favourite dedication
is that of the man who said,
'To my wife,
without whose constant interruptions
this work would have been finished years ago.'
Mine is just the opposite:
To my husband,
without whose help and encouragement
this work would never have been finished.

Contents

PREFACE   19

ACKNOWLEDGEMENTS   23

INTRODUCTION   25

POEMS (titles in quotation marks represent first line of poem)   101

ANONYMOUS: OLD ENGLISH
    1. *from* The Seafarer (prob. 9th or 10th century)   103
    2. *from* The Fortunes of Men (prob. late 8th or early 9th century)   103
    3. *from* The Battle of Brunanburh (937)   104
    4. Riddle 7 (Mute Swan) (poss. 8th century)   104
    5. Riddle 8 (Nightingale) (poss. 8th century)   105
    6. Riddle 9 (Cuckoo) (poss. 8th century)   105
    7. Riddle 24 (Jay:*Higora*) (poss. 8th century)   105
    8. *from* Genesis (prob. end of 7th or beginning of 8th century)   106
    9. *from* The Phoenix (prob. 9th century)   107

ANONYMOUS (c. 1200)
    10. *from* The Owl and the Nightingale   110

ANONYMOUS (13th century)
    11. 'Summer is y-comen in'   117

ANONYMOUS (13th century)
    12. *from* 'Lenten is come with love to town'   118

ANONYMOUS (13th century)
    13. *from* The Bestiary: The Nature of the Eagle   118
    14. *from* The Bestiary: The Nature of the Turtle Dove   120

WILLIAM LANGLAND (c. 1332–c. 1400)
    15. *from* Piers the Ploughman: *from* Passus XI   121
    16. *from* Piers the Ploughman: *from* Passus XII   122

ANONYMOUS (14th century)
    17. *from* The Parliament of the Three Ages   123

ANONYMOUS (14th century)
    18. *from* The Romaunt of the Rose   124

GEOFFREY CHAUCER (c. 1340–1400)
19. *from* The Book of the Duchess   125
20. *from* The Parliament of Fowls   126
21. *from* The Canterbury Tales: *from* The Nun's Priest's Tale   128

SIR THOMAS CLANVOWE (fl. early 15th century)
22. *from* The Cuckoo and the Nightingale   130

JOHN LYDGATE (c. 1370–c. 1450)
23. *from* Devotions of the Fowls   132

ANONYMOUS (15th century)
24. 'As I me walkëd one morning'   134

ANONYMOUS (15th century)
25. Revertere   135

ANONYMOUS (15th century)
26. *from* 'When nettles in winter bear roses red'   136

ANONYMOUS (15th century)
27. 'I have a gentle cock'   137

ANONYMOUS (15th century)
28. 'The false fox came unto our croft'   138

ANONYMOUS (15th century)
29. *from* 'Holly beareth berries'   139

ANONYMOUS (15th century)
30. *from* The Squire of Low Degree   140

ANONYMOUS (late 15th century)
31. *from* The Flower and the Leaf   141

WILLIAM DUNBAR (c. 1460–c. 1520)
32. *from* The Golden Targe   142

JOHN SKELTON (c. 1460–1529)
33. *from* Philip Sparrow   143

ANONYMOUS (early 16th century)
34. 'By a bank as I lay'   151

JOHN HEYWOOD (c. 1497–c. 1580)
35. Of a Daw   152
36. Of Birds and Birders   153
37. The Cock and the Hen   153
38. Of Use   153

ANONYMOUS (mid 16th century)
39. The Lover Compareth Himself to the Painful Falconer   154

ANONYMOUS (mid 16th century)
40. A Poem of a Maid Forsaken   155

ANONYMOUS (1576)
41. 'Even as the raven, the crow, and greedy kite'   156

ANONYMOUS (1578)
42. No Pains Comparable to His Attempt   157

FRANCIS THYNNE (c. 1545–1608)
43. Ingratitude   157

GEORGE GASCOIGNE (c. 1542–1577)
44. 'Of all the birds that I do know'   158

EDMUND SPENSER (c. 1552–1599)
45. Sonnet LXXXIX   160
46. *from* Prothalamion   161

JOHN LYLY (c. 1554–1606)
47. Song   161

SIR PHILIP SIDNEY (1554–86)
48. 'The nightingale, as soon as April bringeth'   162
49. Sonnet LXXXIII   163

NICHOLAS BRETON (c. 1545–c. 1626)
50. 'Upon a dainty hill sometime'   163

THOMAS WATSON (c. 1557–1592)
51. My Love is Past   164

ROBERT GREENE (c. 1558–1592)
52. Verses under a Peacock Portrayed in Her Left Hand   165

ANONYMOUS (late 16th century)
53. *from* An Elegy, or Friend's Passion, for His Astrophel   166

WILLIAM SHAKESPEARE (1564–1616)
54. 'The woosel cock so black of hue'   168
55. *from* Love's Labour's Lost   168
56. *from* The Rape of Lucrece   170

JOSHUA SYLVESTER (1563–1618)
57. *from* Du Bartas: His Divine Weeks and Works:
    from The Fifth Day of the First Week   170

58. *from* Du Bartas: His Divine Weeks and Works:
    from The Seventh Day of the First Week   171

THOMAS CAMPION (1567–c. 1620)
59. *from* 'What harvest half so sweet is'   173

SIR JOHN DAVIES (1569–1626)
60. To the Nightingale   174

THOMAS DEKKER (c. 1570–c. 1641)
61. Song   174

THOMAS HEYWOOD (c. 1575–c. 1650)
62. *from* The Rape of Lucrece   175

RICHARD BARNFIELD (1574–1627)
63. *from* The Affectionate Shepherd: *from* The Second Day's
    Lamentation of the Affectionate Shepherd   176
64. 'As it fell upon a day'   177

ANONYMOUS: MADRIGALS AND LUTE SONGS
65. 'The greedy hawk with sudden sight of lure' (1589)   178
66. 'Sweet nymph, come to thy lover' (1595)   178
67. 'Lady, the birds right fairly' (1600)   178
68. 'A sparrow hawk proud did hold in wicked jail' (1600)   179
69. 'Sweet Philomel in groves and deserts haunting' (1600)   179
70. 'Surcharged with discontent' (1606)   179
71. 'Come, doleful owl, the messenger of woe' (1607)   181
72. 'The nightingale, the organ of delight' (1608)   181
73. 'Well fare the nightingale' (1609)   181
74. 'The white hen she cackles' (1609)   182
75. 'Awake, mine eyes, see Phoebus bright arising' (1611)   182
76. 'The silver swan, who living had no note' (1612)   182
77. For the Hern and Duck (1614)   182
78. 'Sweet Suffolk owl, so trimly dight' (1619)   183
79. 'Pretty wantons, sweetly sing' (1620)   183

MICHAEL DRAYTON (1563–1631)
80. *from* The Muses' Elysium: *from* The Second Nymphal   183
81. *from* Polyolbion (1612): *from* The Thirteenth Song   185
82. *from* Polyolbion (1622): *from* The Twenty-fifth Song   186
83. *from* Noah's Flood   189

WILLIAM DRUMMOND (1585–1649)
84. Madrigal   191

RICHARD BRATHWAITE (c. 1588–1673)
85. 'Jug, jug! Fair fall the nightingal'   192

WILLIAM BROWNE (c. 1591–1643)
86. *from* Britannia's Pastorals   193

PATRICK HANNAY (d. 1629?)
87. *from* Philomela, the Nightingale   194

ROBERT HERRICK (1591–1674)
88. Upon Mrs Eliz. Wheeler, under the Name of Amarillis   195
89. Cock-Crow   196
90. To Robin Redbreast   196

FRANCIS QUARLES (1592–1644)
91. On the Cuckoo   196

THOMAS RANDOLPH (1605–35)
92. On the Death of a Nightingale   197

SIR WILLIAM D'AVENANT (1606–68)
93. Song   197

JOHN MILTON (1608–74)
94. Sonnet I   198
95. *from* Paradise Lost   198

RICHARD CRASHAW (c. 1613–1649)
96. Music's Duel   199

ANONYMOUS (17th century)
97. The Lark   204

GEORGE DANIEL (1616–57)
98. Ode XXIII   205

MARTIN LLUELLYN (1616–82)
99. Cock-Throwing   206

JOSEPH BEAUMONT (1616–99)
100. The Gentle Check   207

RICHARD LOVELACE (1618–c. 1657)
101. The Falcon   208

ABRAHAM COWLEY (1618–67)
102. The Swallow   211

ANDREW MARVELL (1621–78)
103. *from* Upon Appleton House   212

HENRY VAUGHAN (1622–95)
104. Cock-Crowing   214

JOHN BUNYAN (1628–88)
105. Upon the Lark and the Fowler   216
106. Of the Cuckoo   217

JOHN DRYDEN (1631–1700)
107. *from* An Ode on the Death of Mr Henry Purcell   218

MATTHEW PRIOR (1664–1721)
108. *from* The Turtle and the Sparrow   219

ALEXANDER POPE (1688–1744)
109. *from* Windsor Forest   221

JOHN GAY (1685–1732)
110. *from* Rural Sports   222
111. *from* The Shepherd's Week: *from* Thursday; or, The Spell   223
112. The Farmer's Wife and the Raven   224
113. The Turkey and the Ant   225
114. 'The turtle thus with plaintive crying'   226
115. 'Before the barn door crowing'   226

MATTHEW GREEN (1696–1737)
116. The Sparrow and Diamond   226

JAMES THOMSON (1700–1748)
117. *from* The Seasons: *from* Spring   228
118. *from* The Seasons: *from* Autumn   233
119. *from* The Seasons: *from* Winter   234

EDWARD MOORE (1712–57)
120. *from* The Goose and the Swans   235

RICHARD JAGO (1715–81)
121. The Goldfinches   236

GILBERT WHITE (1720–93)
122. The Naturalist's Summer Evening Walk   238

JOSEPH WARTON (1722–1800)
123. Ode: To the Nightingale   240

MARK AKENSIDE (1721–70)
124. Ode XV: To the Evening Star   241

JOHN GILBERT COOPER (1723–69)
125. *from* Epistles to His Friends in Town: *from* The Temper of
Aristippus   244

THOMAS WARTON (1728–90)
126. *from* Ode X: The First of April   245

ERASMUS DARWIN (1731–1802)
127. *from* The Temple of Nature; or, The Origin of Society:
from Reproduction of Life   246

WILLIAM COWPER (1731–1800)
128. On the Death of Mrs Throckmorton's Bullfinch   247
129. The Nightingale and the Glowworm   249
130. The Jackdaw   250
131. Epitaph on a Free but Tame Redbreast   251
132. *from* The Task: *from* The Winter Walk at Noon   252

MICHAEL BRUCE (1746–67)
133. Ode: To the Cuckoo   252

WILLIAM BLAKE (1757–1827)
134. The Blossom   254
135. 'O lapwing, thou fliest around the heath'   254
136. *from* Milton   255

ROBERT BURNS (1759–96)
137. *from* The Humble Petition of Bruar Water to the Noble
Duke of Athole   255
138. On Scaring Some Waterfowl in Loch Turit, a Wild Scene
among the Hills of Oughtertyre   256
139. *from* Elegy on Captain Matthew Henderson   257
140. Hunting Song   258

JOANNA BAILLIE (1762–1851)
141. The Blackcock   258

SAMUEL ROGERS (1763–1855)
142. An Epitaph on a Robin Redbreast   259

THOMAS GISBORNE (1758–1846)
143. *from* Walks in a Forest: *from* Spring   260

JAMES HURDIS (1763–1801)
144. *from* The Favourite Village   261

JAMES GRAHAME (1763–1811)
145. *from* The Birds of Scotland   263

ROBERT BLOOMFIELD (1766–1823)
146. *from* The Farmer's Boy: *from* Summer 267

JAMES HOGG (1770–1835)
147. The Skylark 268

WILLIAM WORDSWORTH (1770–1850)
148. To the Cuckoo 269
149. The Green Linnet 270
150. *from* The Kitten and Falling Leaves 271
151. 'O nightingale! thou surely art' 272
152. To a Skylark 272
153. *from* The Redbreast 273

SIR WALTER SCOTT (1771–1832)
154. 'It's up Glenbarchan's braes I gaed' 274
155. 'Proud Maisie is in the wood' 274

SAMUEL TAYLOR COLERIDGE (1772–1834)
156. The Death of the Starling 275
157. *from* The Nightingale 276
158. 'Sea-ward, white gleaming through the busy scud' 277
159. 'Or wren or linnet' 278
160. 'The spruce and limber yellowhammer' 278
161. Song 278

PERCY BYSSHE SHELLEY (1792–1822)
162. *from* Lines Written among the Euganean Hills 279
163. *from* Prometheus Unbound: Semichorus II 279
164. *from* Prometheus Unbound: *from* Act III, Scene ii 280
165. *from* Charles the First 280
166. *from* The Witch of Atlas 281
167. To a Skylark 281
168. The Aziola 284

JOHN CLARE (1793–1864)
169. The Landrail 285
170. The Lark's Nest 286
171. The Pettichap's Nest 286
172. The Sand Martin 288
173. The Happy Bird 288
174. Early Nightingale 288
175. Hen's Nest 289
176. Autumn Birds 289

JOHN KEATS (1795–1821)
177. *from* 'I stood tip-toe upon a little hill'   290
178. *from* To Charles Cowden Clarke   290
179. Song   291
180. Ode to a Nightingale   291

GEORGE DARLEY (1795–1846)
181. *from* Nepenthe: *from* Canto I   294
182. *from* Nepenthe: *from* Canto II   296

THOMAS LOVELL BEDDOES (1803–49)
183. Song   297

ALFRED, LORD TENNYSON (1809–92)
184. Song – The Owl   298
185. Second Song   298
186. The Dying Swan   299
187. The Blackbird   300
188. The Eagle   301
189. *from* In Memoriam: LXXXVIII   301
190. *from* The Window: Ay   301
191. The Throstle   302

MATTHEW ARNOLD (1822–88)
192. Philomela   303

WILLIAM ALLINGHAM (1824–89)
193. Robin Redbreast   304

GEORGE MEREDITH (1828–1909)
194. The Lark Ascending   305

THOMAS HARDY (1840–1928)
195. Shelley's Skylark   308
196. The Puzzled Game Birds   309
197. The Darkling Thrush   309
198. The Selfsame Song   310

ROBERT BRIDGES (1844–1930)
199. Nightingales   311
200. November   311

GERARD MANLEY HOPKINS (1844–89)
201. 'Repeat that, repeat'   313
202. The Caged Skylark   313
203. The Windhover   314

WILLIAM ERNEST HENLEY (1849–1903)
204. 'Gulls in an aëry morrice'   314

ARTHUR SYMONS (1865–1945)
205. *from* Amoris Exsul: In the Bay   315

WILLIAM BUTLER YEATS (1865–1939)
206. The Wild Swans at Coole   316
207. Leda and the Swan   317

ANONYMOUS: ORAL TRADITION
208. 'As I was walking all alane'   318
209. 'A hoggie dead! a hoggie dead! a hoggie dead!'   319
210. 'Crow, crow, get out of my sight'   319
211. 'The carrion crow sat upon an oak'   319
212. 'All of a row'   320
213. 'One is sorrow, two mirth'   320
214. 'One is a sign of mischief'   320
215. 'One for sorrow, two for mirth'   321
216. 'I crossed the pynot'   321
217. 'A pie sat on a pear tree'   321
218. 'Round about, round about'   321
219. 'Cuckoo, cuckoo'   322
220. 'The cuckoo is a merry bird'   322
221. 'Cuckoo, cherry tree'   322
222. 'Cuckoo, scabbëd gowk'   322
223. 'Of all the gay birds that e'er I did see'   323
224. 'Once I was a monarch's daughter'   323
225. 'Take two-o coo, Taffy!'   323
226. 'I had two pigeons bright and gay'   323
227. 'The dove says, Coo, coo'   323
228. 'Coo-pe-coo'   324
229. 'As I went over the water'   324
230. 'Larikie, larikie, lee!'   324
231. 'Up in the lift go we'   324
232. 'The cock crows in the morn'   325
233. 'Higgledy, piggledy, my black hen'   325
234. 'Lock the dairy door'   325
235. 'Cock, cock, cock, cock'   325
236. 'The cock gaed to Rome, seeking shoon, seeking shoon'   326
237. 'Buy tobacco, buy tobacco'   326
238. 'I went to the sea'   326
239. 'Grey goose and gander'   326

240. 'Here's a string o' wild geese'   326
241. 'Three grey geese in a green field grazing'   326
242. 'A fox jumped up one winter's night'   327
243. 'Goosey, goosey, gander'   328
244. 'Old Mother Goose'   328
245. 'Cackle, cackle, Mother Goose'   328
246. 'Snow, snow faster'   '   329
247. 'O all you little blackey-tops'   329
248. 'Shoo over!'   329
249. 'If the robin sings in the bush'   329
250. 'Crow on the fence'   329
251. 'Wild geese, wild geese, ganging to the sea'   330
252. 'I'm called by the name of a man'   330
253. 'Little Robin Redbreast'   331
254. 'Little Cock Robin'   331
255. 'My dear, do you know'   331
256. 'The north wind doth blow'   332
257. 'Cock Robin got up early'   332
258. 'The wren she lies in care's bed'   332
259. 'The robin and the wren,/They fought'   333
260. 'Says Robin to Jenny, "If you will be mine'   333
261. 'Who killed Cock Robin?'   334
262. 'Kill a robin or a wren'   335
263. 'Malisons, malisons, more than ten'   335
264. 'The robin and the redbreast'   335
265. 'The robin and the wren'   336

SIR JOHN COLLINGS SQUIRE (1884–1958)
266. *from* The Birds   336

SELECTED BIBLIOGRAPHY   339
GLOSSARY OF BIRD NAMES   343
INDEX OF BIRDS   347
INDEX OF POETS   353
INDEX OF FIRST LINES   355

Preface

America and Britain have a great many birds in common. Roger Tory Peterson says that roughly one third of the British birds are the same as the American, one third are similar, and one third completely different.[1] Something like this is probably true in poetry, but when it comes to identification, the reader faces special problems. Since he cannot see the birds, he must depend upon the names. Fortunately, with only a few exceptions, the Americans and the British use the same names for families, such as storks, swifts, woodpeckers, gulls. But with species, it is not always quite so simple. Sometimes the identical bird has different names. (The American bank swallow, for instance, is the sand martin in Britain.) At other times, the same name is used for different birds. The robin of America is really a thrush; the blackbirds belong to a New World family; the wood warblers are completely different from the European warblers; and although the American goldfinch is related to the European, it is quite dissimilar in appearance. Since poets rarely describe birds, this kind of discrepancy usually does not matter. In fact, it is quite possible for Americans to see their own birds in most of what the poets say – the gaudy goldfinch, the robin with the red breast. (But American blackbirds are not musical, and the American robin, which goes south in winter, does not sing in the snow.) More difficult is the fact that in English poetry some birds have multiple names so that what looks like several species turns out to be only one. In the poems in this anthology, for example, about 120 species are represented, but altogether they have more than 200 names. This can be confusing, but, fortunately, most poets prefer the old, simple, unadorned words which are part of everyone's vocabulary, words like hawk, swan, owl, dove. In these poems, for example, crow is used twenty-three times while corbie occurs only once.

If Americans have a complaint, it is not the question of names, it is the fact that among the species which we do not have are three of the most prominent birds in poetry. First there is the cuckoo, which is famous both for its peculiar nesting habits and for its mellow notes which one can recognize instantly because it repeats its name like a cuckoo clock except that the pace is a good deal slower. Second are the skylarks, those singers whose music rains from above as they soar in song flights which

1. Edwin Way Teale, *Springtime in Britain* (New York: Dodd, Mead, 1970), p. 6.

no American bird even begins to approach. Third and most important is
the nightingale, which is so celebrated, with such an aura of poetry and
myth, that it seems more like a legend than a real bird. In the nineteenth
century, attempts were made to establish these and other European
species in America, but they all died out except for the house sparrow
and the starling which spread like weeds from coast to coast. No doubt
there is a melancholy message here, but symbolism aside, it does seem
too bad that this vast continent with its abundance of birds could not
have found place at least for the nightingale. If there is any consolation,
it is that the nightingale we imagine is probably far more beautiful than
the real nightingale. Helen herself could not live up to the Helen of
myth and poem, and many people, when they first hear the nightingale,
find it disappointing.

This book attempts to show the many different ways in which poets
have looked at birds. The Introduction traces the development of bird
poetry, while the anthology gives examples of bird poems from the Anglo-
Saxons to the Victorians. Since it is addressed to the general ·reader,
I have translated all the·Anglo-Saxon poems as well as a few of the Middle
English, namely, the two poems from the Bestiary and the excerpts from
The Owl and theNightingale, *Piers the Ploughman*, and *The Parliament of
the Three Ages*. The punctuation of the poems has been modernized, and
so has the spelling, although I have kept some of the earlier forms. With
the exception of bird names, which are in the glossary, obsolete words are
defined at the foot of the page where they first appear. Stress signs
indicate where the accent should fall, while diacritical marks are used when
silent sounds should be pronounced, as in *walkèd* or *ewë*. Elisions are
meant to be run together – not *th' air*, but *thair*. I have, so far as I know,
eliminated all titles made up by editors. For poems which have no titles, I
have used first lines as substitutes, enclosing them in quotation marks to
distinguish them from true titles. As for the texts, I have chosen the best
versions I could find, using, wherever possible, standard critical works and
original editions, or reprints of the original. The chief source for the
Introduction is the hundreds of bird poems and bird images which I col-
lected from a great variety of poets, ranging from Homer to T. S. Eliot.
Many other books have contributed to this work. Like the threads in a
weaving, it would be difficult to single them out, but there is one person in
particular whom I wish to acknowledge, and that is Edward A. Armstrong,
one of the last of the parson-naturalists who have made such a remarkable
contribution to the study of British birds. I would like to thank him both
for his helpful replies to my letters and for the stimulation of his books,

especially *The Folklore of Birds*[1] which first made me aware of the fact that many literary bird conventions were not the creation of poets but had their origin in earlier beliefs, some of which are thousands of years old. I would also like to thank the staffs of the Vassar College Library, the New York Public Library, and the library of the New York State University College at New Paltz. In addition, I am indebted to many friends, especially the late Professor Robert D. Murray of Princeton University who kindly gave me permission to use his translation of the Greek swallow song; Professor John Jacobson of the college at New Paltz who untangled passages in medieval Latin for me; and Professor Stuart H. L. Degginger of the same college who answered many questions about Anglo-Saxon. My special thanks go to my husband, Hugo Munsterberg, and my daughter, Marjorie, who found books which I said were not available, provided stimulating discussions, read my manuscript, and, most endearing from my point of view and most heroic from theirs, listened to me during all that time I was thinking and talking about birds in poetry.

PEGGY MUNSTERBERG

---

[1]. Edward A. Armstrong, *The Folklore of Birds* (London: Collins, 1958; New York: Dover, 1970).

Acknowledgements

We are indebted to the copyright holders for permission to reprint certain poems:

GERARD MANLEY HOPKINS: from *The Poems of Gerard Manley Hopkins* edited by W. H. Gardner and N. H. MacKenzie, published by Oxford University Press for the Society of Jesus.

Selections from *English Madrigal Verse 1588–1632* edited by E. H. Fellowes, 3rd ed. revised and enlarged by Frederick W. Sternfeld and David Greer, © Oxford University Press 1967. Reprinted by permission of Oxford University Press.

W. B. YEATS: from *Collected Poems of W. B. Yeats* published by Macmillan Ltd. Reprinted by permission of Michael and Anne Yeats and Macmillan Ltd.

Every effort has been made to trace copyright holders. The publishers would be interested to hear from any copyright holders not here acknowledged.

All illustrations are reprinted by permission of the Mary Evans Picture Library, London.

Introduction

I

If Julius Caesar came back to Britain, he would not recognize the coast, the harbours, the land, or the people. Everything is different, but the gulls screaming around the boats would be perfectly familiar, because they are the same today as they were when Caesar arrived, or Stonehenge was built, or neolithic settlers mined the chalk downs for flint. What changes is not the birds, but the way man looks at the birds. One can see this in Anglo-Saxon poetry. The birds are familiar, but the attitude towards them is nothing like ours. In fact, it has much in common with the view of birds in Homer. No doubt some of the similarities are little more than coincidence, but taken as a whole, they represent an early and in some ways quite primitive view of birds. The most obvious parallel is that both use the same general types. By far the most common are fierce flesh-eaters – vulture in Homer, raven in the Anglo-Saxon, eagle and hawk in both. The next sizeable group are birds associated with water, which includes sea birds as well as large, long-necked water birds like the crane and the goose. These two types are among the earliest birds portrayed in art. At Catal Huyuk, a neolithic town site in Anatolia, there are wall paintings of vultures eating corpses which date from about 6000 B.C., and some of the painted Iranian pots of the fourth millennium are decorated with bands of long-necked water birds. The dove, another bird of the Ancient Near East, is also common in Homer. It is not important in Old English poetry, but in some ways the Saxon cuckoo is similar, because like the dove it is a middle-sized bird, has a monotonous voice, and was connected with fertility.

The most striking similarity is that birds are often associated with sorrow and death. A common image in Homer is vultures feasting on corpses, but the negative associations are not limited to the carrion-eaters. To give some examples, a girl is nicknamed Alkyone because her mother wept 'with the sorrow-laden cry of a sea-bird'.[1] In one passage, cranes bring bloodshed and destruction, and in another, Achilles says that he is like a mother bird bringing food to her nestlings, 'but as for herself it is suffering'.[2] The most surprising is the passage where Penelope compares herself to the nightingale, in Greek legend a woman who had been transformed into a bird after she had killed her son.

1. Richmond Lattimore, *The Iliad of Homer* (Chicago: The University of Chicago Press, 1951), p. 213.
2. ibid., p. 206.

> But whenever night comes and slumber seizes them all
> I lie in my bed, and thronging about my throbbing heart,
> The sharp anxieties plague me as I lament.
> As when the daughter of Pandareus, the nightingale of the green,
> Sings beautifully when spring has freshly risen,
> Seated amid the thick foliage of the trees,
> And, often modulating, pours out her loud-sounding song,
> Lamenting her dear son Itylos, child of lord Zethos,
> Whom one day she killed with a sword unwittingly.
>
> (*The Odyssey*, XIX, ll. 515–23)[1]

Here the nightingale functions as a bird of spring, and yet its song expresses not joy but grief, and not life reborn but death.

Similar images occur in Anglo-Saxon poetry. As in Homer, a common figure is the corpse-eating bird, notably the raven and the eagle. The cuckoo announces spring, but his voice is called sad, and in *The Seafarer* he is a bird of ill omen with a mournful cry. The sea birds are predominantly negative. In *Andreas*, the storm brings the gull who is called corpse-greedy, and in *The Wanderer*, the sea birds are associated with sorrow and death. The only bird which is treated in a really positive way is the hawk. It is not the wild hawk, however, it is the hawk trained to hunt, a prized personal possession which was a part of man's world, as in *Beowulf* where the old man, the last survivor, grieves over the loss of his kin:

> . . . There is no music now,
> No plucked harp playing, no good hawk
> Swooping through the hall, no swift horse
> Stamping at the gate. Baleful death
> Has swept all of it into the dark.
>
> (ll. 2262–6)

Another similarity is the virtual absence of song. The birds in Homer almost never sing. The only real exception is the *Odyssey* passage, but Penelope compares herself to the nightingale not because it sings beautifully, but because it fills the night with its lamentations. Anglo-Saxon poets were very interested in bird voices, but like Homer, they had little to say about song. In fact, they do not really distinguish between musical notes and noisy cries. The word sing could be used for any bird – the hoarse raven as well as the nightingale, the clamorous gull, the cuckoo, the swan. (Wolves and trumpets also sing.) In Old English poetry, there are only two descriptions of real song and one, which is in *Riddle 8*, puts so much emphasis upon noise that some scholars think it is not a song which is described but the raucous screams of a jay. The other, which is in *The Phoenix*, is derived from a late classical poem. The Latin makes the

1. Albert Cook, *Homer: the Odyssey* (New York: Norton, 1967), pp. 270–71.

voice melodic by comparing it to the nightingale's song, the music of a pipe, the singing of the dying swan, and the strings of a lyre. The Old English uses the same outline but modifies the images. The phoenix's voice is surpassingly fair, it says:

> It cannot be equalled by trumpets or horns,
> Or the sound of the harp, or any voice
> Of any man, or the musical strain
> Of organ pipes, or the wings of the swan,
> Or any sound which God created
> To gladden man in this mournful world.
>
> (ll.134–9)

The nightingale is dropped; trumpets and horns are added; and the singing of the dying swan is changed to the whistling notes of its wings. Obviously, the poet did not think that bird song should be ranked with the loveliest sounds which God has ever created. This surprises us, but as Edward Armstrong says:

> Primitive people are not interested aesthetically in bird songs ... A bird's supposed magical power or its significance as an omen is that which raises its status for folk of the lower levels of culture. Legends about bird songs, as distinct from bird calls, are the product of sophisticated society.[1]

In Homer, many of the birds are either omens sent by the gods or the gods themselves appearing as birds. There is nothing like this in the Old English. One reason is that the bulk of the extant poems deal with Christian subjects, and while a handful of heathen poems have survived, they are more or less Christianized because they were written down by monastic scribes. Nevertheless, we know that some of the birds were once associated with Germanic gods. The best example is the raven. In its most common role, it is one of the three beasts of battle, the others being the eagle and the wolf. Murderous camp followers, they watch and wait and when the fighting is over, eat their fill of the dead. A good example is the passage from *Judith*.

> ... Battle shields clashed
> With loud clangs. Then the lank wolf
> Rejoiced in the wood, and that black raven,
> The corpse greedy bird. Both of them knew
> That the men who fought would provide them a feast
> Abundant in flesh. Behind them flew
> The hungry eagle: dewy feathered,
> Dusky coated, the horn beak sang
> His battle song ...
>
> (ll. 204–12)

1. Edward A. Armstrong, *The Folklore of Birds* (London: Collins, 1958; New York: Dover, 1970), p. 187.

The same beasts are used in the same way in Old Norse literature. In one of the Gudrun poems, for example, the queen's brother says that the king lies slaughtered beyond the river, given to the wolves.

> Look for Sigurd in the south.
> There you will hear the ravens scream,
> And the eagles scream, exulting in their feast;
> And the wolves howl over your husband.
> (*Gudrunar-kvida in Forna*, ll. 23–6)

Now it happens that these three were all associated with the war god. Take the raven. The Wodan of the Germanic tribes was the god of the raven,[1] and so was the Scandinavian Odin. One of his many names was Hrafnáss, or Raven God, and according to the Eddas, he had two ravens which perched on his shoulders and told him everything they had seen in their daily flights over the world. With the Old Irish war goddesses, the link is even closer. An ominous, bloodthirsty trio, they appear so often as ravens or crows that they seem as much bird deity as goddess. Even more interesting, it is said that they sometimes feasted on the bodies of the slain, presumably in their guise of corvine birds. There is nothing as savage as this in the Old Norse. Various poems say that fallen warriors were *given* to Odin, but it is the beasts of battle who eat them. In Anglo-Saxon poetry, the raven also eats the dead on the gallows, and this, too, suggests a link to the war god. We know that men were sacrificed to both Wodan and Odin by being hanged to death on trees. Odin was called Lord of the Gallows and God of the Hanged, and it is said that he sometimes sat beneath the gallows, called Odin's tree. Both the hanged men and the dead warriors belonged to the war god. He did not devour them himself, but since the flesh-eaters were his attributes, it could be that they represented the god who was taking up his dead through his agents. In Anglo-Saxon poetry, these images are quite conventional, but they have roots in a primitive past where carrion-eating birds were associated with death-hungry gods.

When the Anglo-Saxons became Christians, the deities of the old religion were turned into devils. This meant that their animal associates were still in league with the supernatural. Chief among them was the raven, who was certainly not looked upon as an ordinary bird. In fact, even the raven banner of the Vikings was said to have magical powers. According to the *Annals of St Neots*, a twelfth-century Latin chronicle, if the Danes were to win, the raven on the banner fluttered as if it were alive, but when they were to lose, it hung motionless – 'and this', it

1. Hilda Roderick Ellis Davidson, *Gods and Myths of Northern Europe* (Penguin Books, 1964), pp. 69–70.

says, 'has often been proved'. A second account makes the banner even more wonderful, for in times of peace, it had nothing on it, but when war broke out, the figure of a black raven was always seen on the white silk.[1] In Anglo-Saxon poetry, there are at least two instances where specific reference is made to a bird's uncanny power. One is the passage in *The Seafarer* where the cuckoo foretells the future.

> Then the cuckoo warns in his woeful voice:
> Summer's herald sings, boding sorrow
> Bitter to the breast . . .
> (ll. 53–5)

The other is in an Old English charm against wens.

> Under the wolf's foot, under the eagle's feather,
> Under the eagle's claw, may you shrink forever.
> (ll. 6–7)

There is no doubt that the chief birds in Anglo-Saxon poetry were believed to possess supernatural power. They are often ominous, but in the traditional images, there is no suggestion that they were considered unremittingly evil, the way a Christian would regard a devil. As Edward Armstrong says, it is a characteristic of primitive thought to see the supernatural as expressing itself either benevolently or malignantly. An uncanny bird is sometimes good and sometimes bad. To give an example: in Anglo-Saxon poetry, a raven on a battlefield is a bird of death, but in a different situation he can be quite positive, as in *Beowulf* where the hero sleeps

> Until the black raven, blithe hearted,
> Announced break of day . . .
> (ll. 1801–2)

We are so steeped in the either-or of Christianity that it is difficult to think of supernatural power as fluctuating between good and evil. On the side of the angels, we say, because the heavenly hosts are drawn up against Satan and his cohorts. But in the world of omens, it is as if God were the same person as the devil, now functioning as one and now as the other. If you think of it in terms of natural forces, the paradox makes sense. Fire on the hearth is good, but if it escapes and the room is wrapped in flames, it is evil. So with rain, water, sun – they nourish life but they also bring disaster and death. The same could be true of birds. In *Beowulf*, the blithe-hearted raven is obviously auspicious, but the raven which appears at the end is an evil omen.

1. Charles Plummer, *Two of the Saxon Chronicles* (Oxford: Clarendon Press, 1899), p. 93.

> ... No plucked harp
> Will wake the warriors, but the dark raven,
> Greedy for the dead, will croak to the eagle
> To tell how he fared at the feast of flesh
> When he and the wolf both ravaged the slain.
>
> (ll. 3023–7)

The typical Anglo-Saxon bird image is short and concrete. Sometimes the birds are presented entirely through their voices, as in *The Seafarer* where they sing, call, clamour, and scream. At other times, they are shown in action, as when the carrion birds wheel in the air, waiting for their tribute of flesh. There are brief descriptions, often formulaic. Many of them refer to colour – the grey gull; the black-coated raven; the eagle with the white behind. It is a simple style, sometimes so compressed it is like a telegram, but it can be very effective, a kind of primitive naturalism which creates a strong sense of the real bird, as in this image from *Elene*: 'Hrefen uppe gol,/wan ond waelfel', which translated literally means 'Raven on high screamed,/Black and cruel-to-the-slain'.

The birds in these passages are not what you would call endearing. Ominous, at times even frightening, they seem larger than life and it is easy to believe that they are touched with something uncanny. The Anglo-Saxon bird riddles are very different. More folk-like in character, they suggest the homely world of pre-industrial rural life. A cock treads a hen – a swan flies overhead, its wings whistling. As a whole, they are quite positive – in fact, a few are even cheerful, especially the jay riddle with its lively account of the jay's different voices. In some riddles the bird itself speaks, a device at least as old as the ancient Sumerians, who had little fables with talking animals and birds. Others are presented in the third person, as in *Riddle 57*.

> This air carries these little creatures
> Over mountains, creatures very black,
> Swarthy, dark coated. Full of noise,
> They travel in flocks, loudly shrilling.
> They light on wooded cliffs, sometimes
> On the halls of the sons of men. Name them.

Swallows is the usual answer, but I think that swifts is more likely, because they are dark all over, often dash about in noisy groups, and have a voice which Peterson's *Field Guide* calls a 'shrill, prolonged, piercing screech'.[1]

In *The Phoenix*, a Christian allegory of 677 lines, the focus has shifted from the temporal world to the world of the eternal. Instead of a real

1. Roger Tory Peterson, *et al.*, *A Field Guide to the Birds of Britain and Europe* (Boston: Houghton Mifflin, n.d.), p. 177.

bird familiar to both poet and audience, the subject is the fabulous phoenix. That no one had ever seen it did not matter, because what is important is not the bird but the truth which the bird represents. Sometimes he stands for Christ, and sometimes he is the Christian, as in the part beginning, 'When the wind is still and the weather fair'. Here the tree in which he builds is Christ; the fragrant plants he gathers are his good deeds; the nest is his life; the burning is the fire of Judgement Day; and the rebirth is the resurrection of the body.[1] Like the glass in a lantern, the phoenix is supposed to reveal God's light as a guide to the earnest seeker. Once the symbols are explained, the physical forms should dissolve into the spiritual, just as the glass disappears when the light comes on in the lantern.

As far as bird poetry is concerned, it must be said that all this allegorizing had an unfortunate effect. The birds are lifeless and the poetry is wordy, repetitious, and rambling. Some passages have a naive charm, especially the description of the phoenix which makes him sound like a jewelled bird on a Carolingian Bible cover, but there are parts which are tedious, and the words wash over one, leaving precious little behind. No doubt part of the reason is that the phoenix was to the Anglo-Saxons what the bird of paradise is to us, an exotic creature, so unfamiliar that it has to be explained. But more important, when the poet spoke about the bird, his mind was on the allegory which is spelled out at great length in the second half of the poem. In Anglo-Saxon poetry, the traditional bird symbolism is never explained because it is not an assigned value, it is part of an objective reality. In the battle scenes, the raven is not just a symbol of war and death, he is one of the actors, and he is as real as the warriors hacking at the living flesh. The raven-eagle passages look back to a primitive time when the real could embody the supernatural, but *The Phoenix* is typically medieval in the way it transforms the bird into an arbitrary symbol.

Considering the fact that Old English poetry was predominantly Christian, it is surprising how much of the bird imagery is essentially heathen. The birds of the battlefield are the most obvious, but the mournful cuckoo and the sea birds are also pagan, steeped in a pessimism that broods over mortality. It is no accident, surely, that in the well-known passage from Bede, man's lot in the pagan world is symbolized by a bird. 'But as for herself it is suffering,' Homer said, and so it is with the sparrow who has a moment of safety in a life beset by winter storms. According to Bede, in the year 627, King Edwin of Northumbria asked

1. N. F. Blake (ed.), *The Phoenix* (Manchester: Manchester University Press, 1964), p. 32.

his counsellors whether he should become Christian. The first said yes; a second agreed and then added,

> It seems to me, oh king, that man's life on this earth, as compared to that part which is unknown to us, is like the time when you are sitting at supper with your officers and ministers, and the fire is burning, and the hall is warm, and outside there are storms of rain and snow, and a sparrow comes in and flies swiftly through the room, entering at one door and going out the other. While he is within, he is safe from the storms, but in a minute, the interlude is over, and he vanishes into the winter from which he emerged. So this life lasts for a brief period, but what went before or what comes after, we know not. If, therefore, this doctrine offers us something more certain, I think it would be wise for us to follow it.[1]

Very few birds in Anglo-Saxon poetry are specifically Christian, but those which do occur are treated in a quite different way. The most fundamental change is the introduction of moral judgement. In the battle scenes, the raven is never condemned. He is presented in a matter-of-fact way, as much a part of war as the enemy, as much a part of fate as death. But in the Anglo-Saxon version of the flood story, the raven is called *feond*, meaning enemy, devil, fiend. He is bad because he disobeyed Noah.

> The fiend soon fell upon floating corpses;
> The dark feathered bird did not come back.
> *(Genesis*, ll. 1447–8)

The 'bad' bird is hateful, but the 'good' bird can partake of Christian joy. This results in a much more positive attitude towards birds. To give an example: in *Guthlac*, an Old English poem about an Anglo-Saxon saint who died in 714, the birds in the trees rejoice at his return because often, when they have been hungry, he has fed them from his hand. This loving bond is very different from the pagan world of *The Seafarer*. Here man, like the sparrow, is alone in the midst of mysterious, potentially destructive forces. 'There I heard nothing but roaring sea,/Ice cold surf,' the narrator says.

> Storms beat the stone cliffs where the tern answered,
> Icy feathered, and the wet winged eagle
> Often screamed: no kin to protect me,
> No one to comfort my desolate heart.
>
> (ll. 23–6)

The tern screams an answer to the storm because storm and tern are alike – wild and implacable, beyond the control of man. In *The Life of*

---

1. *Ecclesiastical History of the English People*, Book II, Ch. 13.

St Guthlac, an eighth-century Latin work, not only the birds and the fishes obey the saint, but also the water and the air. One day two swallows fly into the hermitage and, lighting on Guthlac's shoulders, they sing songs with every sign of great joy. When a visitor asks how this could happen, Guthlac says, 'Have you not read that with him who is united with God in a pure spirit all things are joined together in God?'[1] Nature itself is Christianized, and though it still has terrors, it is a radically different world, more joyful, more certain, where man and bird can come together because they are creatures of a loving God.

II

Medieval bird poetry marks a complete break with the Anglo-Saxon. Nightingales are as common as hawks; bird song stands for love and joy; and instead of morally ambivalent birds, there are symbolic bird types so that a given species tends to be either good or bad. Most important, the birds symbolize various aspects of the human state. Generally speaking, in Anglo-Saxon poetry the birds are distinct from man. They may be death omens or heralds of spring, but whatever their role, you do not identify with the birds because they are something other, like storms or gods. Medieval poetry blurs the distinction because it humanizes the birds. They are not only judged by moral standards, they are often characterized by human traits like the false cuckoo or the pious pelican. It is a different world from the Anglo-Saxon, a world of bird symbols and bird types.

In Old English poetry the most typical bird is the raven, with its dark aura of death and doom. What best exemplifies the medieval is the hawk family. Its symbolism was more complex and more all-embracing than that of any other bird. To begin with, the different kinds were ranked in a hierarchy which reflects the whole of medieval society. The eagle is always at the top, the emperor, the king of kings. The upper orders are represented by the hawks trained for hunting, such as the gyrfalcon, the peregrine falcon, the saker, the lanner, the merlin, the hobby, the goshawk, and the sparrow hawk. At the bottom are the buzzard and the kite. Considered inferior because they could not be trained for falconry, they are symbols of everything base, whether it is character or class. 'All one to thee a falcon and a kite,' says a fifteenth-century poet[2] speaking of a peasant, and the two words express a whole

1. Clinton Albertson, *Anglo-Saxon Saints and Heroes* (New York: Fordham University Press, 1967), p. 198.
2. John Lydgate, *The Churl and the Bird*, l. 358.

series of contrasts, such as knight and churl, valour and cowardice, honour and treachery.

In addition to their class symbolism, the birds of prey could typify various aspects of love. For example, in Chaucer's *Parliament of Fowls*, the eagles give voice to the ideals of courtly love, and in *The Squire's Tale*, the noble lovers are a pair of peregrines. Sometimes the falcon and his hawk stand for the lover and his lady. It is a perfect symbol of courtly love because, in order to master the hawk, the trainer had to devote himself to it so completely that he became in effect its servant. A more common image is hawking as the hunt of love. Here the hawk represents the man and the prey the woman. It is a carnal chase, often nothing but the pursuit of sex, as in *Confessio Amantis* where Gower says that a man lusting for a woman eyes her like a hawk about to seize his prey.

> And thus he looketh on the flesh,
> Right as an hawk which hath a sight
> Upon the fowl, there he shall light.
> (Book V, ll. 7070–72)

But the hawk-prey image could also be used for love. When Troilus finally embraces Criseyde, for instance, Chaucer compares the knight to a sparrow hawk and the lady to a captured lark.

> What might or may the seely larkë say,
> When that the sparhawk hath it in his foot?
> (*Troilus and Criseyde*, Book III, ll. 1191–2)

It is not a very attractive image, but no doubt one was supposed to think of the hunter's success rather than the speedy demise of the prey.

Trained hawks like the peregrine were not just arbitrary symbols of the nobility, because in real life they were treated as a kind of aristocracy. Housed in their own quarters, fed on special diets, and equipped with costly trappings, they were cared for by attendants who had a fit if they broke so much as a tail feather. They were at once gentle and fierce, at once civilized and savage. The perfect knight, after all, spent a good deal of his time in brutal killing, and the hawk on his fist, with its bells and feathered hood, was in many ways his animal double.

In medieval bird poetry, the most characteristic device is talking birds. In the debates they argue; in the masses they sing services; in the didactic poems they preach; and in the fables they are characters in stories. For the most part they are little more than substitute people, but in *The Owl and the Nightingale* there is a real fusion of the animal and the human. An anonymous poem of about 1200, this is a debate between two birds who argue about which is better, the nightingale who represents joy or the owl who stands for sterner virtues. The substance of the poem is serious, but the manner is lively and direct, and there are passages which are quite entertaining, especially when the birds become abusive. Here are the nightingale's first words to the owl.

> 'Monster,' she said, 'get out, be quick!
> When I see you, then I feel sick.
> Indeed, because of the noise you make,
> My song I often must forsake.
> My heart flips up and chokes my tongue,
> Whenever I see that you have come.
> I would rather spit than sing,
> When I hear your ghastly scream.'
> (ll. 33–40)

Since both talk incessantly, sometimes at great length, it should be easy to forget that they are birds, but this does not happen because the author maintains a clear distinction between the avian world and the world of men. The birds' role in human affairs is limited strictly to their singing. When they discuss love, for example, the poet does not pretend that they themselves are lovers. The bird experience is summed up briefly by the owl, who says that when the nightingale wishes to copulate she sings in an excited manner, but as soon as she breeds she falls silent. Love is a human experience and the birds are spectators who give support through their songs. They do not fall in love themselves. They live in a bird world, leading bird lives, yet their speech, their reactions, and their values are so intensely human that they function simultaneously as people. What makes them so convincing is that their human character comes out of their bird nature. To give an example, the owl is a year-round resident, therefore she is steadfast; she sings in winter which shows that she never shirks her duty; and her voice is sad because she weeps for the suffering, urges sinners to repent, and gives warning when disaster approaches. It is not what we would call realistic, and yet it is this underlying naturalism that makes them both so vivid as birds.

Chaucer's bird characters are lively and engaging, but they are more like people wearing bird masks than birds with human reactions. Instead of combining the two natures, they tend to shift from one to the other, sometimes so abruptly that it surprises one. If the mix rarely jells, it is because they take on human roles so that sooner or later they begin to act like people. An eagle blushes when a suitor declares his love; a hawk falls on his knees before his falcon. The best example is Chauntecleer in *The Nun's Priest's Tale*. The story opens with a vivid description of the cock. His crowing is like an organ, his feathers are the colour of burned gold, and he lives in a yard with seven hens, one of which, his favourite, is called Pertelote. Almost at once, they start turning into husband and wife. He calls her Madame, she addresses him as Sire, and they have a long discussion about dreams. 'Men may in oldë bookës read,' he says at the beginning, but a hundred lines on, it is he himself who reads, and then, still later, he tells Pertelote to look into Daniel and Joseph in the Old Testament. At this point we are absorbed in them as people, and though it is a bit disconcerting when, in a compliment to his wife, he says her face is beautiful because it is so scarlet red about the eyes, it still comes as a shock when, the minute the conversation is over, he reverts to a cock. Book-reading, Latin-quoting Chauntecleer now struts about the yard, clucking to his hens whenever he finds some corn.

The talking birds are obviously extensions of people, but even birds which do not talk are fitted into a human frame. Sometimes, like heraldic figures, they exist only as signs. A good example is the thirteenth-century English Bestiary where, after a brief account of the bird, the poet tells us what it really means. Take the poem about the eagle. The author begins, 'I will make known the eagle's nature/As I read it in a book' – and then he launches into a wild account of how the eagle renews his youth. First he seeks out a spring, and then he flies up and hovers in the sun which makes his eyes bright. When his feathers fall out he plunges into the water, from which he emerges rejuvenated except for his beak.

> Then he goeth to a stone,
> And he pecketh there-on,
> Pecketh till his twisted beak
> Hath foregone its crooked shape.
> After, with his righted bill,
> Taketh whatso meat he will.

Next comes the moral.

> Just so is man as is this ern: [1]
> Will you all now listen –
> Old he is in his secret sin
> Before he becometh Christian.

The sun is God, the spring is the water of baptism, and the crooked beak is the mouth which cannot nourish the soul until it learns the proper prayers.

The modern reader glances at the moral as if it were a footnote, and then concentrates on the eagle. He sees it hovering in the sun as bald as a plucked goose, and he either dismisses it as absurd, or he enjoys it because it is so naive. But in this kind of work, as in the Anglo-Saxon

1. eagle

Phoenix, the bird is important not in itself but as a manifestation of a deeper truth. The phoenix rising from its ashes is a visible form of the resurrection; the pelican who revives her dead offspring with her own blood is an example of Christ the Redeemer. St Gregory the Great said that allegory is to truth as the chaff is to the grain.

> But to eat the chaff is to be a beast of burden; to eat the grain is to be human. He who uses human reason, therefore, will cast aside the chaff and hasten to eat the grain of the spirit.[1]

From this point of view, it does not matter whether these marvellous creatures are real or imaginary. Like figures painted on a door, they disappear when the door is opened. They are the chaff which the wise man throws away – though judging from the immense popularity of the many medieval Bestiaries, the readers must have been eating the chaff along with the grain. And swallowing symbol with lesson, for most people probably believed in these marvels, just as they believed in mermaids or dragons. If they seem childlike to us because they were so credulous, from their point of view we are Gregory's beasts because we cast out the grain.

The Bestiary birds were part of a learned tradition of bird lore that had been accumulating for centuries. It was a mass of undifferentiated material, a peculiar assortment where the fabulous is mixed with the factual and the phoenix is as real as the barnyard cock. Unlike modern science, it did not develop logically, in an orderly progression. On the contrary, it was a piling up that was essentially static because it was based upon authority. Something from the Bible, or a Church Father, or a Greek or Roman writer, was accepted as truth like a papal pronouncement, and though it might be varied, it was never really challenged. 'As I read it in a book,' says the English Bestiary. We think of this as typically medieval, but it was an attitude which lasted much longer. In his *Animadversions* of 1598, Francis Thynne props up a naive story about the stork by saying, Aristotle said this, and so did Bartholomew, along with many other authors. Even Sir Thomas Browne, in his so-called *Vulgar Errors* of 1646, does not so much reject the authorities as update them. Well into the seventeenth century, names like Aristotle still had considerable weight.

A perfect example of the learned tradition is the bird list in Chaucer's *Parliament of Fowls*, a work which was written about 1380. The poet, who is recounting a dream, wanders through a park where he meets various figures associated with love. At last he comes upon the Goddess of

1. Durant Waite Robertson, Jr, *A Preface to Chaucer* (Princeton: Princeton University Press, 1962), p. 58.

Nature. She is presiding over a vast number of birds, every kind in the world, a parliament of fowls which meet once a year on Valentine's Day in order to choose their mates. 'There mightë men the royal eagle find,' Chaucer begins, and the reader expects a description of those birds at that moment, as they are grouped around Nature. Instead, the noisy crowd freezes into a set piece, and we are given a list of about thirty-five types, each summed up in a word or a phrase. Here are some of the more important.

> The eagle which gazes at the sun;
> The falcon which sits on the king's hand;
> The swan which sings as it dies;
> The owl which announces death;
> The cowardly kite;
> The cock which is the village clock;
> The lecherous sparrow;
> The faithful turtle dove;
> The unnatural cuckoo;
> The stork which avenges adultery;
> The wise raven;
> The ill-ómened crow.

Chaucer's list is almost wholly derivative, a compendium of medieval bird lore so full of echoes, conventions, and allusions that for almost every line, scholars have found at least one literary parallel, and sometimes as many as four or five. The list itself is based on a similar list in *De Planctu Naturae*, a work by Alanus de Insulis who lived in the twelfth century. Much of what Chaucer says can be found in medieval encyclopedists, and they, in turn, often drew upon older sources. Since the material was so familiar, Chaucer could reduce his descriptions to the briefest statements, mere tags which identify the traditions. This makes it difficult for us because we are absolutely ignorant about many of the things that Chaucer expects his readers to know. Two examples will suffice. First, the sun-gazing eagle with which the list begins.

> There mightë men the royal eagle find,
> That with his sharpë look pierceth the sun. (ll. 330–31)

This curious notion goes back to Aristotle who said:

> The sea-eagle is very keen-sighted, and before its young are fledged tries to make them stare at the sun, and beats the one that refuses to do so, and twists him back in the sun's direction; and if one of them gets watery eyes in the process, it kills him, and rears the other.[1]

1. *History of Animals*, Book IX, 620ª, 1–5 (translation by D'Arcy Wentworth Thompson).

Pliny, the first-century Roman writer, echoed this in his *Natural History*, and the belief that the eagle could look at the sun became a part of the learned tradition. Strangely enough, the legend persisted long after the medieval period. In fact, there were sun-gazing eagles in the famous eighteenth-century poem, *The Seasons*, although Thomson eventually removed them. The original lines read:

> High from the summit of a craggy cliff,
> Hung o'er the green sea grudging at its base,
> The royal eagle draws his young, resolved
> To try them at the sun. Strong-pounced, and bright
> As burnished day, they up the blue sky wind,
> Leaving dull sight below, and with fixed gaze
> Drink in their native noon: the father-king
> Claps his glad pinions, and approves the birth.[1]

The second example is the cuckoo. Chaucer calls it 'ever unkind', using a word which in Middle English meant unnatural as well as wicked, ungrateful, and cruel. This idea is based upon its parasitical habits. Instead of building a nest, the female removes an egg from the nest of a victim, always a much smaller bird, and replaces it with one of her own. When the cuckoo is hatched, it gets rid of the foster parents' chicks by pushing them out of the nest. The basic facts were embellished with various misconceptions, the most important being that when the cuckoo was grown, it killed its foster mother either by devouring her, as Pliny says, or by biting off her head.

> Thou murderer of the heysoge[2] on the branch
> That brought thee forth, thou ruthless glutton!
> (*The Parliament of Fowls*, ll. 612–13)

Because of its peculiar domestic habits, it was also a symbol of disreputable kinds of love. To give an example, in *The Cuckoo and the Nightingale*, a love debate long attributed to Chaucer, the nightingale represents the noblest ideals of courtly love while 'that sorry bird', the lewd cuckoo, stands for the lecherous and the false. Chaucer sums up the cuckoo tradition in a single phrase – ever unkind. His audience understood all these cryptic tags because they were familiar with the various types, but today, one cannot get through the bird list without a bank of explanatory notes.

---

1. James Logie Robertson (ed.), *James Thomson: Poetical Works* (London: Oxford University Press, 1951), p. 50.
2. the hedge sparrow, the cuckoo's foster parent

To the modern reader, looking hopefully for a real bird, there is a great difference between the non-realistic types like the pelican and those which are relatively naturalistic. But a medieval reader would not be aware of this distinction. Chaucer uses both types in the *Parliament* list, and there is no attempt to distinguish one from the other. To give an example, when he speaks of the falcon gentle 'that with its feet distraineth [1]/The kingë's hand', he is giving us a realistic glimpse of a king with a peregrine falcon on his fist. But his 'wedded turtle, with her hertë true' comes straight from the Bestiaries, which tell us that if the turtle dove is widowed, she never takes a second mate. The common denominator, not just in the *Parliament* but in all medieval bird poetry, is symbolism. The turtle dove stands for faithfulness; the falcon for nobility. That some bird types are more realistic than others is quite incidental, because all of them function primarily as symbols, and this is as true for *The Owl and the Nightingale* as it is for the various Bestiaries.

If there is one exception to this, it is the treatment of bird song because, although it is used symbolically, one can see a growing interest in the song for its own sake. It starts out as a minor theme, with simple statements which often echo one another because the vocabulary is so limited. If they describe the song at all, they do so in the briefest terms – 'These fowlës merry [2] singeth.' Sometimes the detail is more specific, but it does not really go beyond a simple generalization. A good example is the song lines from *The Land of Cokaygne*.

> There beth [3] briddës many and fale: [4]
> Throstil, thrush, and nightingale,
> Chalander, and wodwale,
> And other briddës without tale, [5]
> That stinteth never by their might
> Merry to sing day and night.
>
> (ll. 95–100)

In *The Romaunt of the Rose*, the fourteenth-century English translation of the thirteenth-century French classic, the treatment of song is much more sophisticated. Instead of brief statements, there are several passages, the longest about forty lines, and the song vocabulary is so extensive that it is safe to say that more different words are used in the *Romaunt* passages than in all of the early images. The birds still sing joyful songs that are

---

1. grasps
2. In addition to glad or gay, the Middle English *merry* could also mean pleasant, agreeable, sweet.
3. be   4. many   5. number

associated with love and spring, but now it is also an accomplished art. This idea is very old. Aristotle says, 'a mother-nightingale has been observed to give lessons in singing to a young bird', and according to Macrobius, a writer of the fifth century A.D. who was well known in the medieval period, birds like the nightingale and the swan 'practise song with almost the technique of an art'.[1] The *Romaunt* adds to the expert singer the idea of the group performance. The birds are not only skilled in the craft of song, they sing together like members of a choir. The poet compares their voices to angels, mermaids, sirens – no mortal man, he says, has ever heard such singing.

> Full fair service and eke full sweet
> These briddis maden as they sete.[2]
> Lays of love, full well souning,[3]
> They songen in their jargoning;
> Some high and some eke lowë song
> Upon the branches green y-sprong.
> The sweetness of their melody
> Made all mine heart in revelry.
> (ll. 713–20)

In *The Book of the Duchess*, one of Chaucer's early works, there is a song passage of some twenty-seven lines which is obviously based on the *Romaunt*. Much of the vocabulary is the same, and there are the same basic concepts – skilled singers, group performance, unique experience, comparison to the supernatural. The birds sing the most festive service that ever man heard, some high, some low, and all of one accord. So sweet a sound was never heard 'But it had be a thing of heaven'.

> For instrument nor melody
> Was nowhere heard yet half so sweet,
> Nor of accord half so meet,
> For there was none of them that feigned
> To sing, for each of them him pained
> To find out merry crafty notes.
> They ne sparëd not their throats.
> (ll. 314–20)

Although the passage has a naive charm, the effect of the whole is rather laboured. Chaucer himself must have been dissatisfied, because the birdsong images of his later work are quite different, more like the simple

---

1. Jack Arthur Walter Bennett, *The Parlement of Foules* (Oxford: Clarendon Press, 1957), p. 51.
2. sat   3. sounding

statements of the thirteenth century than the elaborate style of the *Romaunt*. A nightingale sings lays of love in the moonlight, a lark salutes the dawn, 'And smallë fowlës maken melody'.

The fifteenth century refined and conventionalized the theme of birds as expert singers. In Lydgate, a prolific poet who died about 1450, the birds sing motets, carols, complines, hours, hymns. One of the most charming of the many examples from Lydgate is a passage in *The Churl and the Bird*. Its basic ideas suggest the *Romaunt*, but they are absorbed into the larger theme so that it creates a more unified effect. The bird 'did her pain most amorously to sing', saluting the day star at dawn and going to rest after her compline.

> It was a very heavenly melody,
> Even and morrow to hear the briddë's song,
> And the sweetë, sugared harmony
> Of uncouth¹ warbles and tunës drawn along,
> That all the garden of the noisë rong.
>
> (ll. 71–5)

If medieval bird song has an unearthly beauty, it is because it is part of the dream garden which haunts medieval poetry, that paradise where it is always May, that enchantment of flowers and flowing water where the birds in the trees sing with angel voices. It is a generalized music which is evoked, a heavenly harmony that is not made up of particular voices. In fact, a bird which cannot sing at all will be used in a song group if it fits in symbolically. In the *Romaunt*, the poet elaborates upon the beauty of the sound, but when it comes to the singers, he makes some very odd choices, as in the passage where popinjay and lark sing blissful songs in May. (Both had erotic associations.) A more extreme example is Lydgate's bird mass, *Devotions of the Fowls*. Popinjay, pelican, nightingale, lark, and dove sing a service to glorify God in the Trinity. As a group, it is most peculiar – in fact, it would be easier to find the unicorn than these five birds all sitting in the same tree. (Not to mention the fact that nightingale and lark are tiny compared to the pelican, a huge, grotesque-looking bird about the size of a swan.) As a song group, it is even more peculiar. Popinjay usually meant parrot, but it was also a name for the green woodpecker. Neither is our idea of a song bird, since one is given to harsh squawks and the other has a loud cry that rings out like a crazy laugh. Doves say nothing but coo, and the pelican is silent except in the breeding colony where it utters an occasional groan. Yet Lydgate tells us that their voice is celestial, their hymns are heavenly, and their melody is sweet. This is ridiculous if you think of the actual birds but, obviously,

---

1. strange, marvellous

they are not supposed to be realistic. Each is a symbol of a part of the service. To give an example, the pelican grieves over Christ's suffering and death because she herself is a symbol of loving sacrifice, but the nightingale sings of the resurrection because as a bird of spring, she is associated with renewal and joy.

> The nightingale leap from bough to bough,
> And on the pelican she made a cry,
> And said, 'Pelican, why mournest thou now?
> Christ is risen from death truly,
> Mankind with him to glorify:
> Wherefore sing now as we do,
> *Consurgit Cristus tumulo*.'

In the bird mass in *Philip Sparrow*, a work from about 1505, Skelton combines the typically medieval with elements which belong to the new century. Seventy-five birds are summoned to the funeral of Philip, a pet sparrow who has been killed by a cat. The scope is impressive – in this one scene, there are more different species than either Chaucer or Shakespeare uses in his entire work. Sea birds, shore birds, marsh birds, game birds, doves, domestic fowl, members of the crow family, song birds, birds of prey – like the *Parliament* list, it represents all sorts and kinds of birds. The dominant theme is the mass, but Skelton works in bits and pieces from the grab bag of medieval bird lore.

> The peacock so proud,
> Because his voice is loud,
> And hath a glorious tail,
> He shall sing the Grail.
> (ll. 438–41)

There is the turtle most true, the stork who hates adultery, and the phoenix,

> Of whose incineration
> There riseth a new creation.
> (ll. 540–41)

All this is medieval, but in its use of voices the mass is unmistakably sixteenth-century. In the dream garden, the harsh and the sweet are blended into an ideal harmony. 'Full angel-like these birdis sang their houris,' says Dunbar. It is 'a thing of heaven' like the music of the spheres. Skelton wakes us with a babble of about twenty different voices. Some are only suggested, as when he says that to keep the plain song, the chanters will be the cuckoo, the stock dove, and the culver, all of which

have monotonous calls. But for others, he uses specific sound words –
'The starling with her brabling', for example, or,

> The woodhack, that singeth 'chur'
> Hoarsely, as he had the mur.[1]
>
> (ll. 418-19)

Although the descriptions are very brief, most of them suggest some
general characteristic of the real voice. In fact, if you compare what he
says to Peterson's *Field Guide to the Birds of Britain and Europe*, you
will find a number of examples where the same word, or something similar,
is used for a given voice.

Skelton	*Peterson*
The fleckëd pie to chatter	chattering . . . notes
And robin . . . softly warbëling	warbling phrases
The plover with us to wail	plaintive (grey plover)
	melancholy (golden plover)
The bitter with his bump	deep, booming '*woomp*'
The crane with his trump	strident, trumpeting
The owl . . . to howl	long, wild shriek (barn owl)
And the gaggling gant	gabbling notes (grey lag goose)

In the *Sparrow* mass, the birds still act like people, but when they open
their mouths, they sound like birds.

Skelton's mass is the most impressive of the medieval bird assemblies.
A roll-call, a procession, a motley crowd as varied as a Noah's ark, it gives
you the feeling that all the birds in Christendom have come to the
sparrow's funeral. In English poetry, it is the last really creative ex-
pression of the medieval view of birds. In this way, it brings the period to
a close, but since it also looks ahead, one might say that in Skelton's
Sparrow, Renaissance voices sing a requiem mass for the medieval.

III

The theme of birds as expert singers was perfect for the Elizabethans.
George Sampson says, 'As we should know if we had merely the evidence
that Shakespeare affords, music was a natural activity of Elizabethan man.
Everybody sang, lords and lackeys alike.'[2] In this musical world, the
birds are Nature's singers. Instead of the divine service, with its masses

---

1. a bad cold
2. George Sampson, *The Concise Cambridge History of English Literature* (Cambridge: Cambridge University Press; New York: Macmillan, 1941), p. 189.

and matins, their songs reflect the vocal music of the period which, as Sampson says, 'took two main forms, which we can roughly call the solo and the concerted piece'. The nightingale is most apt to sing solos, as in Sidney's poem where she uses a thorn for a song book. Birds are choristers, the forest's choir. Sometimes they sing part songs, as in William Browne's *Britannia's Pastorals* of 1613. 'A description of a musical concert of birds,' he says in a note in the margin.

> The mounting lark, day's herald, got on wing,
> Bidding each bird choose out his bough and sing.
> The lofty treble sung the little wren;
> Robin the mean, that best of all loves men;
> The nightingale the tenor; and the thrush
> The counter-tenor, sweetly in a bush:
> And that the music might be full in parts,
> Birds from the groves flew with right willing hearts.
> (Book I, Song 3, ll. 197–204)

From the *Romaunt* on, a typical medieval device is to use the poet as a listener who tells us how he reacts to the song. In *The Flower and the Leaf*, a late fifteenth-century poem, the author, listening to the nightingale, says that she stood astounded, 'through ravishëd', with the song,

> Whereof I had so inly great pleasure
> That, as me thought, I surely ravished was
> Into Paradise . . .
> (ll. 113–15)

It is all vague rapture, like a person who says of a concert, 'It was divine! I was simply carried away!' The Elizabethans are much more direct. 'Hark, hark! the lark at heaven's gate sings,' Shakespeare says. The focus is on the song; the *reader* is the listener. Like Skelton, they use specific sound words, but what makes their poetry so distinctive is the rich musical vocabulary which they vary most inventively. Instead of describing the voices, they evoke them in terms of music. To give some examples, Lyly's nightingale sings a 'brave prick-song'; Brathwaite's chants out a 'merry madrigal'; and Breton's sits in a bush, 'Recording of a ground'. There are bird musicians as well as bird singers – Drayton's blackbird plays upon his dulcet pipe; Shakespeare's 'plain-song cuckoo grey' sounds a shrill trumpet for Spenser; and in the lute song beginning 'Surcharged with discontent', the jay blows his hautboy and the woodpecker hammers melody. Although their bird-song vocabulary is more extensive than that of any other period, they also create charming effects with very simple words. 'The sweet birds, O, how they sing!' says Shakespeare.

> In springtime, the only pretty ring-time,
> When birds do sing, hey ding a ding, ding,
> Sweet lovers love the spring
> (*from* 'It was a lover and his lass')

Complex or simple, the musical birds are charming, and it is not surprising that the freshest, loveliest bird-song poems were written between the 1580s and the 1620s, a period which corresponds to the flowering of the English Madrigal School.

In Elizabethan poetry, the dream garden gives way to the woods and fields of a spring landscape. It is a pastoral world, all delicate artificiality, with melodious birds singing madrigals to love-sick shepherds. The lark greets the dawn; the robin covers up the dead with moss and leaves. Most of the bird roles are derived from the medieval, such as the ominous owl, the dove grieving for its mate, and the swan which sings as it dies. But as a rule, they are handled in a less serious way, more graceful, more light-hearted. Take the cuckoo. He can still be evil, but he is more apt to be treated as a bawdy joke, his cuckoo notes taken to mean 'Cuckold, cuckold!' as in Shakespeare's song beginning, 'When daisies pied'.

> The cuckoo then on every tree
> Mocks married men; for thus sings he:
> 'Cuckoo!
> Cuckoo, cuckoo!' O word of fear,
> Unpleasing to a married ear!

If the raven is the bird of the Anglo-Saxons, and the hawks of the medieval, the one which best represents the Elizabethans is the nightingale. She is the only bird with a classical name like those of the shepherds and the shepherdesses. It is Philomela,[1] which means lover of song, and it is always capitalized because it is used as a proper noun. The genius of Arcadia, she is all music, all emotion. As the unrivalled prima donna, she fills the night with her beautiful songs. But she is also Love's singer, and she not only presides over lovers, she devotes herself completely to the passions of love. Sir Philip Sidney said that nature's world is brass and that only the poets create a golden world. The nightingale is a perfect example of their gilding, and yet strangely enough, this exquisite creature was associated with brutal crimes of passion. The key is her name, which comes from one of the most gruesome of the Greek myths. Tereus, the Thracian king of Daulis, was married to Procne. He raped her sister Philomela and then cut out her tongue. Philomela wove her story into a tapestry which she sent to Procne. In revenge, Procne killed her son,

---

1. There are various forms, such as Philomel and Philomele.

Itylus,[1] and with her sister's help, cooked him and served the flesh to his father. After Tereus had eaten his son, Procne proclaimed her revenge, whereupon Philomela burst in, carrying the child's head. Tereus drew his sword, meaning to kill them, but at this point, the gods changed them all into birds. In the Greek, the sister becomes the swallow and the mother the nightingale, but the Elizabethan poets used the Latin version where it is the other way round.

This wild story was a favourite of the Elizabethans, but as a rule, only the Tereus–Philomela part was used in poetry. The central theme is the rape, which forms the ground of the nightingale's complaint.

> Come, Philomele, that sing'st of ravishment,
> Make thy sad grove in my dishevelled hair.
> (Shakespeare, *The Rape of Lucrece*, ll. 1128 9)

Sometimes the rape is ambiguous, more impetuous ardour than the savage violence of the myth. Sidney's nightingale poem is a good example.

> Alas, she hath no other cause of anguish
> But Tereus' love, on her by strong hand wroken,
> Wherein she suff'ring all her spirits' languish,
> Full womanlike complains her will was broken.
> But I, who, daily craving,
> Cannot have to content me,
> Have more cause to lament me,
> Since wanting is more woe than too much having.

Although the word Philomela was bound to suggest the myth, there are many poems where it is used simply as a name for the nightingale. An example is the song 'You spotted snakes' by Shakespeare, where she is asked to join the chorus.

> Philomele, with melody
> Sing in our sweet lullaby;
> Lulla, lulla, lullaby; lulla, lulla, lullaby.

The nightingale can be either happy or sad. As mournful Philomel, she grieves most musically, her breast against a thorn, a curious idea which is a commonplace in Elizabethan poetry. But she is also 'glad Philomela', singing tunes of joy. The most common version of her song is *jug, jug*, to which *tereu* is often added. If you have never heard a nightingale, this conveys absolutely nothing – in fact, it sounds more like a bullfrog croaking than a songbird. But *jug, jug, tereu* is actually a fairly close

---

1. Also Itys.

approximation of two of the nightingale's most characteristic notes. *The Handbook of British Birds*[1] says:

> Most of notes have clear, rich, liquid, now bubbling, now more piping quality . . . Most striking are the extremely rapid, loud 'chooc-chooc-chooc-chooc-chooc – – –' and the fluty, much higher-pitched 'piōō' repeated rather slowly in a magnificent crescendo.
>
> (Vol. II, p. 188)

The *jug* represents the *chooc* note, while *tereu* suggests both the crescendo and King Tereus, as if Philomel in her impassioned lament kept calling out his name.

In Elizabethan poetry the nightingale is not just the emblem of music, she is the essence of love because she symbolizes the full range of passion, from violence at one extreme to joyful fulfilment at the other. Like Helen of Troy, she is a distillation more magic than any experience – she sums up, and at the same time, she transcends.

In the typical medieval poem, the birds represent human traits or human behaviour, but in the Elizabethan, they are more apt to stand for emotion. The widowed dove and the dying swan are symbols of sorrow, while the nightingale can represent either sadness or joy. Sometimes the bird expresses what the poet himself feels, as in Spenser's sonnet which opens with the dove.

> Like as the culver on the barëd bough
> Sits mourning for the absence of her mate,
> And in her songs sends many a wishful vow
> For his return, that seems to linger late;
> So I alone, now left disconsolate,
> Mourn to myself the absence of my love,
> And wand'ring here and there all desolate,
> Seek with my plaints to match that mournful dove.

To use an Elizabethan expression, in this kind of image the birds 'record' the human emotion, meaning that they render it into song. So Philomela, singing out her woes, gives voice to Sidney's grief. It is a kind of counterpoint, at times almost a duet, as in *The Two Gentlemen of Verona* where Valentine says,

> Here can I sit alone, unseen of any,
> And to the nightingale's complaining notes
> Tune my distresses and record my woes.
> (V, iv, 4–6)

1. Harry Forbes Witherby, *et al.*, *The Handbook of British Birds*, 5 vols. (London: H. F. and G. Witherby, 1938–41).

Elizabethan poetry is full of voices, but it has little to say about physical appearances. The poets are most apt to mention colour, but it is usually quite simple, a handful of stock conventions which are limited to a small number of birds. The most common is the image which says, in effect, that the swan is white – milk white; snow white; silver. Doves are also white, and the blackbird and crows are black. Shakespeare's song beginning, 'The woosel cock so black of hue,/With orange-tawny bill', is more visual than usual, because he not only tells us that the blackbird is black, he adds that its beak is yellow, and then he says that the wren is small and the cuckoo grey. When you think how sophisticated the treatment of sound is, it seems strange that the visual conventions were so undeveloped. It was certainly not ignorance. In some ways, their experience of birds was more direct than ours, what with hunting birds with hawks, not to mention all the bird-catching with traps and nets and lime. It could be that their interest in music made them think of birds as voices. Shakespeare knew that the cuckoo was grey, but in 'The woosel cock' it is quite incidental, something slipped in for the rhyme, the point being the voice.

> The plain-song cuckoo grey,
> Whose note full many a man doth mark,
> And dares not answer nay.

Whatever the reason, the fact is that while you can often *hear* the birds, unless you know what they look like, you usually cannot see them.

One would never guess from the poetry that the sixteenth century marks the beginning of a more objective study of birds. Naturalists were starting to look at the real bird but the poets, as Sir Philip Sidney said, disdained to be tied to any such subjection. They 'grow in effect another nature, in making things either better than nature bringeth forth, or, quite anew, forms such as never were in nature'.[1] For all their artificiality, however, Elizabethan birds have a certain underlying naturalism. This is most apparent in their voices. As in Skelton, many of the images evoke some recognizable characteristic of the real voice. The moans of the dove, for instance, suggest its plaintive, monotonously repeated calls, while conventions like *jug, jug* and *tu whit tu who* are echoic words which imitate actual notes. Even the musical group image has a realistic base, and that is that each kind of song bird has a distinctive way of singing. Since the madrigal consists of a polyphonic interweaving of various parts, it is a most ingenious way of suggesting the individual songs, as in Browne's concert where each part represents the voice of a different bird.

1. 'An Apology for Poetry', in Roy Lamson and Hallett Smith (eds.), *The Golden Hind* (New York: W. W. Norton, 1942), p. 563.

As a rule, the singing groups are made up of birds which have true songs. The Elizabethans would not stick in a parrot, not just because of the voice, but because they place birds in a more realistic manner. They thought that the swan was very musical, but they would never have it perched in a tree like Lydgate's pelican, singing with a nightingale and a lark. The swan floats on the water, the lark sings in the sky, the nightingale sits in a bush. The settings are still quite vague, but they are beginning to suggest, if only in the simplest way, the characteristic environment.

Elizabethan bird poetry is touched with a new naturalism, but it is not yet cut off from the rich bird lore of the medieval period. It can still move back and forth, it can still use the old with the new. No one illustrates this more dramatically than Drayton, who was born in 1563, a year before Shakespeare, and who died in 1631 when Milton was twenty-three years old. His work shows a growing interest in real birds, and yet throughout his career he continues to use the birds of tradition. Sometimes he reverts to the medieval; at other times he is typically Elizabethan. The best example of his realism is a passage in the *Polyolbion* of 1622. He starts out with a specific locale, the Lincolnshire fens, and then he writes an account of twenty-six water birds which inhabit the region. It is not just marsh in general, it is deeps, rushes, shallows, and most of the birds are shown in a typical habitat like the wild swan swimming on the pool. Although many of the names are familiar, Drayton did not limit himself to birds which were used in poetry. Take the wild ducks. Of his six different species, the mallard was a minor bird of poetry and the widgeon and the teal were marginal, but Drayton is the first poet to use the goosander,[1] the goldeneye, and the smeath. Only Skelton approaches him in variety, but Drayton's account is not just a list, it is a series of shifting scenes. The eye moves from vast flocks of ducks, covering the water, then darkening the sky, to vignettes of individual birds – the dabchick diving, the heron hunting in the reeds. Elizabethan birds are usually static – they sit and sing – but Drayton gives a sense of almost continuous movement. Ducks flock from mere to mere, gulls search for food. One does not hear these birds, one *sees* them, usually in action but occasionally with a sharp visual detail that is drawn from direct observation. For instance, when Drayton says that the white which the coot has on its forehead the moorhen[2] wears on its tail, he is distinguishing between two black water birds of about the same size and the same shape. His descriptions are not scientifically exact, but they are excellent as general approximations. Take the goosander. 'His head as ebon black, the rest

1. In America, the merganser.
2. In America it is called the common or Florida gallinule.

as white as snow,' Drayton says. This does not agree with the detailed account in Peterson[1] ('pinkish-white breast and under-parts, black back, glossy greenish-black head'), but it is almost the same as the brief description which accompanies the plate – 'Long white body, dark head'.[2] Which is accurate enough for any poet, not to mention a poet of this period!

In *Noah's Flood*, which was published in 1630, Drayton goes back to conventional material which he enlivens with touches of realism. Like Skelton's funeral, the ark scene is a grand assembly which represents all the birds in the world. Some are pure medieval like the 'careful stork' which symbolized filial piety because it was supposed to take care of its aged parents. Others are typically Elizabethan. The most charming example is the scene where, when the small birds hear the nightingale sing,

> They soon set to her, each a part doth take,
> As by their music up a choir to make.
>
> (ll. 899–900)

The birds are conventional, but here and there Drayton handles them naturalistically. This is especially true of the movements – the lark drops down, the kestrel hovers. Occasionally, he shifts to a realistic style so visual, so immediate, that for a moment you see a real bird. The best example is the dove. It finds land,

> And wondrous proud that he a place had found,
> Who of a long time had not touched the ground,
> Draws in his head and thrusteth out his breast,
> Spreadeth his tail and swelleth up his crest,
> And turning round and round with cuttry coo,
> As when the female pigeon and he woo;
> Bathing himself, which long he had not done,
> And dries his feathers in the welcome sun,
> Pruning his plumage, cleansing every quill.
>
> (ll. 857–65)

Obviously, Drayton did not think that realistic birds invalidated the birds of tradition. He not only uses both in the same work, he combines them in peculiar blends, adding naturalistic touches to conventional types. The two are not yet incompatible, and so his Ark can contain a realistic pigeon along with Bestiary types and madrigal singers.

While Drayton was experimenting with realism, other poets went on using the old conventions. The widowed dove is still complaining, and Philomel – 'Most musical, most melancholy' – nightly 'her sad song

---

1. *A Field Guide to the Birds of Britain and Europe.*
2. This has been changed in the second edition (1966).

mourneth well'. The content is still Elizabethan, but there is a tendency, already apparent earlier in the century, towards the mannered, the exaggerated, the excessive. Periphrases become more common. Instead of simple things like sweet birds, there are elegant conceits – happy choristers of air; sirens of the grove; winged choirs. (Sometimes they are a bit too clever, as when Drummond says, 'Wild citizens, Amphions of the trees' when all he means is birds.) The content itself is exaggerated. Carew has the nightingale winter in his lady's throat, and Lovelace takes the swan which sings as it dies and says that for his falcon's funeral, it will die in order to sing. (A most obliging swan.) Even the pelican can be used as an extravagant conceit.

> Down in a garden sat my dearest love,
> Her skin more soft and white than down of swan,
> More tender-hearted than the turtle dove,
> And far more kind than bleeding pelican.
> (*from* 'Down in a garden')

A typical seventeenth-century image is the nightingale which drops dead after losing a contest. The basic idea comes from Pliny who, in discussing the nightingale's song in *Natural History*, said:

> And that no one may doubt its being a matter of science, the birds have several songs each, and not all the same but every bird songs of its own. They compete with one another, and there is clearly an animated rivalry between them; the loser often ends her life by dying, her breath giving out before her song.[1]

> (Book X, xliii, 83)

The idea in itself seems quite fantastic, but in the seventeenth century it was pushed to greater heights, to more bizarre extremes. The birds not only compete with each other, they have contests with human beings. 'Music's first martyr', Benlowes calls the nightingale, an apt description because, since she always loses, she always dies, 'O'ercome by art and grief'. In Crashaw's *Music's Duel*, a brilliant poem about a competition between a nightingale and a lute player, the defeated bird not only dies of grief, she falls on the master's lute which thus becomes her grave. Cowley has Orpheus compete not just with one nightingale but with a number. When they lose, they *all* drop dead, falling in a group on the poor man's lyre. A rain of larks!

> Happy, O happy they whose tomb might be,
> Mausolus, envied by thee!
> (from *Ode I, On the Praise of Poetry*)

1. Translation by Harris Rackham.

James Shirley actually *asks* the birds to die, as if death were an elegant gesture, a mere flourish performed for the effect.

> Ye warbling nightingales repair
> From every wood, to charm this air,
> And with the wonders of your breast,
> Each striving to excel the rest,
> When it is time to wake him, close your parts,
> And drop down from the trees with broken hearts.
>
> (*A Song*, ll. 11-16, from *The Triumph of Beauty*)

Although song is still a theme, the poetry of the mid seventeenth century is no longer preoccupied with birds as musical voices. Lovelace has a poem about a fight to death between a hawk and a heron, while Vaughan turns barnyard cocks into mystical birds of light. The most interesting example is Marvell's *Upon Appleton House*, a long poem believed to date from the early sixteen-fifties. One passage is basically Elizabethan, all music, with winged choirs, nightingale, and doves, but this is not characteristic of the poem. Instead of song, Marvell has realistic glimpses of birds he happens to see as he walks around the estate.

> Then as I careless on the bed
> Of gelid strawberries do tread,
> And through the hazels thick espy
> The hatching throstle's shining eye,
> The heron from the ash's top
> The eldest of its young lets drop.
>
> (ll. 529-34)

No doubt Drayton was familiar with the Lincolnshire birds, but we do not see them through his eyes at a particular moment in time. Take his black-headed white duck which appears with the mallards and teals. It could well represent something he actually saw, but in the poem it stands for the goosander as such, like a bird description in a Field Guide. Marvell is completely different. He gives us the feeling that he really looks at the birds, really watches them, really sees them with his own eyes, and yet no matter how realistic he is, the objective bird is always shaped by his poetic vision. It is not the bird as such, like Drayton's goosander, it is the bird which *Marvell* sees, coloured by his mind, 'that ocean', as he says in *The Garden*, 'where each kind/Does straight its own resemblance find'.

The best example is the halcyon passage, a complex image in which the real kingfisher and the halcyon of fable[1] are fused into Marvell's

---

[1]. Since the legendary halcyon was identified with the kingfisher, poets often called the kingfisher the halcyon.

bird, the resemblance. The sun puts its head behind blushing clouds. As shadows begin to close like black shutters over the river,

> The modest halcyon comes in sight,
> Flying betwixt the day and night.
>   (ll. 669–70)

According to tradition, it is supposed to calm the winter sea as it broods on its floating nest, and in a charming hyperbole, Marvell attributes the sunset calm to the fact that nature, upon seeing the kingfisher, is struck dumb with admiration. Water, air, fishes, even men are all hushed and motionless, caught in the magic spell of the halcyon. The real kingfisher is evoked in two images which turn accurate observation into brilliant metaphor. To understand them, one must envisage the actual bird. James Harting, the nineteenth-century naturalist, says it flies so straight and fast 'that when the sunlight falls upon its bright blue back, it seems as if an azure bolt from a crossbow had been suddenly shot across our path'.[1] Marvell says something quite similar.

> The viscous air, wheres'e'er she fly,
> Follows and sucks her azure dye.
>   (ll. 673–4)

Here the speed is suggested by the image of the blue streak. The second figure combines the same two qualities, swiftness and colour – it moves so fast, it blurs into a hazy blue.

> And men the silent scene assist,
> Charmed with the sapphire-wingèd mist.
>   (ll. 679–80)

To Marvell, the little halcyon calming the winter storms resembles the ideal woman. In one of the dream visions in *The Gallery*, 'halcyons, calming all that's nigh', dart around his lady who sits like Venus in her pearly boat, and in *A Poem upon the Death of His Late Highness the Lord Protector*, Cromwell's daughter is one of the 'halcyons kind' because whenever she appears to her father, she 'calms his growing cares'. In the *Appleton* poem the halcyon symbolizes Lord Fairfax's daughter, whom Marvell had tutored when he lived at Appleton House. As the kingfisher charms the sunset river scene, so Maria hushes the world, herself a halcyon.

The birds in *Appleton House* are very different from those in the usual seventeenth-century poem. What makes them so remarkable is not just

1. James Edmund Harting, *The Ornithology of Shakespeare* (London: John van Voorst, 1871), p. 276. Reissued as *The Birds of Shakespeare* (Chicago: Argonaut, 1965).

the fresh visual detail, but the subjective way in which Marvell uses it. Drayton at his most realistic sounds like a naturalist, but Marvell is a birdwatcher-poet, transmuting what he sees into images of rich complexity.

In the second half of the seventeenth century, there was a marked increase in the development of science. Compare, for example, Sir Thomas Browne's *Vulgar Errors* of 1646 with his *Notes on the Natural History of Norfolk* written some twenty years later. The first takes us back to what William Dunn calls 'that region of half-lights and uncertain ground in which the seventeenth century made its reluctant, groping transition from age-long modes of thought to the ruling conceptions of the modern world'.[1] To give some examples, Browne accepts the fable of the halcyon, but he cannot decide how it happens that the winds cease and the waves are calm so long as the birds are in their nest. He does not believe that swans sing as they die, however. In fact, he doubts that the swan is capable of song because it has a flat bill and no flat-billed bird was ever commended for its note. But he thinks that there might be some truth in the old story about the pelican. (There is, of course, none.)

> A possibility there may be of opening and bleeding their breast, for this may be done by the uncous and pointed extremity of their bill: and some probability also that they sometimes do it for their own relief, though not for their young ones; that is, by nibbling and biting themselves on their itching part of their breast, upon fullness or acrimony of blood.

If *Vulgar Errors* is full of half lights, the Norfolk *Notes* read like the jottings of a naturalist. Instead of the halcyon, he has 'that handsome coloured bird', the kingfisher, which abounds on rivulets, becks, and streams and builds in holes 'wherein is to be found great quantity of small fish bones'.[2] A paragraph on the wild swan discusses its winter migrations, and the bleeding pelican has been replaced by a real pelican which was shot in 1663 and 'which stuffed and cleansed I yet retain'.

> It was 3 yards and half between the extremities of the wings, the jowl and beak answering the usual description; the extremities of the wings for a span deep brown, the rest of the body white. A fowl which none could remember

1. William P. Dunn, *Sir Thomas Browne* (Minneapolis: University of Minnesota Press, 1950), p. 4.
2. Kenneth Richmond says, 'The Kingfisher's domestic arrangements are apt to become highly insanitary . . . as anyone who has tried putting his nose to the entrance will know. Very often a thin trickle of slime exudes from the underground passage, and inspection of the interior shows that the nest-chamber is a mess of decomposed fish-bones' (*Birds in Britain* (London: Odhams Press, 1962), p. 128).

upon this coast. About the same time I heard one of the King's pelicans was lost at St. James, perhaps this might be the same.

The 1670s saw the publication of Francis Willughby and John Ray's *Ornithologia*, a monumental work which laid the foundation for the scientific study of birds. A new world was opening, but its effect upon bird poetry was very negative. The old traditions began to collapse, and as Richard Fogle says, 'The Royal Society's drive for denotative accuracy of language struck at the validity of poetic imagery and figure.'[1] A poet brought up on the music of the dying swan might well be discouraged by Mr Ray's description of its wind-pipe.

> The wind-pipe after a strange and wonderful manner enters the breast-bone in a cavity prepared for it and is therein reflected and after its egress at the divarication is contracted into a narrow compass by a broad and bony cartilage, then being divided into two branches goes on to the lungs.[2]

Strange and wonderful it no doubt is, but it was not the stuff that poetry was made of. As Marvell says in his poem on the death of Cromwell,

> Who now shall tell us more of mournful swans,
> Of halcyons kind or bleeding pelicans?
>
> (ll. 79–80)

Who, indeed, if the swan cannot sing, if the pelican gouges itself because it itches, and the beautiful kingfisher, instead of floating on the winter sea, nests in a hole which is stuffed with stinking fish bones. The Marvell lines actually refer to Cromwell and his daughter,[3] but taken out of context they sound like a lament for the old bird lore, that rich lode which poets had mined for centuries.

Bird poetry retreated to a perfunctory conventionalism. While naturalists were describing birds according to specific distinctions, poets used a vocabulary which is an impoverished version of the Elizabethans'. For the most part, everything is colourless, generalized, unreal. A good example is Dryden. He has several hundred images using specific birds, but the bulk of them are either in his translations or in the swallow fable in *The Hind and the Panther*. The rest of his poetry has a relatively small

1. Alex Preminger (ed.), *Princeton Encyclopedia of Poetry and Poetics* (Princton: Princeton University Press, 1965), p. 231.
2. Charles Earle Raven, *John Ray, Naturalist, his Life and Works* (2nd edn, Cambridge: Cambridge University Press, 1950), p. 328.
3. Both are swans because they knew that they were dying; she is a halcyon and he a pelican because his grief for his daughter, who died three weeks before he did, hastened his own death.

number, most of them completely conventional. There are sun-gazing eagles, new-born phoenixes, doves from the Ark. In one poem, poets mount like eagles – another says that at the Last Judgement they will rise like mounting larks. In 1630, Drayton could combine realistic observations with poetic conventions. His Ark represents a world which is still whole, but the new science split it apart, leaving a gulf between the poets' birds and the birds of the ornithologists.

IV

The eighteenth century narrowed the gap by using conventions which were a reasonable approximation of the real bird. It was a period of deflation, a general scaling down in which the wilder excesses were weeded out. With some birds, the old symbolism was retained but it was expressed in more naturalistic terms. The robin covering up the dead, for example, turns into the friendly winter visitor, while the halcyon, instead of magically calming the seas, becomes the blue-coloured bird of the peaceful summer river. Where a tradition was more complex, the changes are less noticeable. Take the nightingale. She no longer sings with her breast against a thorn, nor does she throw herself into those contests which lead inexorably to her death. The rape also disappears, leaving an aura of unhappy love, but she is still Philomel, still the songstress of the night, still the solace of the lonely and the lovelorn. At the opposite extreme is the pelican. It was practically identified with its bleeding, perhaps because, since there were no pelicans in Britain, it had become in effect a legendary bird. In the seventeenth century it functioned both as a religious emblem and a fashionable conceit, but in the eighteenth it all but disappeared, no doubt because, to 'eyes of sense and reason', its legend is not only grotesque, it is patently absurd, a relic of the medieval, a remnant of the Bestiaries.

If the pelican could not survive, there were birds which flourished in the new climate. A good example is the lark. A bird of middling rank, it rose to a dominant position because it could be perfectly adapted to eighteenth-century poetry. Unlike the bleeding pelican, which is the essence of the anti-rational, the lark of the poets had always been basically realistic. From Chaucer on, it was a sky singer associated with spring and dawn, so that it not only had an old tradition which was sanctioned by the best poets, it also combined the conventional with the naturalistic. Samuel Johnson said that an intelligent reader sickens at the sight of words like crook or sheep, which it is not necessary to mention because the poet 'ought to show the beauties without the grossness of the country life'.[1] But no one could object to the lark. On the contrary, it was a model of what the eighteenth century called elegance. Simple, tasteful, correct, it was an ideal adornment for the rural scene, as in the lovely lines from Gray's *Ode on the Pleasure Arising from Vicissitude.*

> But chief, the skylark warbles high
> His trembling thrilling ecstasy;
> And, lessening from the dazzled sight,
> Melts into air and liquid light.
>
> (ll. 13–16)

The eighteenth century not only trimmed the birds of tradition to reasonable shapes, it also introduced a certain order into the confusion of bird names. Seventeenth-century poets used a rich variety of words. The most common were simple generic terms, such as eagle or swan, but there were also specific names like sparrow hawk, as well as various literary, folk, and regional names. What makes it confusing is that some birds had more than one name. The most extreme are the robin, which in seventeenth-century poetry had five names – ruddock, redbreast, robin redbreast, robin, robinet – and the blackbird which had three: blackbird, merle, and ouzel, sometimes spelled woosel. There was very little sense of one kind of word being preferable to another. To give some examples, Mildmay Fane has Philomel in a group of birds which includes 'little washdish or wagtail'. In the *Appleton House* poem, Marvell uses a poetic name, halcyon, in one passage, and in another, he calls the green wood-pecker the hewel, which is a variant of the provincial name hickwall. Even more curious, in Sylvester's *Du Bartas*, Madge, a folk name for the barn owl, appears in the midst of an imposing array of birds which represent the fowl of the air which God created on the fifth day: 'The scritch owl, used in falling towers to lodge,/Th' unlucky night raven, and thou lazy Madge.'

Eighteenth-century poets used language in a much more restrictive way. Their standards were correctness, elegance, propriety – the right word in the right place. They did not mix up different kinds. As a rule, they chose simple common names, avoiding the rare, the archaic, and the provincial. With the exception of a few literary words like Chanticleer, most birds had only one name. Where variations exist, they are almost always self-explanatory, as when throstle is used for thrush, or the owl is called the screech owl. Folk names were limited to certain kinds of poetry, usually the fable. No one writing a serious poem would have used a name like little washdish. In fact, the chances are that no one would have used

1. George Birkbeck Hill (ed.), *Lives of the English Poets* (Oxford: Clarendon Press, 1905), Vol. III. p. 356.

wagtail because, although it is a perfectly valid name, still standard today, to ears attuned to elegance it would sound too coarse, something which Dr Johnson would pounce on with disgust.

The choice of bird names was dictated by the standards of poetry, but it also reflects a more scientific terminology because, except for literary words like Philomel, almost every name which poets used was also used by naturalists. Blackbird instead of ouzel or merle; redbreast instead of ruddock. (The chief exception is halcyon, which poets preferred to king-fisher.) A reader familiar with British birds will recognize practically every name in eighteenth-century poetry, which is not true of the sixteenth and seventeenth centuries where a number of names are now obsolete or dialectal.[1] Even the periphrases are often marked by an accuracy which at times approaches the scientific. Seventeenth-century periphrases are chiefly musical, the most common words being chorister and choir. The key word in the eighteenth century is feathered. It is often used with musical terms, particularly choir, but what is most characteristic is the combination of feathered with an abstract noun denoting a large group – legions, throng, race, tribe, nation. The seventeenth-century figures have a certain charm, but all these feathered tribes and feathered races strike us as ridiculous, no doubt because at the back of the mind there is a lurking image of people with glued-on feathers, tarred and feathered without the tar. To borrow a phrase from Dr Johnson, we can scarce check our risibility, which prevents us from seeing what these images are supposed to do. Generally speaking, the seventeenth century defined birds as singing animals. Since man also sings, this makes them a kind of supporting cast, singing along with men. The typical eighteenth-century phrase forces the reader to think of birds in terms of their most characteristic trait, the only one they possess which is unique to birds. It is not their song, not even their flight, but the fact that they are covered with feathers instead of naked skin or fur or scales. Words like nation and race heighten the sense of birds as a distinct group, separate not just from man but from fishes and beasts. All this seems obvious to us, but in the eighteenth century it was part of a new way of looking at birds.

The interest in real birds is most apparent in those conventions which were developed in the eighteenth century. The most striking is the bird-shooting scene. In the seventeenth century an increasing number of sportsmen used firearms to kill birds,[2] but as a rule, poetry did not reflect

1. Such as pavone, queest, gripe, haysugge, staniel, nope, elk, hecco – meaning the peacock, the wood pigeon, the vulture, the hedge sparrow, the kestrel, the bullfinch, the whooper swan, and the green woodpecker.

2. George Macaulay Trevelyan, *Illustrated English Social History* (London and New York: Longmans, Green, 1950), Vol. II, p. 137.

this until the eighteenth century when the gun displaced the falcon.[1] By far the most brilliant scene – and the one which had the greatest influence – is in Pope's *Windsor Forest*, which was published in 1713.

> See! from the brake the whirring pheasant springs,
> And mounts exulting on triumphant wings:
> Short is his joy; he feels the fiery wound,
> Flutters in blood, and panting beats the ground.
> Ah! what avail his glossy, varying dyes,
> His purple crest, and scarlet-circled eyes,
> The vivid green his shining plumes unfold,
> His painted wings, and breast that flames with gold?
>
> (ll. 111–18)

And a few lines later:

> With slaught'ring guns th'unwearied fowler roves,
> When frosts have whitened all the naked groves;
> Where doves in flocks the leafless trees o'ershade,
> And lonely woodcocks haunt the wat'ry glade.
> He lifts the tube, and levels with his eye;
> Straight a short thunder breaks the frozen sky:
> Oft, as in airy rings they skim the heath,
> The clam'rous lapwings feel the leaden death:
> Oft, as the mounting larks their notes prepare,
> They fall, and leave their little lives in air.
>
> (ll. 125–34)

After the endless parade of conventional images, it is startling to come upon something so fresh, so direct, so visual. This is especially true of the pheasant with its sharp pictorial detail. Compare what Pope says to a description in a modern bird book.

> Burnished copper-coloured male, with his metallic dark green head and neck, red wattles surrounding eye, and ear-like tufts at back of crown . . . Flight . . . begins with rapid wing-beats, causing loud whirring as bird rises . . .[2]

By these standards Pope is not entirely accurate, but it is a vivid portrait and at that period it was remarkable for its close observation.

Although the pheasant is the most striking, all the birds are treated quite realistically both in their behaviour and their habitat, which ranges from the woods to the open country. By showing the birds in new ways, Pope eliminates much of the automatic symbolism that clusters around

1. The bird-shooting scene in Sylvester's *Du Bartas*, published in the 1590s, is of particular interest, partly because it is so early and partly because it foreshadows Pope. (See p. 173.)
2. *The Handbook of British Birds*, Vol. V, p. 234.

the traditional types. Take the woodcock. In poetry it stood for a fool, because it was supposed to be exceptionally stupid. 'O this woodcock, what an ass it is!' Shakespeare says. Pope by-passes the traditional bird by evoking a real woodcock. He does this partly by using a typical habitat – a wet woodland glade – and partly by characterizing it in terms of its actual behaviour. As *The Handbook of British Birds* says, the woodcock is among the least sociable of the waders, 'practically always seen singly, birds behaving quite independently even when a number are present in one covert'.[1] Pope intensifies this by calling it lonely, and as a result it takes on an elegiac beauty, not Shakespeare's ass but the potential victim, unaware of the slaughtering guns. Of all these birds, only the lark is used conventionally. Pope varies it by showing it in winter, a realistic touch since it sings for most of the year, but it is still the poets' lark, symbol of dawn, the bird that sings at heaven's gate. No doubt Pope uses it because his sympathies lie with the birds, and to end with such an appealing victim makes the hunter seem more brutal. It is one thing to shoot game birds, but to gun down larks seems pointlessly cruel, more a massacre of innocents than a sport.

The most important realistic bird poetry of the eighteenth century is in Thomson's poem, *The Seasons*, which came out in 1730 and was substantially revised in the edition of 1744. There are bird passages in all the Seasons, but the most significant is in *Spring*, which contains a long section of 216 lines. Thomson himself announces that he is writing on a new subject, or as he puts it, he will 'touch a theme/Unknown to fame – the passion of the groves'. It is an unfortunate phrase and quite misleading, because the real subject is altogether different. Dr Johnson said, 'The reader of *The Seasons* wonders that he never saw before what Thomson shows him.'[2] In this passage, it is the round of activities set off by the spring songs – the courtship; the nest building; the brooding; the care and feeding of the young. Thomson calls it the passion of the groves because he endows the birds with human emotions. It is love, exalting love, which inspires their behaviour. At times they sound like a kind of people, with lovers, and connubial leagues, and parents instructing their feathered youth.

> . . . Oh, what passions then,
> What melting sentiments of kindly care
> On the new parents seize! . . .
>
> (ll. 674–6)

To us, all these raptures are rather trying, but no doubt they helped his

---

1. *The Handbook of British Birds*, Vol. IV, p. 186.
2. *Lives of the English Poets*, Vol. III, p. 299.

readers to accept what for poetry was a radically new approach. One can see it most clearly when he is not being sentimental. A good example is the nest-building passage. Having chosen their sites – a hedge, a grassy dale, the bank of a woodland brook,

> They frame the first foundation of their domes – [1]
> Dry sprigs of trees, in artful fabric laid,
> And bound with clay together. Now 'tis nought
> But restless hurry through the busy air,
> Beat by unnumbered wings. The swallow sweeps
> The slimy pool, to build his hanging house
> Intent. And often, from the careless back
> Of herds and flocks, a thousand tugging bills
> Pluck hair and wool; and oft, when unobserved,
> Steal from the barn a straw – till soft and warm,
> Clean and complete, their habitation grows.
>
> (ll. 650–60)

Sir Philip Sidney said that the poet could improve upon nature, but the eighteenth century, in its enthusiasm for science, was fascinated by the workings of the real world. It is this interest which Thomson expresses when he tells his readers what materials are used in the nests, or how the dam broods on the eggs until the young 'their brittle bondage break'. From our point of view he is much too anthropomorphic, but this does not change the fact that he is writing about birds as birds. For centuries poets had used birds as accessories to the human scene. They are symbols, metaphors, even servants in the sense that their actions are often treated as if they were performed for the benefit of man. When Pope says, ' Is it for thee the lark ascends and sings?' the answer for poetry in general is obviously *yes*. He announces dawn, he wakes people up. But in *The Seasons*, the answer is no. Thomson's birds do not stand for something else. They are themselves, birds, immersed in activities that have nothing to do with man. What made Thomson unique was not his specific detail. He has nothing as sensitive as Marvell's kingfisher, nothing as visual as the pheasant in Pope. His great contribution lay in his larger views. No doubt the most popular was the idea that birds are motivated by love.

> 'Tis love creates their melody, and all
> This waste of music is the voice of love.
>
> (ll. 614–15)

But more important, Thomson gives an objective account of how birds actually function, especially in *Spring*, which gives the full round of bird life from the first songs to the young adults who take off on their own,

1. house, home

next year's parents who will repeat the same cycle. In the poem as a whole, he shows how the complex pattern of bird life fits into the larger pattern of the seasons, from the vast migrations set off by autumn to the breeding cycle which begins in spring. Thomson's birds are a part of nature. If at times they are too sentimental, at their best they can be quite strong, as in the passage from *Autumn* which suggests the lonely grandeur of huge flocks remote from man.

> Or, where the Northern Ocean in vast whirls
> Boils round the naked melancholy isles
> Of farthest Thule, and the Atlantic surge
> Pours in among the stormy Hebrides,
> Who can recount what transmigrations there
> Are annual made? what nations come and go?
> And how the living clouds on clouds arise,
> Infinite wings! till all the plume-dark air
> And rude resounding shore are one wild cry?
>
> (ll. 862–70)

Thomson's greatest influence came towards the end of the eighteenth and the beginning of the nineteenth century. In fact, so many poets borrowed from *The Seasons* that it became a kind of source book. As Dwight Durling says,

> And even when poets began turning to natural history, to close knowledge of birds, flowers, trees, and animals . . . Thomson was still their guide . . . They learned to see, partly by seeing through his eyes.[1]

Although *The Seasons* was very popular, the bird passages are not typical of eighteenth-century bird poetry, which was not only quite conventional but was also much more generalized. Johnson sums up the standards in his famous dictum from *Rasselas* which was published in 1759.

> The business of a poet . . . is to examine, not the individual, but the species; to remark general properties and large appearances: he does not number the streaks of the tulip, or describe the different shades in the verdure of the forest. He is to exhibit in his portraits of nature such prominent and striking features, as recall the original to every mind; and must neglect the minuter discriminations, which one may have remarked, and another have neglected, for those characteristics which are alike obvious to vigilance and carelessness.
>
> (Ch. X)

By these standards, Drayton's ducks are the streaks on the tulip. Instead of describing wild ducks in general, he presents individual species – the huge flocks of mallards, the bunches of dabbling teals, the goosander

1. D. L. Durling, *Georgic Tradition in English Poetry* (New York: Columbia University Press, 1935), p. 124.

with its black head. In the eighteenth century, however, poets not only simplified the bird names, they also simplified the birds. Where two or more are closely related – swallow and martin, buzzard and kite – they usually concentrated on one (swallow; kite). So with the ducks: instead of using different species, they almost always said 'wild duck', the old name for the mallard which, as Kenneth Richmond says, most people think of as *the* wild duck.[1] Ornithologists were still discovering new species, but eighteenth-century poets actually used fewer birds than the seventeenth-century poets had because they preferred the general to the specific.[2]

If Drayton's ducks are the streaks on the tulip, Pope's pheasant is too detailed because it has those 'minuter discriminations' which would not be obvious to the careless. Pope himself must have come to the same conclusion, because after *Windsor Forest*, he shifted from realistic birds to stereotypes. Yet interestingly enough, once the pheasant was sanctioned by Pope, other writers imitated it. Gay borrowed a single detail – 'the red-eyed pheasant'. But there were others who helped themselves more generously.

> See from the brake the lonely pheasant fly,
> Mark his rich plumage and his scarlet eye!
> (Samuel Boyse, *Retirement*,
> Part I, ll. 249–50)

> Ah! see the pheasant fluttering in the brake,
> Green, azure, gold, but undistinguished gore!
> (Edward Lovibond, *On Rural Sports*,
> ll. 13–14)

It is still realistic, but the sharp details have been reduced to a few over-simplified generalizations. (Red eye is not the same as red *circled* eye.) Pope's pheasant has been turned into a convention like the halcyon of the river.

Although Johnson's dictum says nothing about stereotypes, one of the dominant traits of eighteenth-century bird poetry is its use of conventions. Poets not only concentrate upon the same small number of birds, they use them in the same way over and over, again and again and again. The eagle is the sovereign of the sky; the owl shrieks in graveyards and ruins. It is like a repertory company where the same actors are always playing the same roles. The three most common are the lark

---

1. *Birds in Britain*, p. 48.
2. Shakespeare used at least 60 different birds, Drayton over 90, but Thomson, 'the poet of nature', has barely 35.

at dawn, the amorous dove, and the nightingale singing at night. So in Joseph Warton's poem, *The Enthusiast, or the Lover of Nature.*

> . . . The shrill lark,
> That wakes the wood-man to his early task,
> Or love-sick Philomel, whose luscious lays
> Soothe lone night-wanderers, the moaning dove
> Pitied by listening milk maid . . .
>
> (ll. 38–42)

We see this as an impoverishment, but actually it is part of what Johnson called general properties and large appearances. The eighteenth-century naturalist Gilbert White said that the number of bird species known in Great Britain was 252. Of these, however, only about thirty were used with any frequency in poetry. Presumably, they stand for various types of birds, exhibiting characteristics which were common knowledge, such as the fact that the lark sings in the sky. But even the best conventions have limits, and the more often they were repeated, the more stagnant they became. Mad Christopher Smart sounds eminently sane when he says, 'For nature is more various than observation though observers be innumerable.' Naturalists were exploring this variety, but the poets had locked themselves up in a world of stereotypes.

Gilbert White is a good example of this dichotomy. A clergyman who was passionately interested in nature, he described himself as 'an outdoor naturalist, one that takes his observations from the subject itself, and not from the writings of others'. His *Natural History of Selborne*, based on letters written over a twenty-year period and published in 1789, is a classic which still charms the reader today. Although White limits himself to the district around his village, he creates a world which suggests the inexhaustible variety of Smart's nature. Instead of large generalities, it is filled with those particulars which Johnson said are not the business of the poet. Even when he generalizes, he keeps recording the most exact details, as in his image of the swallow hunting.

> When a fly is taken a smart snap from her bill is heard, resembling the noise at the shutting of a watch-case . . .
>
> (Barrington, Letter XVIII)

His eye is so sharp, he can make even the ordinary seem fresh.

> Thus an hen, just become a mother, is no longer that placid bird she used to be, but with feathers standing on end, wings hovering, and clocking note, she runs about like one possessed.
>
> (Barrington, Letter XIV)

If White is still read today, it is because he has an extraordinary ability to make the reader see and hear. So, for example, in his description of the evening manoeuvres of the rooks.

> Just before dusk they return in long strings from the foraging of the day, and rendezvous by thousands over Selborne-down, where they wheel round in the air, and sport and dive in a playful manner, all the while exerting their voices, and making a loud cawing, which, being blended and softened by the distance that we at the village are below them, becomes a confused noise or chiding; or rather a pleasing murmur, very engaging to the imagination, and not unlike the cry of a pack of hounds in hollow, echoing woods, or the rushing of the wind in tall trees, or the tumbling of the tide upon a pebbly shore. When this ceremony is over, with the last gleam of day, they retire for the night to the deep beechen woods of Tisted and Ropley.

(Barrington, Letter LIX)

C. J. Horne says that prior to Wordsworth, 'the most truly poetic response to the life of the plant and animal world' is to be found in Gilbert White's *Selborne*.[1] Needless to say, this is not true by eighteenth-century standards. In fact, White himself would have been astonished, because in his own verse, he eliminated practically every sign of what Horne calls his poetic response. Here are some lines from his poem, *Selborne Hanger*.

> Return, dear nymphs; prevent[2] the purple spring,
> Ere the soft nightingale essays to sing;
> Ere the first swallow sweeps the fresh'ning plain,
> Ere love-sick turtles breathe their amorous pain.

(ll. 29–32)

These are not the birds which White saw in Selborne, they are Birds of Poetry, part of that limited group which had become as static as if it had been turned into a canon. In *The Naturalist's Summer Evening Walk*, White tried something different. The title itself is an announcement – he appears in his own person, the outdoor naturalist, and instead of stereotypes, he has realistic pictures of birds in action. Yet interestingly enough, the effect is quite conventional, because everything is bathed, at times even drowned, in that elevated language, the so-called poetic diction, which is characteristic of certain kinds of eighteenth-century poetry.

> While high in air, and poised upon his wings,
> Unseen, the soft enamoured wood lark sings.

In the context, one hardly notices these lines, because the 'soft' wood lark blurs into the 'soft quail' at the beginning of the poem, not to

---

1. 'Literature and Science', in *The Pelican Guide to English Literature*, ed. Boris Ford (Harmondsworth: Penguin Books, 1965), Vol. IV, p. 201.
2, come in advance of

mention the 'soft nightingale' of *Selborne Hanger*. White must have been pleased with the lines because he used them in another poem. But pleased or not, when he put the *Summer Evening Walk* in *Selborne*, he added a footnote which restates the image in prose.

> In hot summer nights wood larks soar to a prodigious height, and hang singing in the air.
>
> (Pennant, Letter XXIV)

Obviously, what White said as a poet did not satisfy him as a naturalist, but what he saw as a naturalist, he could not say as a poet. Hence the footnote, simple and exact, appended to the vague image of the poem. The crux of the dilemma is language. In his prose, White has a vivid style, lively and clear, but it is filled with plain words which he could not use in his verse because he was writing in a conventional manner. Prose could be a pig's ear but poetry had to be silk. In *Selborne* the owls 'sally forth' and 'beat the fields over like a setting-dog',[1] but the owl in the *Summer Evening Walk* 'skims round the grassy mead'. No doubt this was more poetic, but it is so general that one could substitute swallow without noticing the difference. In *Selborne Hanger*, the elegant, rather artificial language is perfectly suited to the stylized birds. The one expresses the other. But to use the same manner in a more realistic work is like trying to do a pencil sketch with a broad-tipped brush. In its content, the *Summer Evening Walk* anticipates the nineteenth century, but White could not work out an appropriate form because as a poet he was still bound by the dictums of the eighteenth century.

V

In the bird poetry of the Romantic period, the restrictive conventions were opened up. It was an age of contrasts – the objective and the subjective, the literal and the imaginative. If at one extreme there are bird poems which faithfully describe the outer reality, at the other extreme there are birds which are part of an inner world like Poe's hallucinatory raven or Coleridge's albatross in *The Rime of the Ancient Mariner*. Romantic is a poor name because it does not apply to all of the poetry, although there are, of course, romantic elements in the realists. Their love of birds was part of the romantic involvement in nature, and one might say that in their use of new material, they reflected the interest in the strange and the unfamiliar. If there is a common thread in this diversity, it is perhaps the desire to explore, whether it is Clare examining a bird's nest or Keats looking at himself through the nightingale.

1. setter

Although the famous birds were still the most common, there were also birds which had never been used in poetry and therefore had no echoes, no symbolism, no tradition – Scott's snowy ptarmigan; Darley's hoopoe; Wordsworth's restless stonechat. There was a marked increase not only in the species but also in the names. In fact, the eighteenth-century pool was so liberally restocked, it rivals the seventeenth century in its richness. Old words like ern reappear. In addition to the new species, there are names of foreign birds like condor and flamingo, and there are also a good many provincial names, some of which are quite unusual. Readers who recognize practically every name in eighteenth-century poetry will find the going more difficult, what with words like lintwhite, cushat, and glede, not to mention bumbarrel or butter-bump![1] As in the seventeenth century, some birds have more than one name. To give an example, Gilbert White's churn owl, Wordsworth's dor-hawk, and Clare's fern owl are all names for the common European nightjar.[2] Obviously, the Birds of Poetry were no longer an exclusive club to which only the right names were admitted.

Generally speaking, the bird poetry of the Romantic period reflects a more accurate knowledge of birds. As Durling says, a taste for natural history became fashionable in the late eighteenth century – 'intellectuals studied botany and ornithology, and poets heeded Aiken's admonitions to "studying in fields and woods".'[3] So Robert Burns, writing to a friend about his *Elegy on Captain Matthew Henderson*, speaks of having 'read your Aiken on the poetical use of natural history, a favourite study of mine, the characters of the vegetable and the manners of the animal kingdoms'.[4] Gilbert White's *Selborne* was surprisingly successful, and so was the two-volume *History of British Birds* which came out in 1797 and 1804. Illustrated by Thomas Bewick with wood engravings which are remarkable both for their accuracy and their excellence, it was so popular that today some of the earlier editions are very rare because they were 'torn up or worn out with incessant use'.[5]

A good example of this more scientific interest is *The Birds of Scotland* by James Grahame. Published in 1806, the bulk of its considerable length is devoted to birds, describing the behaviour and habitat of twenty-three different species. The influence of *The Seasons* is everywhere

1. Linnet, wood pigeon, and kite – long-tailed tit and bittern.
2. Meredith calls it the eve-jar, Hardy the nighthawk.
3. *Georgic Tradition in English Poetry*, p. 124. The reference is to John Aiken's *Essay on the Application of Natural History to Poetry*, published in 1777.
4. John De Lancey Ferguson (ed.), *The Letters of Robert Burns* (Oxford: Clarendon Press, 1931), Letter 410, Vol. II, p. 33.
5. *Encyclopaedia Britannica*, 11th edn, art. 'Ornithology', p. 305.

apparent, in both small echoes and larger themes. A recurrent subject is what Thomson called 'the passion of the groves'. Instead of a general summary, however, Grahame describes specific nesting sites, sometimes giving accurate descriptions of the nest and, on occasion, the eggs. The framework is Thomson's, but in his approach he resembles Gilbert White. Grahame says in his preface:

> What I have written is the result of my own observation. When I consulted books, my object was not information so much as correction; but as in these pages I have not often travelled beyond the limits of my own knowledge . . . I may, without arrogance, assert, that when I did consult books, I very seldom found myself either corrected or informed.

This is part of a new realism. Not even Thomson could have made such a claim – Thomson who was called the naturalist's poet. (Sometimes he used his own observations and sometimes he borrowed from others, as in the migrating bird image which is based on a description in an eighteenth-century travel book.[1]) Grahame sounds like an outdoor naturalist, and indeed, parts of his poem are really popular ornithology, as in these lines about the lark.

> On tree or bush no lark was ever seen:
> The daisied lea he loves, where tufts of grass
> Luxuriant crown the ridge; there, with his mate,
> He founds their lowly house, of withered bents,
> And coarsest speargrass; next, the inner work
> With finer and still finer fibres lays,
> Rounding it curious with his speckled breast.[2]
> (Part I, ll. 31–7)

The poem is filled with small, concrete details, and no doubt Durling is correct when he calls Grahame one of the keenest observers in English poetry. But his language is against him. Although occasionally he is quite graphic, his verse keeps softening, keeps spreading out, blurred and diffuse, in a pallid poetical diction. Plumy tribes. The fond parental eye. The habitation of the wedded pair. To make it worse, he indulges in bouts of sentimentality because he uses his factual descriptions as a stage for pathetic little dramas. The wedded pairs have much to suffer. School-boys plunder their nests:

1. Alan Dugald McKillop, *The Background of Thomson's Seasons* (Minneapolis: University of Minnesota Press, 1942), pp. 132–3.
2. *The Handbook of British Birds* says, 'Nests always on ground in depression in grass or growing crops . . . *Nest.* – Said to be made by hen only, with cock in attendance. Built of bents and grasses, lined finer grasses, sometimes a little hair' (Vol. I, p. 181).

> . . . Ah, little think
> The harmless family of love, how near
> The robber treads! . . .
>
> (Part I, ll. 72–4)

And then, of course, there are the hunters with their guns which Grahame calls tubes.

> Alas, he comes! yes, yonder comes your foe,
> With sure determined eye, and in his hand
> The two-fold tube, formed for a double death.
>
> (Part I, ll. 190–92)

Grahame tried to make poetry out of facts by sentimentalizing both the content and the language. He was not successful, but *The Birds of Scotland* has a certain charm, if only as a period piece.

Despite his sentimentality, Grahame is an objective realist. His birds are part of an external nature, something which exists in itself and which is described for its own sake. Even when he steps into the poem, he does not add anything of himself to what he describes. It is like a photograph which shows the shadow of the photographer – he is still recording, only he lets us see him as the recorder. With the Romantics, it is just the opposite. They were not interested in the factual minutiae of ornithology. They did not consult books either for information or correction, they consulted themselves because what they wrote about was not the bird as such but their reaction to the bird. It is an approach which is intensely subjective. In his poem, *To the Nightingale*, Coleridge says,

> O! I have listened till my working soul,
> Waked by those strains to thousand phantasies,
> Absorbed hath ceased to listen! . . .

To the realist, the external object is the end point, but to the Romantic it is a beginning, an opening, an entrance to his own experience. Stephen Spender says, 'The Romantic finds everywhere in nature his own image.'[1] This may be an exaggeration, and yet there are poems where the bird is so steeped in the poet's sensibility that it seems more akin to the poet than to the real bird. In *Prometheus Unbound*, for example, the nightingales are pure Shelley, swooning with voluptuous bliss. 'I die! I faint! I fail!' he says in *The Indian Serenade*, and so one nightingale,

> Sick with sweet love, droops dying away
> On its mate's music-panting bosom.

That is a Shelley nightingale, unmistakably.

1. *A Choice of English Romantic Poetry* (New York: Dial Press, 1947), p. 8.

In the typical Romantic bird poem, both the bird and its role are usually quite conventional. In Shelley's poem, *To a Skylark*, the lark is warbling in the sky; in Keats's *Ode to a Nightingale*, the nightingale is singing at night to a solitary listener. The basic patterns are no different from the eighteenth century. But while the eighteenth-century bird image is usually a two-dimensional stereotype, in the Romantic poems the conventions are so enlarged, so enriched, so deepened that they are utterly transformed, as if the stereotypes had been projected through a magic lantern. What makes them seem so new is the way the poet explores the experience. In 105 lines, Shelley tells us no more about the lark itself than Gray does in four. But he showers us with a cascade of images that become an ecstatic equivalent of the song. (An American poet, on first hearing the skylark, said that Shelley sang a better song to the lark than the lark sang to Shelley.[1]) As for Keats, he says almost nothing about the nightingale. He tells us only how he reacted to its singing, and yet he transforms his experience into something so impassioned, so alive, that everything seems impregnated with that marvellous song, as if one were feeling the music rather than hearing it.

That the Romantics preferred conventional birds was not primarily a question of knowledge. Wordsworth knew a good deal about birds, yet he seldom ventured beyond the familiar. All his bird poems are about famous birds except for one which uses a very minor bird of poetry, the green linnet. Occasionally, he has a line or two about a new bird, but I have found only a single instance where he describes one at any length, and that is in *The Kitten and Falling Leaves* where he has a charming passage about the blue-cap. Since the Romantics were rebelling against traditional poetry, it may seem strange that they did not throw out the old order of birds. But it was not just poetry which had made them famous – some went back to the ancient world; others had roots in folklore. For a poet, such birds have obvious advantages. The names are not only familiar, they have so rich an ambiance of symbol and association that the word itself can be a powerful evocation. A bird like the nightingale is not just a convention, it is an archetype. If the poet can revitalize it, then its ambiance will enrich the poem, giving it a resonance and a depth which it would not have with a new bird. Take Keats's *Ode*. If he had addressed it to the blackcap, which is also a beautiful singer, he could not have written the same poem because part of the effect depends upon the nightingale's fame, especially in the stanza beginning, 'Thou wast not born for death, immortal bird!'

Despite their radical differences, the romantic and the realistic bird poems have certain things in common. Most important is the individual

1. Sarah Piatt, *A Word with a Skylark*.

'I'. In the one, it is the I-who-reacts, 'This *I* so much alive' – in the other, it is the I-who-observes. For all their objectivity, the realists put a high value on their own experience. They look for themselves; they tell us what they see. Grahame consulted books because he wished to be accurate, but he made it quite clear that the real source of the poem was his own knowledge, his own observation, his own experience. Even when there is no first person, the fresh detail often reveals the observer. So in Crabbe's description of the petrel in the stormy sea.

> Far off, the petrel in the troubled way
> Swims with her brood, or flutters in the spray:
> She rises often, often drops again,
> And sports at ease on the tempestuous main.
> (*The Borough*, Letter I, ll. 214–17)

If the realists value the individual eye, the Romantics take their flight from a real nature. In fact, sometimes they remain quite earth-bound, and when they fix their eye on the object, they can be as precise as any realist. As Spender says, 'The Romantics themselves are romantics only intermittently.'[1] An interesting example is Coleridge. At one extreme, he is pure magic, as in the song from *Zapolya* with its fairy-like bird which twinkles in a sunny shaft and sings, 'Adieu! Adieu!' But in *This Lime-Tree Bower My Prison*, he reveals a quite different side. The poem closes with a realistic description of a rook in flight which includes the phrase 'flew creaking'. When the poem was published, Coleridge added a footnote which said,

> Some months after I had written this line, it gave me pleasure to find that Bartram had observed the same circumstance of the Savanna Crane. 'When these Birds move their wings in flight, their strokes are slow, moderate and regular; and even when at a considerable distance or high above us, we plainly hear the quill-feathers: their shafts and webs upon one another creak as the joints or working of a vessel in a tempestuous sea.'

The note adds nothing to the poem. In fact, it rather spoils the mood, but apparently Coleridge could not resist the chance to show us that in his own observation, he could be as acute as any naturalist.

Objective realism comes to a climax in the work of John Clare, the peasant poet who was born in 1793, a year after Shelley, and who died in 1864 when Tennyson was fifty-five years old. Although Clare descends in a direct line from Thomson and his followers, his mature work was strikingly original because he drew completely from his own experience. 'I found the poems in the fields/And only wrote them down,' he said. Grahame diluted his realism with poetic clichés, but Clare cut through the

1. *A Choice of English Romantic Poetry*, p. 27.

conventions by keeping an absolute focus on the real bird. One can see this in his titles, which are terse and factual, mere statements of the subject. Here are some typical examples: *Clodhopper*; *Crows in Spring*; *The Green Woodpecker and the Wryneck*; *The Moorhen's Nest*. Many of his bird poems are about species which were either new to poetry or very rare. The best example is the warblers. The entire family had been virtually ignored by poets, but Clare wrote poems on at least six different kinds – the blackcap, the whitethroat, the reed warbler, the sedge warbler, the chiffchaff, and the willow warbler, which Clare calls the pettichap and sometimes the willow-biter.

If Clare was a peasant poet, he was also something of a peasant naturalist. In Gilbert White the two were separate, but in Clare they were one, and he made poetry out of ornithology because to him the facts were an integral part of his experience. This is most apparent in his many poems about birds and their nests. Written in an unpretentious style which is very vivid and direct, they contain a wealth of ornithological material, some of it so specific that a bird watcher could use it as a Guide. Compare a modern account of the nest and eggs of the song thrush with what Clare says in the small compass of a sonnet.

Nest. – Well built, by hen alone, of grasses, roots and at times moss, leaves and twigs, solidified with earth, and lined with smooth coating of rotten wood or dung mixed with saliva. *Eggs.* – ... Colour blue with slight greenish tinge, scantily spotted black ...

(*The Handbook of British Birds*, Vol. II, p. 116)

> I watched her secret toils from day to day –
> How true she warped the moss to form a nest,
>   And modelled it within with wood and clay;
> And by and by, like heath-bells gilt with dew,
>   There lay her shining eggs, as bright as flowers,
>   Ink-spotted over shells of greeny blue.
>
> (from *The Thrush's Nest*)

Clare's best work combines a remarkable clarity with a strong sense of the immediate experience. The poem about the willow warbler is a good example.

> Beside a mole hill thickly topt
>   With wild rock-roses' lemon blooms,
> I stooped and out a something popt,
>   A very mouse in russet plumes;
> So low and nimble was its flight
>   It rather seemed to run than fly,
> And in a furze bush out of sight
>   It in a moment left my eye.

A lapt-up[1] ball of withered grass
   Appeared its little tiny house,
And sure enough my early guess
   Thought it the dwelling of a mouse;
At length I found a little hole
   I scarce could get a finger through,
And eggs, a dozen on the whole –
   I wanted them to tell it true –

As large as is a large white pea,
   And less than wrens' in hovels are,
With spots scarce big enough to see
   Most finely freckled here and there.[2]
The woodmen call them, in their way,
   The willow-biters 'cause they see
Them biting in the month of May
   The young shoots of the willow tree,
But what they are in learning's way
   Is all unknown to them or me.

The conclusion is an anti-climax, but in its naive honesty, it is typical of Clare. 'Poor idle tales of idle minds/Who never seek for truth,' he says in a disparaging remark about poets who used the old traditions about the nightingale. To Clare, truth meant a straightforward account of what he himself had experienced, and *not* knowing was as much a part of the truth as knowing.

But whether it the fern owl be,
   Or as may hap a stranger-bird,
Is still a hidden mystery
   Whose truth as fact I've never heard.
          (from *The Fern Owl*)

Clare saw nature in sharp particulars, and he tried to translate them as exactly as possible into words. The yellowhammer's eggs are 'pen-scribbled o'er with ink' – the nightingale's are 'deadened green or rather olive brown'. (The *Handbook* has 'pencilled with fine hair lines' and 'olive-green or olive-brown'.) The best example of his realism is the way he handled voices. Most poets suggest them, but Clare, like Skelton, tried to approximate actual sounds. One method was to use short, echoic words, some standard like caw, and others dialectal, such as quawk, chitter, and chelp. The nuthatch makes 'a skreeking noise' – the young birds 'cree and crow'. But this kind of word is rather general, and Clare tried to push closer to reality by making up his own words, pure sound nota-

    1. wrapped up
    2. The *Handbook* says, 'Some finely freckled light red'.

tions which imitate specific notes. It is a risky venture because it is apt to sound like baby talk, but sometimes he makes a brilliant hit. 'The sailing puddock's[1] shrill "peelew"' is excellent, and so is the flycatcher who 'sings "eejip, eejip" all the day'. But the effect can be quite naive, almost comical, as in *The Progress of Rhyme* where he imitates the nightingale with a string of words like *chew-chew chew-chew, woo-it woo-it, wew-wew wew-wew*.

Although Clare is a master realist, in his love of nature he is quite romantic.

> Lost in such ecstasies, in this old spot
> I feel that rapture which the world hath not,
> That joy like health that flushes in my face
> Amid the brambles of this ancient place.
> (*The Robin's Nest*, ll. 17–20)

Compared to Wordsworth, Clare is much closer to the natural world. Wordsworth may chance upon a nest, but Clare hunts them out with a tireless ardour. He crawls on his hands and knees through matted thorn; he searches woods so lonely that footprints 'seem like miracles'; he explores the marshy flats 'where man nor boy nor stock hath ventured near'.

> For when a boy a new nest meets,
> Joy gushes to his breast,
> Nor would his heart so quickly beat
> Were guineas in the nest.
> (from *The Landrail*)

When Wordsworth really looks at a bird, it is usually either more or less tame like the common swan or it is a bird which he watches in his garden.

> In this sequestered nook how sweet
> To sit upon my orchard-seat!
> And birds and flowers once more to greet,
> My last year's friends together.
> (from *The Green Linnet*)

More typically, Wordsworth listens to a bird which he does not actually see.

> I heard a stock dove sing or say
> His homely tale, this very day.
> (from 'O nightingale!
> thou surely art')

Wordsworth wrote three poems about the cuckoo, which was one of his favourites, but to him it was only a voice, 'echo's self', because although he had hunted for it as a boy, he had never seen it.

1. Buzzard – but sometimes Clare used it to mean kite.

> Thrice welcome, darling of the spring!
> Even yet thou art to me
> No bird, but an invisible thing,
> A voice, a mystery.
>
> (from *To the Cuckoo*)

This is a common experience since the cuckoo is quite furtive, but needless to say, it was no mystery to Clare – in fact, in a poem where he says that he has watched it sing for half an hour, he was so close to it that he could see the colour of the inside of its mouth.

When Wordsworth recollected in tranquillity, he transformed the bird into something larger. One is always conscious of him shaping his experience. The blue-cap is described not for itself but. because, like the kitten, it is an example of baby innocence. The cuckoo not only evokes Wordsworth's boyhood, it is also 'a hope, a love;/Still longed for, never seen', which has overtones of that mystical presence with which Wordsworth felt that nature was infused. Clare's world was much simpler. He did not transform what he perceived, he transcribed it, fresh and sharp, with all the vividness of direct experience. A crane cranking its melancholy cry; a ground lark's[1] nest fixed snugly into the footprint of a horse – to Clare, all these particulars were meaningful in themselves. Sometimes he is too factual, too much the naturalist, but at his best his work is charged with a kind of wonder and joy, as if he were saying: Look! This *is*, this is *true*! It was Wordsworth who attacked the poetry between *Paradise Lost* and *The Seasons* because it contained scarcely an image of external nature 'from which it can be inferred that the eye of the poet had been steadily fixed upon his object'. Yet Wordsworth himself looked only in glimpses. It was Clare who had the steady eye, who stood and stared. If he lacked Wordsworth's larger vision, it must be said that Wordsworth did not have Clare's genius for graphic description. Clare has a special appeal for bird lovers, but there will always be readers who prefer Wordsworth's more complex, more contemplative view of nature.

By the 1830s, descriptive bird poetry had fallen out of fashion. It was not that readers had lost interest in this kind of material – on the contrary, there was still a great demand for it – but prose was winning out over poetry as the medium for popular nature writing. Clare himself could not find a publisher after the poor sales of his fourth book, which came out in 1835, and masses of his poems, including most of his bird-nest series, remained unpublished until the twentieth century. No doubt there were many reasons for the decline of descriptive nature poetry. Durling thinks that the most important was the triumph of the Romantics, who made

---

1. meadow pipit

Thomson and his followers seem outdated. Another reason, surely, was the growing sophistication of the audience. At the beginning of *Jane Eyre*, the heroine, at that point aged ten, pores over Bewick's *History of British Birds*. It was the pictures which fascinated her, especially the settings which she interpreted in a very romantic way, yet since she also read parts of the text, she must have absorbed a good deal of information. In fact, because Bewick's *Birds* was used in nurseries and school-rooms, a bright ten-year-old in the nineteenth century probably had a more accurate knowledge of birds than the adults who read *The Seasons* in the 1730s. Thomson could enthrall his readers with simple facts, but Grahame, writing some seventy-five years later, had to be much more specific to give his audience fresh material. Clare went even further, but there is a limit to the load which poetry will carry. It is more like a skiff than a barge, and although Clare packs in a surprising amount of detail, even his densest verse seems sketchy when you look at his prose.

> Long-tailed titmouse and chaffinch and redcap[1] make a most beautiful outside to their nests of grey lichen. Linnets and hedge sparrows make a loose ruff outside of coarse green moss, wool and roots. The first are like the freestone fabrics of finished elegance, the latter like the rough plain walls of a husbandman's cottage, yet equally warm and comfortable within. Pinks[2] use cow hair and some feathers for their inside hangings. Redcaps get thistle down. Hedge sparrows use wool and cow hair intermixed. Linnets use wool and cow hair and the furze linnet uses rabbit down.[3]

In the long run, it was inevitable that as nature writers became more specific, they would work in prose.

Victorian bird poetry contains both Romantic and realistic elements, but there are no longer such pronounced extremes because the two are merged into a more moderate middle ground. If on the one hand the poetry is less subjective, with the focus more on the bird than the poet, on the other hand there is very little of what you might call the bird-nest complex where ornithological detail is described for its own sake. Accurate information is no longer presented as something special. It is a part of a general knowledge, something which is assumed rather than displayed. There are no John Clares, and yet the level of realism is generally high, with a good deal of personal observation. To give an example: in a note to the image, 'As careful robins eye the delver's toil', Tennyson's son says,

This line was made one day while my father was digging, as was his wont then,

1. European goldfinch
2. chaffinch
3. Eric Robinson and Geoffrey Summerfield (eds.), *Selected Poems and Prose of John Clare* (London: Oxford University Press, 1967), p. 109.

in the kitchen garden at Farringford, when he was much amused by the many watchful robins round him.

He looked at the bird rather than himself, but then he transformed what he saw so that the realism is unobtrusive.

The eagle is a typical Romantic subject, but most characteristic of the Victorian period are birds like the seagull, the blackbird, and the thrush. Widespread, year-round residents, what they have in common is that they are all highly visible. Only the most intrepid naturalist could observe the eagle at first hand, but anyone can watch gulls at the sea shore and blackbirds and thrushes in the garden. Victorian poetry is filled with just this kind of observation. Not the expert describing the nest, but the amateur who watches the bird life around him like Tennyson with the robins.

A perfect illustration of the Victorian approach is the song thrush. From the medieval period on, its role was that of a minor nightingale. Romantic period poets add a certain amount of detail but with a few exceptions, notably Clare, they always present it in more or less the same way. Keats says 'The thrush/Began calm-throated', and Wordsworth has,

> The thrush is busy in the wood,
> And carols loud and strong.
> (*The Idle Shepherd-Boys*, ll. 25–6)

In the Victorian period, the thrush becomes much more important. Although it is still treated as a songbird, it is presented in a variety of ways which, taken together, give a good general view of its habits. Unlike the earlier realists who describe and explain, the poets take for granted that the reader is as knowledgeable as they are. In his *Home-Thoughts, From Abroad*, Browning alludes to the fact that the song thrush, when singing, repeats each phrase two or more times.

> That's the wise thrush; he sings each song twice over
> Lest you should think he never could recapture
> The first fine careless rapture!

Its singing is so loud that, according to the British *Handbook*, it 'carries a quarter-of-a-mile in ordinary conditions and much more on occasions'. This is what Hopkins means by 'rinse and wring' in the poem beginning 'Nothing is so beautiful as spring'.

> Thrush's eggs look little low heavens, and thrush
> Through the echoing timber does so rinse and wring
> The ear, it strikes like lightnings to hear him sing.

The thrush falls silent in late summer. In autumn you can hear its sub-

song, which the *Handbook* describes as 'a low warbling and twittering'.[1]
Sir Lewis Morris uses both these points in the poem called *On a Thrush
Singing in Autumn*. 'Where is thy liquid voice/That all day would rejoice?'
It grew dumb in summer,

> Yet now, when leaves are sere, thy ancient note
> Comes low and halting from thy doubtful throat.

The thrush does not always survive the winter. Gilbert White says:

> When birds come to suffer by severe frost, I find that the first that fail and die
> are the redwings, fieldfares, and then the song thrushes.
>
> (Barrington, Letter V)

Hardy sees a starving thrush trying to reach a rotten berry. Bridges has
one frozen on the ground, and in a rhyme from *Sing-Song*, Christina
Rossetti says,

> Dead in the cold, a song-singing thrush,
> Dead at the foot of a snowberry bush –
> Weave him a coffin of rush,   .
> Dig him a grave where the soft mosses grow,
> Raise him a tombstone of snow.

Yet it sings in winter, as in Hardy's poem, *The Darkling Thrush*, which
was written in December of 1900. The poet is gloomily contemplating the
landscape, which strikes him as the century's corpse, when all at once a
thrush bursts into 'a full-hearted evensong/Of joy illimited'.

> So little cause for carolings
>   Of such ecstatic sound
> Was written on terrestrial things
>   Afar or nigh around,
> That I could think there trembled through
>   His happy good-night air
> Some blessëd hope, whereof he knew
>   And I was unaware.

They sing in winter but, as Kenneth Richmond says, they 'wait until
February before they become full-throated'.[2] So in Meredith's poem,
The Thrush in February.

> I know him, February's thrush,
> And loud at eve he valentines
> On sprays that paw the naked bush
> Where soon will sprout the thorns and bines.

1. *The Handbook of British Birds*, Vol. II, pp. 115, 116.
2. *Birds in Britain*, p. 147.

Tennyson's *Throstle* is set in the same season. A charming, light-hearted poem, it imitates the song both by its rapid rhythms and by its repetitions of short phrases and single words.

> 'Summer is coming, summer is coming.
>   I know it, I know it, I know it.
> Light again, leaf again, life again, love again,'
>   Yes, my wild little poet.
>
>   . . .
>
> 'Here again, here, here, here, happy year!'
>   O warble unchidden, unbidden!
> Summer is coming, is coming, my dear,
>   And all the winters are hidden.

The Throstle is not realistic in the way that Clare is. Yet, simple as it seems, it is the result of careful observation. Tennyson's son says,

> My father had been writing his poem, *By an Evolutionist*, between severe attacks of gout in the winter of 1889. He fed the thrushes and other birds as usual out of his window (at Farringford). Towards the end of February he sat in his kitchen-garden summer-house, listening attentively to the different notes of the thrush, and finishing his song of *The Throstle*, which had been begun in the same garden years ago.

In Victorian poetry, there is a steady erosion of bird traditions. The more bizarre disappeared almost at once. (An example is the bleeding pelican which had been resurrected by the Romantics.) Others had a kind of half life, still well known but rarely used, like the singing of the dying swan. The only conventions which continued undiminished were those which are realistic, such as the thrush as songbird or the cuckoo as herald of spring. Minor birds with little or no tradition began to be used as subjects of poems instead of being limited to incidental images. A look at some of the titles gives an idea of the growing diversity.

The Rookery, Charles Tennyson-Turner
Ode to Mother Carey's Chicken (*On Seeing a Storm-Petrel in a Cage on a Cottage Wall and Releasing it*), Theodore Watts-Dunton
The Puzzled Game Birds, Thomas Hardy
The Woodlark, Gerard Manley Hopkins
Flycatchers, Robert Bridges
The Sea-Snipe, A. C. Benson
The Nightjar, Sir Henry Newbolt
To a Sea Gull, Arthur Symons

Even when the bird is famous, it is more apt to be handled freshly, in some unexpected way. The best example is the nightingale. No subject could be more hackneyed, and yet some of the finest nightingale poems come from this period. Perhaps George Sampson was right when he said, 'The truth is that the past and its themes are never exhausted; it is only poets that are exhausted.'[1] Whatever the case, some new wine was poured from the old bottles. To give some examples, Arnold's *Philomela* deals with the myth, but instead of using the Latin version, he goes back to the Greek where the nightingale is the mother. As H. J. Rose says, this account makes more sense because it explains why the nightingale mourns (she is lamenting her child) and why the swallow twitters (she has no tongue and keeps trying to tell her story).[2] But a mother who butchers her child is a bit difficult to handle, especially if she is supposed to be the emblem of love. Arnold solves this by leaving out everything connected with the murder. First we see the mother perusing the tapestry 'with hot cheeks and seared eyes' – next, she is changing into a bird. In Ovid's *Metamorphoses*, the murder is a masterful scene, gruesome yet pitiful, but Arnold omits the horrors because his theme is not the crime, it is the emotions which surround it – love and hate; triumph and agony; passion and pain.

> How thick the bursts come crowding through the leaves!
> Again – thou hearest?
> Eternal passion!
> Eternal pain!

In *Itylus*, Swinburne uses the familiar Latin roles, but he gives the story a new twist by treating the bird behaviour as if it were human character. The nightingale is a secretive, solitary bird. During its song period it sings night and day, often hidden in thick cover. The swallow is gregarious. It skims about in the open, its flight graceful and swift, its voice a rapid twitter. In the poem, the one is faithful and the other is shallow and pleasure-seeking. The central theme is the son, Itylus, and the nightingale accuses the swallow of having forgotten him.

> O sweet stray sister, O shifting swallow,
> The heart's division divideth us.
> Thy heart is light as a leaf of a tree;
> But mine goes forth among sea-gulfs hollow
> To the place of the slaying of Itylus,
> The feast of Daulis, the Thracian sea.

---

1. *The Concise Cambridge History of English Literature*, p. 713.
2. Herbert Jennings Rose, *A Handbook of Greek Mythology* (London: Methuen, 1958), pp. 262–3.

> O swallow, sister, O rapid swallow,
>> I pray thee sing not a little space.
>> Are not the roofs and the lintels wet?
> The woven web that was plain to follow,
>> The small slain body, the flowerlike face,
>> Can I remember if thou forget?
>
> O sister, sister, thy first-begotten!
>> The hands that cling and the feet that follow,
>> The voice of the child's blood crying yet.
>> *Who hath remembered me? who hath forgotten?*
>> Thou hast forgotten, O summer swallow,
>> But the world shall end when I forget.

In *Nightingales*, Bridges breaks with both the classical and the English tradition. It is a dream-like poem, full of magic, but it is based upon fact. A summer visitor, the nightingale arrives in England from Africa, where it spends the winter. 'Beautiful must be the mountains whence ye come,' the poet begins. He imagines starry woods and valleys bright with streams, but the nightingales deny this.

> Nay, barren are those mountains and spent the streams:
> Our song is the voice of desire, that haunts our dreams,
>> A throe of the heart,
> Whose pining visions dim, forbidden hopes profound,
> No dying cadence nor long sigh can sound,
>> For all our art.

Tennyson's poem, *In the Garden at Swainston*, is a lament for a dead friend. While the master lies in his coffin, the nightingales are singing in his woods. Here the birds are used as a contrast. Inside the house there is death, but outside is life, and the nightingales represent the impassioned concerns of the living. The mourners weep, but the birds sing.

> Nightingales sang in his woods:
>> The Master was far away:
> Nightingales warbled and sang
>> Of a passion that lasts but a day;
>> Still in the house in his coffin the Prince of courtesy lay.

In Hopkins's *The Nightingale*, the bird is associated with both love and death. It is a weak poem, poorly developed, about a lover who drowns at sea while his girl, at home in bed, is having an imaginary conversation with him. But it contains an extraordinary description of a nightingale singing. It is not the ravishing, erotic music which had been associated with the nightingale ever since the Elizabethans. In fact, it is not even beautiful, it is nothing but naked volume, almost unbearable in its loudness. The nightingale of poetry is nearly always female, but here, the singer is a male.[1] The use of the pronoun 'he' heightens the sense of power – it is a force, a storm, somehow frightening in its strength. Hopkins exaggerates, but it is true, as Kenneth Richmond says, that 'for sheer power of delivery . . . the Nightingale is supreme'.[2] What makes the Hopkins unique is that it focuses entirely upon this one trait.

> 'For he began at once and shook
> My head to hear. He might have strung
> A row of ripples in the brook,
>   So forcibly he sung,
> The mist upon the leaves have strewed,
> And danced the balls of dew that stood
> In acres all above the wood.

> 'I thought the air must cut and strain
> The windpipe when he sucked his breath
> And when he turned it back again
>   The music must be death.
> With not a thing to make me fear,
> A singing bird in morning clear
> To me was terrible to hear.

Along with the more individual approach went a marked increase in the use of personal symbolism. The lark is an interesting example. Since its role is realistic, it was still used as a sky singer, but its song flight was constantly re-interpreted. To Frederick Tennyson, it is the victorious poet singing alone. Meredith (*The Lark Ascending*) sees it as the essence of nature, a 'spirit voice' which speaks to man because it is selfless. To Francis William Bourdillon, it is like the violinist whose music reveals heavens we have never seen. William Watson says that the lark has two worlds, sky and ground, but that he has only one, this vexed earth, home of tears. Bridges contrasts a day of mournful mist with the sunlight which the larks find above the clouds.

> Sweet birds, far out of sight
> Your songs of pleasure
> Dome us with joy as bright
> As heaven's best azure.
>   (from *Larks*)

The most brilliant is Hopkins's poem, *The Sea and the Skylark*. Written in his mature style, it is dense, knotty, difficult. Here is the lark stanza.

1. In real life, only the male sings.
2. *Birds in Britain*, pp. 149–50.

> Left hand, off land, I hear the lark ascend,
> His rash-fresh re-winded new-skeinéd score
> In crisps of curl off wild winch whirl, and pour
> And pelt music, till none's to spill nor spend.

In this poem, sea and lark are used as a reproach to fallen man. Their voice is aeons old, and yet it is always new because they have never lost their primal freshness. They shame us in our sordid times.

The individualism of Victorian bird poetry was counterbalanced by a strong current of the conventional. One can see this most clearly in their choice of birds. Consider the following passage from Kenneth Richmond.

> Which is the most numerous British bird? The farmer, aghast at the monstrous regiments which descend on his cabbage fields, might be inclined to say it was the Wood Pigeon. The townsman might plump for the House Sparrow. Is it really the Robin, as many people think, or the Chaffinch, or the Starling, or the Meadow Pipit, or the Willow Warbler?[1]

In Victorian poetry, of course, it is none of these. For all its realism, for all its scope and variety, it was still dominated by conventional birds. The most common was probably the skylark, but the most important was the nightingale, which had been the reigning bird of poetry ever since the fifteenth century. In evaluating Victorian poetry, Sampson says its most striking trait is its originality while its chief fault is that it tends to be over-literary. This is certainly true of the nightingale. It was handled with surprising freshness, and yet the fact remains that of the birds of poetry, the nightingale is the most literary. As Edward Armstrong says, it owes its fame not to peasants but to poets – and a long line it is, stretching back some 2,700 years. By the Victorian period, it had accumulated a wealth of literary associations. It was the essence of rich romance, not just the chief bird of poetry but the Poet's bird, conjuring up spring and song, passion and death. 'O nightingale! thou surely art/A creature of a "fiery heart"'! In the most successful poems, its image is revitalized because qualities of the real nightingale are infused into the nightingale of poetry, yet no matter how freshly it is treated, it still has a literary flavour.

It is difficult to sum up Victorian poetry, no doubt because, as W. H. Auden says, 'To a degree hitherto unknown, each poet sets out ... to create a personal style; he invents a particular genre of poem suited to his cast of temperament – the Tennyson idyll, the Browning dramatic monologue, the Patmore ode; for each poem he tries to find the form uniquely suited to its subject and vice versa.'[2] The players evolved their own game

1. *Birds in Britain*, p. 20.
2. *Poets of the English Language* (New York: Viking Press, 1950), Vol. V, pp. xviii-xix.

and yet, nevertheless, they had one thing in common – all of them, including Hopkins, were still thinking in terms of rules. Something similar can be said about their treatment of birds. Take the five nightingale poems. Arnold, Swinburne, Bridges, Tennyson, and Hopkins each created his own version of the nightingale, and yet the mere fact that they chose it as a subject shows that they were still working within definite limits. It was a tethered ball, not yet completely free.

VI

Unlike poetry, which was breaking away from the old restraints, the oral rhymes of the folk tradition were still completely traditional. The best nineteenth-century poems are marked by a strong sense of the individual poet, but the folk rhymes are more like a group production because they were shaped by many people over long periods of time. Although they cannot be dated, most of them survive in a relatively modern form because they were first collected in the nineteenth century. In 1826 Robert Chambers published *Popular Rhymes of Scotland*, which was revised and enlarged in later editions, and in 1842 James Orchard Halliwell brought out *The Nursery Rhymes of England* which was also revised and enlarged and which remained the standard work in its field for more than one hundred years. Both books include bird rhymes and so does Halliwell's *Popular Rhymes and Nursery Tales*, which was published in 1849.

To turn from poetry to the rhymes of the oral tradition is like dropping into another world. There are no arbitrary symbols, no literary conceits, no precise, closely observed details. Even the birds seem different. For the most part they are common, everyday birds, the kind you would see in and around a village.

> Titty cum tawtay,
> The ducks in the water:
> Titty cum tawtay,
> The geese follow after.

Some of the famous literary birds are never even mentioned. Take the nightingale: poetry gives you the feeling that there is a nightingale in every bush in England, but the rhymes go to the opposite extreme – practically speaking, there are no nightingales at all. And there are no eagles, no falcons, no phoenix, no halcyons, no pelicans; very few songbirds; and only an occasional hawk, not specified except for the kite. The goose displaces the swan; the crow all but ousts the raven. No one pretends that the lark wakes up the ploughboy, because it is the rooster which is the village clock.

> The cock doth crow
> To let you know,
> If you be wise,
> 'Tis time to rise.

Despite the differences, there are a handful of birds which are prominent in both traditions. The most important are the robin, the cuckoo, the dove, and the owl. Yet even when the same birds are employed, the result is very different. In poetry, the major birds are used in such distinctive ways that each has its own particular character. The cuckoo is disreputable, the owl is ominous, the robin is friendly, and the dove is a faithful soul who mourns when she is widowed. Of course the roles are not always consistent. In Shakespeare's winter song, for instance, the owl has a merry note, but nevertheless, until the stereotypes began to disintegrate, each of the birds had an unmistakable identity. This is not true in the oral rhymes. There are very few bird types or bird roles, and when they do exist they are not only much simpler, they are also far less binding. The owl illustrates the difference. In poetry, it is predominantly negative. A bird of ill omen, it is associated with darkness, disaster, and death. Its voice is usually frightening, sometimes in a general way and sometimes as a portent of evil.

> Now the wasted brands do glow,
>   Whilst the screech owl, screeching loud,
> Puts the wretch that lies in woe
>   In remembrance of a shroud.
> (*A Midsummer Night's Dream*, V, i, 382–5)

In folklore, the owl is also unlucky. Charles Swainson says, 'In France, in Germany, in Italy, in England, its appearance forbodes misfortune, its shriek foretells woe and ill.'[1] Edward Armstrong quotes an old man who, upon hearing of the death of an acquaintance, said,

> It weren't no more nor I expected. I come past his house one night, and there were a scret owl on his roof, scretting something horrible. I always reckon to take note of them things.[2]

Despite these superstitions, the owl of the rhymes has almost nothing of the character which it developed in poetry. In fact, it has no really coherent character, because the rhymes reflect a variety of unrelated

1. Charles Swainson, *The Folk Lore and Provincial Names of British Birds* (London: published for the Folk Lore Society by Elliot Stock, 1886), p. 126.
2. *The Folklore of Birds*, pp. 114–15.

traditions. In one rhyme it is gay; in another, it is foolish; in still another, it is wise. Even its voice can be treated light-heartedly, as in the couplet from Halliwell where its notes are rendered,

> To whoo – to whoo!
> Cold toe – toe!

The most interesting is the idea that the owl was once a woman, a belief which Shakespeare refers to in *Hamlet* when mad Ophelia says:

> Well, God dild you! They say the owl was
> a baker's daughter. Lord, we know what we
> are, but know not what we may be.
>   (IV, v, 41–3)

In the rhymes, she is a king's daughter, as in this song from the North.

> Oh! o o o, o o;
> I once was a king's daughter,
> And sat on my father's knee,
> But now I'm a poor hoolet,
> And hide in a hollow tree.

Compared to poetry, the birds of the rhymes are very inconsistent. In this way, they are more complex, because they are not cut from single patterns. If there is one exception, it is the robin. The hero of songs, rhymes, and anonymous poems, he has a very definite character. No doubt it reflects the fondness which the British feel for the robin. He is everybody's favourite, and there are a number of rhymes where he is treated with real affection, as if he were an outdoor pet.

> Little Bob Robin,
> Where do you live?
> Up in yonder wood, sir,
> On a hazel twig.

Part of his character comes from the story of the babes in the wood, one version of which was a very popular ballad called *The Children in the Wood*.

> No burial this pretty pair
> From any man receives,
> Till Robin Redbreast piously
> Did cover them with leaves.

'Who . . . is there in whose oldest memory the legendary tale of the "Babes in the Wood" does not forever dwell . . .?' asks the Reverend F. O. Morris in the 1850s,[1] and no doubt it helped create a special feeling

1. Francis Orpen Morris, *A History of British Birds* (London: Groombridge, n.d.), Vol. IV, p. 14.

for the robin. This is most apparent in the winter rhymes, some of which express a compassion which is unique in the bird rhymes of the oral tradition. 'And what will poor Robin do then,/Poor thing.'

> When the snow is on the ground,
>   Little Robin Redbreast grieves;
> For no berries can be found,
>   And on the trees there are no leaves.
>
> The air is cold, the worms are hid,
>   For this poor bird what can be done?
> We'll strew him here some crumbs of bread,
>   And then he'll live till the snow is gone.

The most charming are the rhymes about the courtship and marriage of the robin and the wren, a group which consists of little story poems with humanized birds. Here is one from Halliwell.

> Little Jenny Wren fell sick upon a time,
> When in came Robin Redbreast, and brought her bread and wine;
> 'Eat, Jenny, drink, Jenny, all shall be thine!'
> Then Jenny she got better, and stood upon her feet,
> And says to little Robin, 'I love thee not a bit!'
> Then Robin he was angry and flew upon a twig,
> 'Hoot upon thee, fie upon thee, ungrateful chit!'

The poet's robin is a sophisticated version of the little Bob Robin of the folk. Once his character is set, it never varies. He is loving and good, so therefore he cannot be bad. In the folk world, however, there is a dark side to the robin. This is hinted at in a number of cautionary rhymes which say that if you kill one, you will suffer dire consequences.

> Cursëd is the man
> Who kills a robin or a wren.

But even if you never touched him, he could still be malevolent. Edward Armstrong says, 'The friendly regard for the robin has not prevented its being widely considered a bird of ill omen.' Here are some robin portents.

In Suffolk an intruding robin was an omen of death, and it was believed in Wales that a robin singing on the threshold presaged illness or death. At Hurstpierpoint School there is a tradition that if a robin sings on the altar of the chapel one of the boys will die. By a coincidence this sequence actually occurred some years ago ... A robin tapping on a window was widely regarded as a portent of disaster ... In Bucks the plaintive piping of a robin was thought to foretell death, and in other parts of the country it was considered ominous for a sick person to hear the bird singing.[1]

1. *The Folklore of Birds*, p. 169.

In 'Proud Maisie', Scott uses the ominous robin of the folk, but this is very exceptional. The poet's robin is a dear little bird, but in the folk tradition he is sometimes sweet and sometimes malignant.

Unlike poetry, the oral rhymes are variable. Part of a spoken tradition, people learned them by ear much as children today pick up game rhymes by hearing them recited. There was no correct form because there was no printed original. If someone misquotes Shelley, he has made a mistake, but with the folk rhymes, a 'mistake' meant a new variation. It was a fluid tradition, a series of multiple images rather than set forms. Words were changed and lines were added, or dropped, or transferred to other poems as if they were moveable parts. Many of the countless variations are quite minor, but where a rhyme was widespread some of the regional versions may be so different that they are more like a group of related rhymes than a single rhyme with variations. The best example is probably the cuckoo calendar.

> The cuckoo comes in April,
>   Sings a song in May;
> Then in June another tune,
>   And then she flies away.
>   (Gloucestershire)

> In April,
> The cuckoo shows his bill;
> In May,
> He sings both night and day;
> In June,
> He altereth his tune;
> In July,
> He prepares to fly;
> Come August,
> Go he must.
>   (Norfolk)

> The cuckoo comes of mid March,
>   And cucks of mid Aperill;
> And gauns away of Midsummer month
>   When the corn begins to fill.
>   (Northumberland)

> In March,
> The guku beginth to sarch;
> In Aperal,
> He beginth to tell;
> In May,
> He beginth to lay;

> In June,
> He altereth 'is tune;
> In July,
> Away a dith vly.
> (Devon)

Despite its variations, the oral tradition was astonishingly conservative. In poetry, every period has a distinctive style. It is a history of change, of movements, of fashions, with periodic breaks where one generation cast off the style of another. But the great currents which shaped poetry had practically no effect on the oral tradition, where rhymes might last for centuries without any significant change. This makes them very hard to date, because even if there is an early printed version there is no way of telling how old it was when it was first written down. Andrew Lang said that oral rhymes were stones worn smooth by the constant friction of tongues. What gets rubbed off are the period marks, all those little peculiarities which print preserves. To give an example, there is a riddle song which was collected in the nineteenth century. Halliwell says that several versions were common in the North, one of which he quotes.

> I have four sisters beyond the sea,
>   Para-mara, dictum, domine.
> And they did send four presents to me,
>   Partum, quartum, paradise, tempum,
>   Para-mara, dictum, domine!
>
> The first it was a bird without e'er a bone,
>   Para-mara, dictum, domine.
> The second was a cherry without e'er a stone,
>   Partum, quartum, paradise, tempum,
>   Para-mara, dictum, domine!

The refrain sounds like a garbled Latin which suggests that it is old but proves nothing about the song lines because they might have been a later addition. It would have been impossible to date them were it not for the fact that similar lines appear in a manuscript of about 1440.

> I haue a yong suster fer beyondyn the se,
> Many be the drowryis that che sentë me.
> Che sentë me the cherye withoutyn ony ston;
> And so che dedë dowë[1] withoutyn ony bon.

The riddle song goes back at least 500 years, and the Opies, the leading authority on children's rhymes, think that it may well have been old when

1. dove

it was written down in the fifteenth century.[1] Today, such persistence seems incredible. So far as we know it did not appear in print until 1838, which means that in order to have survived, it had to be passed on orally in a continuous chain, generation after generation, for 400 years.

Although the folk rhymes cannot be dated, there are rhymes which embody attitudes and beliefs that are closer to the primitive than they are to English poetry. For one thing, it was believed that certain birds possessed magical powers. As in Anglo-Saxon poetry, these birds could be either good or bad. The magpie is a perfect example. In both England and Scotland, meeting magpies was an omen whose luck depended upon how many you encountered. The widespread magpie rhymes, some of which go up to twelve, explain what each number foretells. They do not always agree, but practically every rhyme says that to meet one magpie is bad, while two is good. Here is a version which goes back at least to the eighteenth century.

> One for sorrow,
> Two for mirth,
> Three for a wedding,
> Four for death.

Another similarity is the absence of moral judgement. This is most apparent with the cuckoo. In poetry he is vilified because of his parasitical breeding habits. In the medieval period, the nightingale displaced him as herald of spring, which left him all bad, without any positive role. He was murderous, licentious, false, an odious figure, bawdy at one extreme and pure evil at the other. The folk cuckoo is completely different. There is no judgement, no vilification. For the most part its domestic life is ignored, but when it is mentioned, it is accepted in a matter-of-fact way, as in the folk song where its habit of destroying its victims' eggs is treated with a kind of cheerful callousness.

> She sucks little birds' eggs
> To make her voice clear,
> That she may sing Cuckoo!
> Three months in the year.

As in Anglo-Saxon poetry, the folk cuckoo is the bird of spring. A summer visitor, it arrives in England in April, and evidence suggests that to the pre-Christian Saxons the cuckoo was not just the herald, it was the magical bearer of spring like the swallow in the Greek folk song.

1. Iona and Peter Opie (eds.), *The Oxford Dictionary of Nursery Rhymes* (Oxford: Clarendon Press, 1952), p. 387.

> It's come, it's come, the swallow
> Bringing the lovely season
> And lovely years
> On its white belly
> And on its swarthy back.

There is nothing as primitive as this in the folk, but all over Britain and Europe the spring cuckoo was looked upon as a bird of omen with prophetic powers. There were a host of cuckoo superstitions, many connected with its first call, which could be a good or a bad sign depending upon the circumstances. The cuckoo was also used for divination. Gay mentions one such practice in *The Shepherd's Week*. If you want to know whom you will marry, take your shoe off when you hear the first cuckoo and you will find a hair the same colour as that of your future spouse.

> Upon a rising bank I sat adown,
> Then doffed my shoe, and by my troth, I swear,
> Therein I spied this yellow frizzled hair,
> As like to Lubberkin's in curl and hue,
> As if upon his comely pate it grew.

The poets condemned the cuckoo because they judged it by moral standards, but in the folk tradition it was accepted as it is, a part of nature, no more to be judged than rain or sun.

A striking parallel to the primitive is the absence of song. As in the Anglo-Saxon riddles, the birds in the oral rhymes talk. There is no conception of the voice as music, no feeling for what Gray calls the 'trembling thrilling ecstasy'. Whether the notes are musical like the wren's or harsh like the crow's, they are interpreted as human speech. In this way, they are like the talking birds of the medieval period. But in the medieval poems, the birds are simply a mouthpiece for the poet. To a certain extent this is true in the oral rhymes, because what the birds say is bound to reflect the peasant. It is vigorous talk – concise, robust, salted with country humour. Love is almost never mentioned. If there is a common denominator, it is the preoccupation with practical matters which are often put in human terms. The hen is upset because she has no shoes – the yellowhammer cries, 'Little bit of bread but no cheese!' Even the dove has a down-to-earth character. When she complains, it is never about love, it is because she is fussing over domestic problems – her skimpy nest, her difficulties in raising her young. The content is human but in the oral tradition, unlike poetry, the bird's speech often mimics its voice. Sometimes specific notes are verbalized, as in the lapwing rhyme which opens with an imitation of its wailing cry.

> Peese weep, peese weep!
> Harry my nest and gar me greet![1]

At other times, real words are used as approximate equivalents of the notes. What Tennyson did in *The Throstle* had long been common among country folk. Chambers says that the lonely shepherd, listening to the croaking of a pair of crows, 'amuses his fancy by forming regular dialogues out of their conversation'.[2] His examples come from different regions, but they are so similar that they are obviously variations of a formula. Here is one from Tweeddale.

> Sekito says, There's a hog dead!
> Where? where?
> Up the burn! up the burn!
> Is't fat? is't fat?
> 'T's a' creesh! 't's a' creesh![3]

Such a poem must be spoken to be effective, because the pitch and tempo of the voice is part of the imitation. A good example is the cock and hen rhymes, some of which are supposed to alternate between a rapid run and a scream. Here is one which Halliwell collected.

> *Hen.*   Cock, cock, I have la-a-a-yed!
> *Cock.* Hen, hen, that's well sa-a-a-yed!
> *Hen.*   Although I have to go barefooted every da-a-y!
> *Cock.* Sell your eggs, and buy shoes,
> Sell your eggs, and buy shoes!

Obviously, this kind of rhyme was an amusement. The Opies point out that as early as 1606, 'to "mocke the cockes" by giving words to their crowing was a common game with children'.[4] But there are indications that certain birds were once thought to speak in a semi-human tongue. There is a suggestion of this in Chambers's rhyme about the stonechat. A small bird, it has a peculiar voice which Peterson's *Guide* calls 'a persistent scolding "*wheet, tsack, tsack,*" like hitting two stones together'. In some districts of Scotland it was believed that the bird had a drop of the devil's blood and that its eggs were incubated by the toad. Chambers says that its nest was never robbed because it was supposed to be always pronouncing a curse. In the version he gives, there are repeated echoes of the notes.

1. Rob my nest and cause me grief!
2. Robert Chambers (ed.), *Popular Rhymes of Scotland* (London and Edinburgh: W. & R. Chambers, 1870), p. 195.
3. grease, fat
4. *The Oxford Dictionary of Nursery Rhymes*, p. 129.

Stane-chack!
Deevil tak!
They wha harry my nest
Will never rest,
Will meet the pest!
De'il brack their lang back,
Wha my eggs wad tak, tak!

One of the great pleasures of country boys was hunting out nests to steal the eggs. There was even a name for it, bird-nesting, and it was a common theme in poetry from Thomson on. That the stonechat's nest was spared shows that the bird must have been regarded with a superstitious dread. Edward Armstrong says,

> Perhaps the stonechat and the wheatear became associated with the devil because their calls, suggestive of pebbles being knocked together, heard by timorous people in desolate places, may have aroused apprehension of unseen, evil presences moving close at hand . . . As we have noted in connexion with several species, quasi-human bird utterances are commonly regarded as uncanny and devilish; because the devil is conceived as the personification of evil and a being with partly human and partly animal characteristics, birds which seem to partake of two natures are associated with it.[1]

Lucky or unlucky, the birds of the folk were treated with a peculiar intimacy. Among the host of provincial names which Swainson collected (well over 2,000), there are a number of slangy nicknames. Here are some of the more colourful: huck muck; mealy mouth; feather poke; nicker pecker; dun pickle; skitty; thick knee; flopwing; cawdy mawdy. Even more surprising, some birds had Christian names. A few, like Jenny Wren, are still familiar, but there were a good many others, some of which are quite entertaining. Here is a sampling, again choosing the more colourful – and there is plenty of colour to choose from.

Mizzly Dick (mistle thrush)
Meg cut-throat (whitethroat)
Blue Tom (hedge sparrow)
Bessie ducker (dipper)
Peggy dishwasher (pied wagtail)
White wisky John (great grey shrike)
Sweet William (goldfinch)
Jemmy lang legs (heron)
Cornish Jack (chough)

Sometimes only a personal name was used. The wren could be called

1. *The Folklore of Birds*, pp. 195–6.

Kitty, the sparrow Philip, the hawfinch Kate. This is what Swift means when he says:

> . . . Pies and daws are often styled
> With Christian nicknames like a child.[1]
> (*The Description of a Salamander*, ll. 3-4)

This sounds charming when you read about it, but no one could use names like that today without feeling ridiculous. We give names only to those creatures which we know as individuals. It may be a pet python or a duck bought to lay eggs, but it is one particular animal with which we have established a personal relationship. We could call a dove in a cage Dorothy, but we would not transfer the name to every dove we saw. The species is anonymous – only the individual can have a name. In this way, no doubt, we are cut off from nature. We can enjoy animals in the wild. We can watch and admire, but we cannot relate to them unless they step in from the outside, unless they become a part of our world, unless they take on a human identity. Obviously, this was not true of the folk. An entire species could be treated as a kind of collective individual, as if it were a family of look-alike children.

One of the most striking characteristics of the oral rhymes is the direct relationship between person and bird. It was a common device in poetry for the poet to address the bird, as in the sonnet where Milton says,

> O nightingale, that on yon bloomy spray
> Warbl'st at eve . . .

No one supposes that Milton went out to the bloomy spray and started talking to the nightingale, but in the oral tradition this was not at all uncommon. A number of rhymes were actually spoken to the bird. The most widespread were probably the bird-scaring songs. In country districts, boys were used as living scarecrows to protect the newly planted fields. Armed with a clapper, they made banging noises and sang or recited a 'shooing rhyme'. The versions I have seen are all addressed to the birds. Here is one which, according to Halliwell, was 'the universal bird-shooer's song in the midland counties'.[2]

> Away, birds, away,
> Take a peck
> And leave a seck,[3]
> And come no more today!

1. Jack Daw and Mag Pie – also Madge, Magot, and Maggoty.
2. J. O. Halliwell (ed.), *Popular Rhymes and Nursery Tales* (London: J. R. Smith, 1849), p. 179.
3. Take a bit and leave a sackful

Some threaten the birds, as in this rhyme from the vicinity of Cheltenham.

> Shoo! all 'e birds,
> Shoo! all 'e birds,
> I'll up wi' my clappers,
> And knock 'e down back'ards,
> Shoo! all 'e birds.

Another type consists of rhymes which were said upon seeing a particular bird. A charming example is the couplet which country children addressed to the whitethroat.

> Pretty Peggy Whitethroat,
> Come, stop, and give us a note.

The most curious is the one which Chambers calls a 'rhyme of reproach'. Boys in the North of Scotland, he says, addressed it to the yellow yorling or yellowhammer – though more likely they shouted and screamed it, since the poor bird was 'cursed by the causeless hate/Of every schoolboy'. Like the stonechat, it had devil-toad associations. It was supposed to say 'De'il, de'il, de'il tak ye!' but it cursed in vain because children not only destroyed its nest, in some districts they strung up every nestling they could lay their hands on. Here is the taunt with which they greeted it.

> Half a paddock,[1] half a toad,
> Half a yellow yorling:
> Drinks a drap o' the de'il's bluid
> Every May morning.

A number of rhymes addressed to birds were superstitious formulas. In *English Folk-Rhymes*, published in 1892, Northall says that in the northern counties, when a crow flew across their path, peasants exclaimed,

> Crow, crow, get out of my sight,
> Or else I'll eat your liver and lights.

In Shropshire, on seeing a magpie, they spat three times and said,

> Devil, devil, I defy thee,
> Magpie, magpie, I go by thee.

The most intriguing are the divination rhymes where the cuckoo was asked a question. It was either when shall I marry or when shall I die, and the number of times he called was the answer. In nineteenth-century England it survived only as a children's game, but we know that it was once practised by adults. What makes it so interesting is that here, the person not only speaks to the bird, he assumes that the bird will answer.

1. toad

> Cuckoo, cherry tree,
> Good bird, tell me,
> How many years have I to live.

As soothsayers, as weather prophets, as calendars, the birds of the folk were directly involved in human affairs. You could speak to them, even call them by personal names, because there was a kind of communication between man and bird. They were less cut off, less on the outside. All this made them more meaningful than they are today. No doubt this is another way of saying that in the pre-industrial world, country people were close to nature. Sometimes we envy this, but it must be said that the intimacy could cause a good deal of uneasiness. Thiselton Dyer says, 'An old writer quaintly remarks, that "many an old woman would more willingly see the devil, who bodes no more ill-luck than he brings, than a magpie perching on a neighbouring tree."'[1] Wordsworth communed with a benign nature, but in the folk world it was more apt to be malignant. As W. Carew Hazlitt says, 'in all ages ... the bad omens fill a catalogue infinitely more extensive than that of the good'.[2]

The folk rhymes do not elaborate the birds, they present them baldly, sometimes simply by name. There is none of that word embroidery so characteristic of poetry. In fact some rhymes are so compressed, with so much left out, that unless you are familiar with the context you cannot understand them, as in the tiny verse which Scots children said when they heard the chaffinch.

> Weet-weet!
> Dreep-dreep!

(The first line imitates the bird, and the second the sound of rain drops, because the *wheet wheet* cry of the chaffinch was supposed to predict rain.) Compared to the wine of poetry which is served in such a dazzling array of glasses, the oral rhymes are like drinking water out of a tin cup. They are small and plain, but they clear your head after the wordy heights of the poets.

By the time the folklorists appeared, the oral traditions were already dying out. In 1849 Halliwell said:

> It may be that little of this now remains in England ... Many of the fragments in the preceding pages are, in fact, rather indications of what formerly existed than complete specimens of their class. It is beyond a doubt that, two centuries ago, our rural districts were rich in all kinds of popular and traditional literature, in legends and ancient rhymes.[3]

1. T. F. Thiselton Dyer, 'Birds', Ch. III in *English Folk-Lore* (London: W. H. Allen, 1884), pp. 82–3.
2. W. Carew Hazlitt, *Faiths and Folklore* (New York: Benjamin Blom, 1965: re-issue of 1905 ed.), Vol. II, p. 460.   3. *Popular Rhymes and Nursery Tales*, p. 275.

A similar situation existed in poetry. John Ray, writing in the 1670s, deplored the fact that the subject of birds was entangled with 'hieroglyphics, emblems, morals, fables, presages',[1] but by the end of the nineteenth century the rich fabric had almost completely disintegrated. Like folklore, it was an accretion which had developed over thousands of years, so convoluted, so layered that there are images which contain whole time spans like the raven as death bird, which goes back to the Ancient Near East. If the folk rhymes were smoothed by countless tongues, the oldest traditional birds were shaped and re-shaped by an endless stream of writers, beginning with the unknown Sumerians whose poems were inscribed upon clay tablets. Folklore was doomed by the spread of industrial society, but the main cause of the decay of the bird traditions was modern science. One can see this beginning as early as the seventeenth century, when Sir Thomas Browne measured the wing span of the dead pelican. The popular interest in ornithology created an audience of knowledgeable readers, and poets looking at real birds began to treat them less conventionally. Their individual approach and their use of a personal symbolism hastened the decline, and as the twentieth century unfolded, the bird traditions were gradually forgotten so that today, only bits and pieces survive. The modern period lies outside the scope of this book, but, generally speaking, it ushered in a kind of egalitarianism, opening the door to all sorts and kinds of birds, obscure or famous, foreign or fabulous, exotic or imaginary. With no generally accepted traditions and no single, readily comprehensible view of nature, poets are at once more isolated and more private than they were in earlier periods, and yet as far as their bird poetry is concerned, it does not represent a radical departure so much as an intensification of Victorian individualism. Fragmented realistic impressions, often very vivid and sharp, are combined with complex personal reactions. The measured Victorian view becomes intense, strange, difficult, unique.

In the time between the Anglo-Saxons and the present, a period of more than one thousand years, countless numbers of bird poems have been created. The primitive and the folk were preoccupied with the actual bird, because it had a direct bearing upon their lives. Medieval poets looked for revelations, reading birds as if they were signs which God had created to make his many teachings visible. The Elizabethans and their followers embellished nature with elegant exaggerations. The eighteenth century sought a middle ground, using reasonable conventions, while from the nineteenth century on, poets have explored both the objective bird and their own reactions. Each period believed in the basic

1. Charles Earle Raven, *John Ray, Naturalist*, p. 309.

validity of its birds, and yet still the view kept changing. So where, one might ask, is the true bird? The simplest answer would be with the realists, but their descriptions do not encompass the whole bird. Besides, if one looks ahead, if one tries to imagine what bird poetry will be like in a hundred years, or five hundred, or a thousand, the only thing one can say with absolute certainty is that the conceptions will keep changing. All these nets cast, all these webs of shining words, all these insights, these visions, these fantasies, these truths! Yet the real bird, the bird in its totality, escapes every net. What these poems really record is man's changing view of his world, and in this sense, the subject is man himself.

THE
POEMS

Anonymous: Old English

1 · *from* THE SEAFARER

(prob. 9th or 10th century)

... That man cannot know,
He who on shore leads a sheltered life,
How wretched I was on the ice cold sea,
Winter locked on the trackless waves,
Deprived of comrade and kin,
Ship hung with icicles, frozen hail flying.
There I heard nothing but roaring sea,
Ice cold surf. Sometimes the swan's song
Served to distract me, with gannets' clamour
And curlews' cries instead of laughter,
Seamews singing instead of mead.
Storms beat the stone cliffs where the tern answered,
Icy feathered, and the wet winged eagle
Often screamed: no kin to protect me,
No one to comfort my desolate heart.

(ll. 12–26)

2 · *from* THE FORTUNES OF MEN

(prob. late 8th or early 9th century)

Another shall hang from the gallows' height,
Dangling dead until the bone-chamber,
His bloody body, is broken to bits.
The dark coated raven rips out his eyes,
Tears at the flesh of the lifeless corpse,
But his hands cannot beat off the hateful bird,
That black winged ghoul, for his life is gone,
And he, past hope, past despair,
Dead on the gallows endures his fate.

(ll. 33–41)

Another shall tame that proud wild bird,
The hawk on his hand, until the sword-swallow

Is subdued. He puts on straps,
And feeds the fettered, wing-bold bird,
Tempting the sky-speeder with bits of food
Until the falcon, growing gentle
In all his deeds, obeys the food-giver,
Taught to sit on his trainer's hand.

(ll. 85–92)

3 · *from* THE BATTLE OF BRUNANBURH

(937)

Then the Northmen fled in their nailed ships,
Blood stained survivors on Dynges sea.
Over deep waters they hastened to Dublin,
Back to Ireland, disgraced in defeat.
So, too, the brothers, king and prince,
Both together, exulting in war,
Went back to their home in the West Saxon realm.
They left behind them the butchered bodies,
Flesh for the raven, the black coated bird
With the horny beak, food for the grey feathered,
White tailed eagle, carrion to glut
The greedy war-hawk[1] and that grey beast,
The wolf in the wood . . .

(ll. 53–65)

4 · RIDDLE 7 (MUTE SWAN)

(poss. 8th century)

My clothes are silent when I walk on the earth,
Or rest at home, or ride the waters.
Sometimes my wings and this lofty air
Lift me high above houses of men,
And the heavens carry me far and wide
Over the world. My feathered wings
Whistle loudly, singing a shrill
And melodious song when, moving high,
I pass like a soul over land and sea.

1. eagle

5 · RIDDLE 8 (NIGHTINGALE)

(poss. 8th century)

I talk through my mouth with many tongues,
Vary my tone, and often change
The sound of my voice. I give loud cries,
Keep my tune, make songs without ceasing.
An old evening singer, I bring pleasure
To people in towns. When I burst
Into a storm of notes, they fall silent,
Suddenly listening. Say what I'm called
Who like a mimic loudly mock
A player's song, and announce to the world
Many things that are welcome to men.

6 · RIDDLE 9 (CUCKOO)

(poss. 8th century)

When I was born, my mother and father
Abandoned me. I had no breath,
No pulse of life, but a kind hearted creature
Covered me up and kept me close,
Just as she would if we were kin.
A stranger, I was cosseted and cared for
Until in the warmth of that welcome breast,
I was brought to life. After that,
My foster mother fed me and then,
When I was strong enough to set out on my own,
I deserted her, so of daughters and sons,
She had fewer in spite of all she had done.

7 · RIDDLE 24 (JAY : *HIGORA*)

(poss. 8th century)

I am a wonder. I vary my voice,
Sometimes bark like a dog, sometimes bleat like a goat,
Sometimes honk like a goose, sometimes shriek like a hawk.
Sometimes I mimic the dusky eagle,
That war-bird's cry, sometimes I mock

The kite's voice, sometimes the gull singing
Where I sit glad. G suggests me,
Also A and R, with O,
H and I. Now I am named,
As these six letters clearly say.

8 · *from* GENESIS

(prob. end of 7th or beginning of 8th century)

The son of Lamech let a black raven
Fly out of the Ark on the empty flood.
Noah believed that if in his flight
He did not find land, the bird would be forced
To search the wide expanse of the sea
For the ship. But his hopes were all deceived:
The fiend soon fell upon floating corpses;
The dark feathered bird did not come back.
   After seven days and seven nights,
Noah let a grey dove out of the Ark
To follow the raven over the water,
And find out whether the foamy sea,
That high flood, had drawn back its waves
From any ground of the green growing earth.
The dove in her will flew far and wide,
But nowhere found rest. Because of the flood,
She could not set foot on any land,
Nor could she light on a leafy tree
Because of the streams. The highest hills
Were covered with water. When evening came,
The dove flew over the darkened waves,
Back to the ship, and hungry and faint,
She fell to the holy hero's hand.
   After a week, the dove was sent forth
A second time. Exulting in flight,
She flew far and wide until she found
A place to sit. She settled herself
In the midst of a tree, glad at heart,
Rejoicing because at last she could rest,
Perched on a branch of the beautiful tree.
She shook her feathers and flew off again,
Back with her gift, for she brought in her flight

The green leaved twig of an olive tree
To the hands of Noah. He knew at once,
The lord of the ship, that comfort had come,
Relief from trial. The happy man,
When three weeks passed, let the wild dove
Fly out of the Ark. She did not return,
For she came upon land with green leaved groves.
Never again would the glad dove appear
Under the black coloured, pitch painted roof
Of the well nailed Ark, when there was no need.

(ll. 1441–82)

9 · *from* THE PHOENIX

(prob. 9th century)

When the sun comes up from the salt sea,
That radiant bird, in all his brightness,
Flies from his branch in the forest tree,
And moves in swift winged flight through the air,
Singing melodious songs to the sun.
The phoenix's voice is surpassingly fair,
Inspired by his spirit's blissful joy.
His notes are sung in the clearest tones,
More marvellously than ever child of man
Heard under heaven since the Highest King,
The Maker of Glory, created the world
With earth and sky. The sound of that singing
Is sweeter and lovelier than any music,
More lyrical and delightful than any song.
It cannot be equalled by trumpets or horns,
Or the sound of the harp, or any voice
Of any man, or the musical strain
Of organ pipes, or the wings of the swan,
Or any sound which God created
To gladden man in this mournful world.

(ll. 120–39)

When the wind is still and the weather fair,
And the bright sun burns like a brilliant jewel,
And the clouds are gone, and the restless waves
Are calm on the waters, and every storm

Is still beneath the sky, and the candle,
The sun's flame, sheds its warmth from the south,
The phoenix begins to build in the branches,
Preparing his nest. Impelled by desire,
He is filled with passionate fervour, longing
To receive new life, to exchange old age
For the gift of youth. From far and near,
He brings the sweetest plants he can find,
Pleasant spices and forest herbs,
Gathering everything fragrant and fresh,
Everything scented and sweet and fair
That God, the Father of all beginnings,
The King of Glory, created on earth
As a gift for the sons of men. The phoenix
Carries his treasures to his lofty tree,
And there in the wild that wondrous bird,
High above ground, builds for his house
A beautiful bower in which he sits,
Sheltered from sun, his feathers suffused
In the fragrance that rises all around,
The aroma of bloom and spice and herb
That scents the shadows of the leafy shade.
He waits, eager to set out. Sky's gem,
The hottest sun of the summer tide,
Shines on the shadows as it moves in its course,
Looking on all the world. The house
Is heated by the rays of the burning sun.
The spices glow, the green hall fills
With fragrant fumes, then bursts into fire
That spreads its embrace over nest and bird.
The pyre is kindled, and flames enfold
The shrivelling house, raging in leaping
Yellow tongues. The ancient phoenix,
Worn with the weight of his many years,
Burns in the fire. His life fares forth,
And flesh and bone, doomed to die,
Are devoured in the fury of the funeral flames.
Yet out of that death his life returns,
In due time, after the embers fade,
And as soon as the cinders start to knit,
Shrinking to a ball. His lovely bower,
The bright nest sweet with scented leaves,

Is burned to ash, and the body of the phoenix,
That frail vessel, is wholly destroyed.
   The clump of cinders cools, and then,
In the lifeless ash, an apple is found.
Out of it slips a wondrous worm,
As fair as if it were formed in an egg
And hatched from the shell. There in the shade
It grows to a bird as beautiful at first
As the eagle's young. Still he thrives,
Flourishing until he is like the form
Of a full grown eagle. All his feathers
Blossom in beauty as shining and bright
As they were at the beginning, and then the phoenix
Is wholly restored, born again,
Free from sin . . .

                    (ll. 182–242)

The phoenix is fair, his breast all dappled
With different colours, artfully diverse.
Behind his head is a beautiful green,
Wonderfully glossed with purple glints,
And his tail is a glory of variegation,
Part dusky, part crimson, cunningly speckled
With shining spots. His wings underneath
Are snowy white, and his neck is green
In front and in back, and his beak glistens
Like glass or gem, and his throat is brilliant
Inside and out. The nature of his eye
Is piercing and strong, in looks most like
A glittering stone which the skill of a smith
Has put in a mounting of precious gold.
Around his neck, like a circle of sun,
The feathers are formed in a radiant ring.
His belly is beautiful, strangely fair,
Glorious and bright. A wonderful crest
Arches like an ornament over his back.
His legs are covered with shining scales,
His feet are yellow. In beauty nothing
Can match this bird, though as books have said,
He is best compared to a glorious peacock.
The phoenix is never lazy or wanton,
Never slothful like birds which fly

On sluggish wings, moving slowly.
He is nimble and swift and very light,
Unique in beauty, gloriously marked.
Eternal is the Prince who grants such bliss.

(ll. 291–319)

Anonymous
(c. 1200)

10 · *from* THE OWL AND THE NIGHTINGALE

When I was in a summer valley,
In a very secret cranny,
I overheard a violent quarrel
Of a nightingale against an owl.
Their fight was fierce and sharp and tough,
Sometimes soft, then loud and rough,
And each against the other swelled,
And all her evil anger boiled,
And each about the other said,
The very worst things that she could,
But most of all, about their singing,
They disagreed with loud haranguing.
  The nightingale began the clash,
Safe in the corner of a bush.
She sat upon the fairest bough
(About her there were blossoms enow),
Within a thick and close set hedge,
Entangled with reeds and green with sedge.
She was the gladder for the sprays,
And sang in many different ways.
Rather seemed the sound to rise
From harp and pipe than otherwise;
It seemed that it was shooting out
From harp and pipe instead of throat.
  There stood an old stump there beside,
From which the owl sang her tides.[1]

1. canonical hours

It was with ivy all begrown,
And there the owl made her home.
    The nightingale now looked at her,
And gave a very scornful stare.
She thought much evil of the owl,
For all regard her as hateful and foul.
'Monster,' she said, 'get out, be quick!
When I see you, then I feel sick.
Indeed, because of the noise you make,
My song I often must forsake.
My heart flips up and chokes my tongue,
Whenever I see that you have come.
I would rather spit than sing,
When I hear your ghastly scream.'
    The owl waited until it was dark,
And all at once she could not hold back,
For anger swelled up in her heart,
So her breath shot out both quick and short,
And the words came flying off her tongue.
'Now what do you think about my song?
Do you suppose that I cannot sing
Because I do not trill and twang?
You think by lying you can harm me:
You only speak to vex and shame me.
If I could get my claws on you,
I swear I'd teach you a thing or two!
If you came out from that bushy screen,
Then you would sing another tune!'
    Quickly the nightingale replied,
'If I stay put upon this side,
And guard myself in my retreat,
Then I can laugh at every threat.
If I remain within my shelter,
Then all your talk is turned to bluster.
I know that you are cruel to those
Too small and weak to defend themselves.
Whenever you can, you treat them badly,
For you are just a wretched bully,
And that is why the birds all hate you,
And that is the reason they always chase you.
When you appear, they screech and yammer,
And mob you with a shrieking clamour.

The titmouse herself, though small and puny,
Would tear you to bits and do it gladly.
Oh, you are horrible to behold!
Your ugliness is many-fold:
Your body is short, your neck is small,
And your ugly head is biggest of all,
With eyes as black as coal and broad,
Just as if they were dabbed with woad.
You glare as if you wished to bite
All that you with your claws can smite.
Your bill is strong and sharp and hooked,
Just like an awl whose shape is crooked,
And with it you clack both often and long,
And that is one of your ways of song.
Also you threaten me with force:
You wish to crush me in your claws.
Better for you to make your meal
On the frog that sits by the old mill wheel.
Mouse and many a nasty creature,
You eat because it is your nature.
You sit by day and fly at night,
So monstrous that you shun the light.
You yourself are horribly unclean,
And now it is your nest I mean,
As well as your nasty, filthy brood,
Fed by you on the vilest food.
You know what they do, a loathsome thing:
They foul their nest right up to their chin.

(ll. 1–96)

The owl listened all this while,
And her anger came to a sudden boil.
'Your name is nightingale,' she said,
'But chatterbox would do instead,
Because you're such a gabby pest!
Let your tongue have a little rest!
You think that the day belongs to you,
But I must have what is my due.
Give me my turn, don't interrupt:
I'll wreak my revenge, so please shut up.

(ll. 253–62)

And yet you say another thing,
You tell me that I cannot sing,
That all my songs are so weird and sad,
Whoever hears them feels afraid.
It is not the truth: though my voice is plain,
Its sound is full, with a ringing tone.
You think that every song is dreadful
That differs from your piping babble.
My voice is bold and clear and strong:
Its note is like a mighty horn,
But yours is as weak as a little pipe,
Made of a puny reed unripe.
My song is better, to say the least:
You chatter like an Irish priest.
I sing at eve at the proper hour,
Then later, when it is time to retire,
And again, my third, at middle-night,
So all my songs are ordered right.
When I see rising from afar
The break of day or the morning star,
I sing again, just as I should,
To wake men up for their own good.
But you sing all the livelong night,
From eve until the dawning light,
And ever sing your only song,
In length the same as the night is long,
And ever crow your wretched cry,
Which never ceases night or day.
With your piping you assail
The ears of men who near you dwell.
You make your song so cheap and worthless
That in the end it has no purpose.
Every delight which we enjoy
Can last too long and then annoy,
For harp or pipe or bird's sweet song
Displeases if it is too long.

(ll. 309–44)

The nightingale within her heart
Held all of this and carefully thought
What she should say in her reply,

For the nightingale could not deny
That the owl had made some excellent points,
And argued well in her defence.

(ll. 391–6)

'Owl,' she said, 'Please tell me why
You sing all winter "Wellaway!"
You sing just like a hen in snow,
And all she sings it is for woe.
In winter you sing in anger and gloom,
In summer you are always dumb.
It is because of your spiteful nature
That you cannot enjoy our pleasure.
When spring comes back with all its bliss,
You're eaten up with bitterness.
You act just like an evil man:
Every joy displeases him.
He grouches and scowls, burning mad,
Whenever he thinks that men are glad,
But he is happy if he sees
Tears in everybody's eyes,
Nor would he care if wool tufts were
A tangled snarl of thread and hair.
And this is the way that you respond:
When snow lies thick in all the land,
And every creature lives in sorrow,
You sing from eve until the morrow.
But I all gladness with me bring,
And men rejoice to hear me sing.
They are filled with joy when I appear,
For they wait for my coming every year.
The blossoms begin to spring and spread,
Both on the trees and in the mead.
The lily with her fair white hue
Welcomes me – and that you know!
Bids me with her lovely face
That I should fly to where she is.
The rose as well, with her radiant red,
She that comes out of the thorny wood,
Calls me, too, that I should sing
For love of her a joyful song,
And this I do both night and day –

The more I sing, the more I may –
Giving pleasure with my song,
Which never, I tell you, lasts too long,
For when I see that men are glad,
I do not go on, lest they be bored.
When what I wish to do is done,
I am wise enough to leave again.
When the thoughts of men are on their sheaves,
And brown has stained the green hued leaves,
Then I set out and say farewell,
For I do not care for winter's spoil.
When I can see hard weather come,
I travel back to my winter home,
And take with me both love and thanks,
That here I came and did my works.
When my mission is accomplished,
Should I stay on? No, I have finished,
And he is neither wise nor clever
Who lingers when his task is over.'

  The owl listened and laid up a hoard
Of all this speech, word for word,
And then she thought how she could best
Find answers that would fit the case,
For he does well to collect his thoughts,
When he is afraid of the other's tricks.

  The owl said, 'You ask me why
In winter I always sing and cry.
The custom is among good men,
And has been since the world began,
That everyone should cherish his friends,
And rejoice with them at certain times,
Within his house and at his board,
With friendly speech and friendly word.
At Christmas time, most of all,
When rich and poor, great and small,
Sing their part songs night and day,
I give them all the help I may.
But also I think of more serious things
Than pleasing myself or making songs.
A ready answer I have for this,
A fitting reply to help my case.
Summer time is all too gay,

And many a man is led astray.
He does not care for what is chaste,
For all his thoughts are filled with lust.
The beasts themselves are hot for sex,
And mount upon their females' backs.
The very stallions in the stud
Are wild because they're mare-mad,
And you are the same as all the rest:
Your songs are full of wantonness,
For you, whenever you wish to breed,
Are very excited and very bold.
As soon as you have had your way,
Then you have nothing more to say,
But pipe the way a titmouse does,
With choking sounds in a grating voice.
Then you sing worse than the poor hedge sparrow,
Who flits on the ground amid the stubble,
For when your lust is over and done,
Then your singing is also gone.
In summer time the peasants are crazed,
And corrupt themselves in a carnal rage:
It is not for love, nonetheless,
But only the fierce assault of lust,
For when a man has finished the deed,
All his boldness begins to fade.
Once he has stung beneath the dress,
Then his love no longer lasts.
And so it is with your own mood:
As soon as you have started to brood,
Your song goes sour, your tune awry,
For you behave in the self-same way:
When you are done with all your vices,
Your voice begins to go to pieces.
But when the nights come hard and fast,
And bring the freezing winter frost,
Then for the first time it is seen
Who is active, who is keen.
When days are bitter, then you find
Who goes forth, who lags behind.
In times of need I know at last
Who will take the difficult task.
As for me, I play and sing,

And amuse myself with a merry song.
I am never deterred by winter,
For I am not a flabby creature.
Also I comfort many a soul
Who suffers because he is poor and cold.
Full of care, miserable, drear,
They desperately crave a little cheer,
And so I sing again and again,
To lessen some of their bitter pain.

(ll. 411-540)

Anonymous
(13th century)

· 11 ·

Summer is y-comen in,
Loudë sing, cuckoo!
Groweth seed and bloweth mead
And spring'th the woodë now:
Sing, cuckoo!

Ewë bleateth after lamb,
Low'th after calfë cow,
Bullock starteth, buckë farteth,
Merry sing, cuckoo!
Cuckoo, cuckoo,
Well singës thou, cuckoo,
Ne swik[1] thou never now.

Sing, cuckoo, now! Sing, cuckoo!
Sing, cuckoo! Sing, cuckoo, now!

1. cease

Anonymous
(13th century)

· 12 ·

Lenten[1] is come with love to town,
With blossoms and with briddës' rown,[2]
That all this blissë bringeth:
Dayës-eyës[3] in these dales,
Notës sweet of nightingales;
Each fowl song singeth.
The thrustle-cock him threteth oo;[4]
Away is theirë winter woe,
When woodërovë springeth.
These fowlës singeth ferly fele,[5]
And wliteth in their wunnë wele,[6]
That all the woodë ringeth.

(First of 3 stanzas)

Anonymous
(13th century)

from THE BESTIARY

13 · *The Nature of the Eagle*

I will make known the eagle's nature
As I read it in a book:
How he reneweth his youthfulness,
How he cometh out of his age,
After his limbs have grown unwieldy,
After his beak is all distorted,

1. spring   2. birds' song   3. daisies   4. scolds always
5. marvellously many   6. whistle in their wealth of joy

After his flight is all enfeebled,
And his eyes are dim.
Hear how he reneweth him:
A well he seeketh that springeth ay,
Both by night and by day.
There-over he flyeth and up he goeth,
Till at last the heaven he seeth,
And through sky six and sky seven,
Up he cometh to heaven.
There as well as he can,
He hovereth in the sun.
The sun scorcheth all his flight,
And yet it maketh his weak eyes bright.
His feathers fall off in the heat,
And down he droppeth to the wet,
And falleth into that deep well,
Wherein he would be sound and whole,
And cometh out all new,
Were not his beak untrue.
His beak is still distorted wrong,
Although his limbs are sound and strong,
So he cannot eat a bit of food
To do him any good.
Then he goeth to a stone,
And he pecketh there-on,
Pecketh till his twisted beak
Hath foregone its crooked shape.
After, with his righted bill,
Taketh whatso meat he will.

MEANING

Just so is man as is this ern:
    Will you all now listen –
Old he is in his secret sin
    Before he becometh Christian.
And thus this man reneweth him,
    When he goeth to church;
Before he had considered this,
    His eyes were filled with dark.
He forsaketh Satan there,
    And every sinful deed;
Taketh him to Jesus Christ,

For he shall be his meed.
Believeth on our dear Lord Christ,
    And learneth priestly lore;
From his eyes now fadeth the mist,
    While he stayeth there.
All his hope is turned towards God,
    And of his love he learneth:
That is surely like the sun,
    And thus his sight he mendeth.
Naked, he falleth in the font,
    And cometh out all new,
But for a little – what is that?
    His mouth is still untrue.
His mouth is still all unacquainted
    With pater noster and creed;
Fare he North or fare he South,
    Learnen he shall his need,
And offer up his prayers to God,
    So that his mouth is cured,
And he can take the food for his soul,
    Through the grace of our dear Lord.

14 · *The Nature of the Turtle Dove*

In a book the life of the turtle dove
Is written in rhyme, how faithfully
She keepeth her love throughout her life time.
If she once should have a mate,
    From him she will not go.
Women think about her life:
    I will tell it to you.
By her mate she sits a-night,
    A-day they goeth and flyeth;
Whoso says that they are sundered,
    I say that he lieth.
But if this mate of hers were dead,
    And she widow were,
Then flyeth she alone and fareth;
    None other will she more,
But alone goeth and alone sits,
And for her old love ever waits,

In her heart holding him night and day,
As if he were alive ay.

MEANING

Listen, faithful men, here-to,
    And here-of often think:
Our soul when at the church's door,
    Chooses Christ for her mate.
He alone is our soul's spouse,
    Love we him with might,
And turn we never away from him,
    By day or by night.
Though he be from our vision gone,
    Be we to him all true,
No other Lord should we espouse,
    Nor any lover new.
Believe we that he liveth ever,
    Up in heaven's kingdom,
And he from there shall come again
    And be to us all useful,
For to judge the souls of men,
    Not all of them the same:
His hated foes to hell shall fare,
    His lovers to his realm.

William Langland

(c. 1332–c. 1400)

from PIERS THE PLOUGHMAN

15 · from *Passus XI*

Birds I beheld building nests in the bushes
Which no man has the wit even to begin to work.
I wondered where and from whom the pie could have learned
To put together the sticks in which she lays and broods,
For there is no craftsman, I know, who could construct her nest,

And it would be a wonder if any mason had made such a mould.
  And yet I marvelled even more at how many birds
Concealed their eggs which were carefully secreted
In marshes and moors so that men could not find them,
And their eggs lay hidden when they flew up in fear
Because of other birds or of beasts of prey.
And some trod their mates and bred in the trees
And brought forth their broods high up from the ground,
And some conceived by breathing through their beaks,
And others coupled, and I took note how the peacocks bred.
I marvelled much over what master they could have had,
And who taught them to timber so high in the trees,
Where neither man nor beast could get near their birds.

(B Text, ll. 336–53)

16 · from *Passus XII*

As for the birds and the beasts, the men in bygone times
Took them as examples and parables, as did the poets
Who said that the fairest fowl is the foulest engendered
And feeblest in flight of any that fly or swim.
That is the peacock and the peahen. They betoken the rich and the proud,
For the peacock, when someone pursues him, cannot soar up high
Because of the trailing of his tail, and so is soon overtaken.
His flesh is foul flesh, and so are his feet,
And he has a hideous voice, which is horrible to hear.
  So with the man who is rich: if he hangs on to his wealth
Until the day of his death, it is the tail of all sorrow.
As the feathers of the peacock hinder him in his flight,
So the coffers of golden coins are a cause of pain
To all who possess them, until their tail is plucked.
Though the rich man begins to repent, and berues the time
When he gathered a fortune so great, and gave up so little,
Though he cries out to Christ and calls on him, I believe
That his prayers in our Lord's ears are like the chattering of a pie.
And when his carcass shall come to be cast in the pit,
I think that its foul fumes will stink up the field,
And its stench will corrupt all the graves that lie in that ground.
As for the peacock's feet, they betoken, as I have found in fables,
The executors, those false friends who do not fulfil his wishes
As they were written out, though they were witnesses to his will.
Thus the poets show that the peacock is admired for his plumage,

Just as the man who is rich is made much of for his wealth.
   The lark that is a little fowl is lovelier of voice
And faster by far of wing, swifter than the peacock,
And of flesh by many-fold fatter and sweeter.
To men of lowly life, the lark is compared.
Aristotle, the great author, has told such tales,
For in his *Logic*, he used even the least of birds.

(B Text, ll. 236–67)

Anonymous
(14th century)

17 · *from* THE PARLIAMENT
OF THE THREE AGES

When the water fowl are found, the falconers hasten
To untie the leashes and let the hawks loose.
They snatch off their hoods and cast them from their hand,
And the hottest in haste quickly soar up high,
With their bells so bright ringing blithe and bold,
And there they hover aloft like angels in heaven.
Then the falconers furiously rush to the river
Where at the water they rouse up the fowl with their rods,
Raining blows all around them to service their hawks.
Then the tercelets[1] swiftly strike down the teals,[2]
And the lanners and lannerets swoop to the ducks,
Meeting the mallards and striking down many.
The hawks in the air hurtle down from on high,
And they hit the heron, whooped up by the falconers,
Buffet him, beat him, and bring him to the ground,
And assail him savagely and boldly seize him.
Then the falconers set out in hasty pursuit,
And run up hurriedly to give help to their hawks,
For with the bit of his bill the heron slashes about.
They drop down to their knees and crawl in cautiously,

1. male hawks   2. a kind of duck

Catch hold of his wings and wrench them together,
Burst open the bones and break them apart.
He picks out the marrow onto his glove with a quill,
And whoops them to the quarry that they crushed to death.
He feeds them and quiets them, and then loudly calls out,
Encouraging those on the wing to give up the hunt,
Then takes them on his hand and slips on their hoods,
Tightens up the thongs that secure their caps,
And loops in their leashes through rings of silver.
Then he picks up his lure[1] and looks to his horse,
And leaps up on the left side as called for by custom.
The carriers quickly put up the game fowl,
And wait for the tercelets that often are troublesome,
For some choose the chase, though others are better.
The mud-splashed spaniels keep springing about,
Bedraggled from their dunking when the ducks took to the water.

(ll. 210–45)

Anonymous

(14th century)

18 · *from* THE ROMAUNT OF THE ROSE

There is no place in paradise
So good in for to dwell or be
As in that garden, thoughtë me,
For there was many a brid singing,
Thoroughout the yard all thronging;
In many places were nightingales,
Alpës, finches, and wodëwales,
That in their sweetë song delighten
In thilkë[2] places as they habiten.
There mightë men see many flocks ˈ
Of turtles and of laverocks.
Chaláundrës felë[3] saw I there,
That weary, nigh forsongen[4] were;

---

1. device for recalling hawks   2. such   3. many   4. worn out with singing

And throstles, terins, and mavís,
That sangen for to win them praise,
And eke to súrmount in their song
That other briddës them among.
By notë madë fair servíse[1]
These briddës, that I you devise;
They sang their song as fair and well
As angels do espiritual.
And trusteth well, when I them heard,
Full lustily and well I fared,
For never yet such melody
Was heard of man that mightë die.
Such sweetë song was them among
That me thought it no briddis' song,
But it was wonder like to be
Song of mermaidens of the sea,
That, for their singing is so clear,
Though we mermaidens clepe[2] them here
In English, as is our usánce,
Men clepen them siréns in France.

(ll. 652–84)

Geoffrey Chaucer
(c. 1340–1400)

19 · *from* THE BOOK OF THE DUCHESS

Me thoughtë thus: that it was May,
And in the dawening[3] I lay
(Me mettë[4] thus) in my bed all naked,
And lookëd forth, for I was wakëd
With smallë fowlës a great heap
That had affrayed me out of my sleep,
Through noise and sweetness of their song.
And, as me mette, they sat among

1. service   2. call   3. dawn   4. dreamed

Upon my chamber roof without,
Upon the tiles, over all about,
And sangen, each one in his wise,
The mostë solempnë[1] servíse
By note, that ever man, I trow,
Had heard; for some of them sang low,
Some high, and all of one accord.
To tellë shortly, at one word,
Was never heard so sweet a steven,[2]
But it had be a thing of heaven,
So merry a sound, so sweet entewnës,[3]
That certës, for the town of Tunis,
I nold but I had heard them sing;[4]
For all my chamber gan to ring
Through singing of their harmony.
For instrument nor melody
Was nowhere heard yet half so sweet,
Nor of accord half so meet,
For there was none of them that feigned
To sing, for each of them him pained
To find out merry crafty notes.
They ne sparëd not their throats.

(ll. 291–320)

20 · *from* THE PARLIAMENT OF FOWLS

There mightë men the royal eagle find,
That with his sharpë look pierceth the sun,
And other eagles of a lower kind,
Of which that clerkës well devisë can.
There was the tyrant with his feathers dun
And grey, I mean the goshawk, that doth pyne[5]
To briddës for his outrageous ravýne.[6]

The gentle falcon, that with its feet distraineth
The kingë's hand; the hardy sparhawk eke,
The quailë's foe; the merlioun, that paineth

1. festive   2. voice   3. tunes   4. F. N. Robinson says that these two lines mean,
'Certainly, even to gain the town of Tunis, I would not have given up hearing them sing.'
5. pain   6. plundering, rapine

Himself full oft the larkë for to seek;
There was the dovë with her eyën meek;
The jealous swan, against his death that singeth;
The owl eke, that of death the bodë[1] bringeth;

The crane, the giant, with his trumpet's sound;
The thief, the chough; and eke the jangling pie;
The scorning jay, the eelë's foe, herón;
The falsë lapwing, full of treachery;
The starë, that the counsel can bewry;[2]
The tamë ruddock, and the coward kite;
The cock, that orloge[3] is of thorpes lyte;[4]

The sparrow, Venus' son; the nightingale,
That clepeth forth the greenë leavës new;
The swallow, murderer of the fowlës small[5]
That maken honey of flowers fresh of hue;
The wedded turtle, with her heartë true;
The peacock, with his angels' feathers bright;
The pheasant, scorner of the cock by night;

The waker[6] goose; the cuckoo ever unkind;
The popinjay, full of delicasy;
The drakë, 'stroyer of his ownë kind;
The stork, the wreaker of avoutery;[7]
The hotë cormorant of gluttony;
The raven wise; the crow with voice of care;
The throstle old; the frosty fieldëfare.

(ll. 330–64)

1. omen   2. betray   3. clock   4. little villages   5. bees   6. watchful   7. adultery

21 · *from* THE CANTERBURY TALES

from *The Nun's Priest's Tale*

His comb was redder than the fine corál,
And batailled¹ as it were a castle wall;
His bill was black, and as the jet it shone;
Like azure were his leggës and his toon;²
His nailës whiter than the lily flow'r,
And like the burnëd gold was his coloúr.
This gentle³ cock had in his governánce
Seven hennës, for to do all his pleasánce,
Which were his sisters and his paramours,
And wonder like to him, as of coloúrs;
Of which the fairest huëd on her throat
Was clepëd fair damoiselle Pertelote.
Courteous she was, discreet and debonair,
And companionable, and bore herself so fair,
Since thilkë⁴ day that she was seven night old,
That truëly she hath the heart in hold
Of Chauntecleer, locken in every lith;⁵
He loved her so that well was him therewith.
But such a joy was it to hear them sing,
When that the brightë sunnë gan to spring,
In sweet accord, 'My lief is faren in land!'⁶

1. notched 2. toes 3. of excellent breed 4. that 5. limb
6. My love has gone away

For thilkë time, as I have understond,
Beastës and briddës couldë speak and sing.
  And so befell that in a dawening,
As Chauntecleer among his wivës all
Sat on his perchë, that was in the hall,
And next him sat this fairë Pertelote,
This Chauntecleer gan groanen in his throat,
As man that in his dream is drecchëd¹ sore.
And when that Pertelote thus heard him roar,
She was aghast, and saidë, 'Heartë dear,
What aileth you, to groan in this manére?
Ye been a very sleeper; fie, for shame!'
  And he answerd, and saidë thus: 'Madame,
I pray you that ye take it not agrief.
By God, me mette I was in such mischíef
Right now, that yet mine heart is sore afright.
Now God,' quoth he, 'my sweven² recche aright,³
And keep my body out of foul prisón!
Me mette how that I roamëd up and down
Within our yard, whereas I saw a beast
Was like an hound, and would have made arrest
Upon my body, and would have had me dead.
His colour was betwixë yellow and red,
And tippëd was his tail and both his ears
With black, unlike the remnant of his hairs;
His snoutë small, with glowing eyën tweye.⁴
Yet of his look for fear almost I die;
This causëd me my groaning, doubtëless.'
  'Avoy!' quoth she, 'fie on you, heartëless!⁵
Alas!' quoth she, 'for, by that God above,
Now have ye lost mine heart and all my love.
I can not love a coward, by my faith!
For certës, what so any woman saith,
We all desiren, if it mightë be,
To have husbandës hardy, wise, and free,
And secret, and no niggard, ne no fool,
Ne him that is aghast of every tool,⁶
Ne none avauntour,⁷ by that God above!
How dar'st ye say, for shame, unto your love

---

1. troubled 2. dream 3. interpret favourably 4. two 5. coward 6. weapon
7 . braggart

That anything might makë you afeared?
Have ye no mannë's heart, and have a beard?
Alas! and can ye been aghast of swevenys?
Nothing, God wot, but vanitee in sweven is.

(ll. 39–102)

Sir Thomas Clanvowe

(fl. early 15th century)

22 · *from* THE CUCKOO AND
THE NIGHTINGALE

But as I lay this other night wakíng,
I thought how lovers had a tokening,
And among them it was a common tale,
That it were good to hear the nightingale
Rather than the lewdë cuckoo sing.

And then I thought, anon as it was day,
I wouldë go some whither to assay
If that I might a nightingalë hear,
For yet had I none heard of all this year,
And it was tho¹ the thridde² night of May.

And then, anon as I the day espied,
No longer would I in my bed abide,
But unto a woodë, that was fastë by,
I wentë forth alonë, boldëly,
And held my way down by a brookë side,

Till I come to a land of white and green;
So fair one had I never innë been;
The ground was green, y-powd'red with daisy,
The flowers and the grass alikë high,
All green and white; was nothing elsë seen.

There sat I down among the fairë flowers,
And saw the briddës trip out of their bowers

1. then   2. third

Thereas they had them rested all the night.
They were so joyful of the dayë's light
That they began of May to do their hours![1]

They coudë[2] that servícë all by rote;
There was many a lovely strangë note;
Some songë loudë, as they haddë pleyned,[3]
And some in other manner voice y-feigned,
And some all out, with all the fullë throat.

They preenëd them, and maden them right gay,
And dancëden, and lepten on the spray,
And evermorë two and two in-fere,[4]
Right so as they had chosen them to-year[5]
In February, on Saint Valentine's day.

And eke the river, that I sat upon,
It madë such a noisë as it ran,
Accordant with the briddës' harmony,
Me thought it was the bestë melody
That mightë been y-heard of any man.

And for delight there of, I wot never how,
I fell in such a slumber and a swow,[6]
Not all asleepë, ne fullý waking,
And in that swow me thought I heardë sing
That sorry bird, the lewëdë cuckoo.

And that was on a tree right fastë by;
But who was then evil apayd[7] but I?
'Now God,' quoth I, 'that diëd on the cross
Give sorrow on thee and on thy lewdë voice!
For little joy have I now of thy cry.'

And as I with the cuckoo thus gan[8] chide,
I heardë, in the nextë bush beside,
A nightingalë so lustily sing
That with her clearë voice she madë ring
Throughout all the greenë woodë wide.

'A! goodë nightingalë!' quoth I then,
'A little hast thou been too lóngë henne,[9]

1. to sing their matins 2. knew 3. complained 4. together 5. this year 6. swoon
7. ill pleased 8. *Gan* can mean *began*, but here, as in most of these poems, it is an
auxiliary for past time, in the sense of *did*. 9. hence

For here hath been the lewëdë cuckoo,
And sangen songës rather than hast thou:
I pray to God that evil fire him brenne!'[1]

(ll. 46–105)

John Lydgate
(c. 1370–c. 1450)

❧

23 · *from* DEVOTIONS OF THE FOWLS

Then I heard a voice celestial,
Rejoicing my spirits inwardly,
Of diverse souls both great and small,
Praising God with sweet melody,
In all his works full reverently,
With an heavenly hymn and an wholesome
Conditor alme siderum.

The popinjay alone gan sing,
And said, 'This is my property,
With *ave* or *kyrie* salute a king,
As scripture maketh mention of me,
In books of nature who list to see:
Wherefore me think I do not amiss,
To welcome the king of heavenë bliss,

That from the seat of the high Trinity,
Into a virgin's womb immaculate,
Descended this time of free voluntee,
And so became man incarnate,
To restore him to his first estate:
Wherefore I sing of his nativity,
A solis ortus cardine.'

The pelican sang with mourning cheer,[2]
'Of Christ's compassion I do complain,

1. burn 2. expression; mood

That mankind hathë bought so dear,
With grievous hurts and bitter pain,
And yet man cannot love him again:
Wherefore I sing as I was wont,
Vexilla regis prodeunt.'

The nightingale leap from bough to bough,
And on the pelican she made a cry,
And said, 'Pelican, why mournest thou now?
Christ is risen from death truly,
Mankind with him to glorify:
Wherefore sing now as we do,
Consurgit Cristus tumulo.'

The lark alsó full naturally,
Christ's ascension in humanity
Commended with song specially,
And said, 'Blessed be thou, Lord of felicity,
That hast called man to so high degree,
That never deserved of equity,
Eterne rex altissime.'

The dove alsó that is so white,
In heart both meek and beauteous,
Unto the earth she took her flight,
And sang a song full gracious,
Of all songs most virtuous,
And as I perceived, she sangë thus:
Veni Creator Spiritus.

The briddës present upon a tree
Were gathered together as covenant was,
Praising one God in Trinity,
That all this wide world doth embrace;
And thus they sang, both more and less,[1]
This melodious hymn with great solace,
O lux beata Trinitas.

(ll. 15–70)

1. great and small

Anonymous

(15th century)

· 24 ·

In what state that ever I be,
Timor mortis conturbat me.[1]

As I me walkëd one morning,
I heard a bird both weep and sing,
This was the tenor of his talking:
Timor mortis conturbat me.

I asked this birdë what he meant;
He said, 'I am a musket[2] gent;[3]
For dread of death I am nigh shent,[4]
Timor mortis conturbat me.

'Jesus Christ, when he should die,
To his Father loud gan he cry,
"Father," he said, "in Trinity,
Timor mortis conturbat me."

'When I shall die, know I no day;
In what place or country, can I not say;
Therefore this songë sing I may:
Timor mortis conturbat me.'

1. The fear of death discomfits me   2. male sparrow hawk   3. noble
4. destroyed

Anonymous
(15th century)

25 · REVERTERE

In a time of a summer's day,
   The sun shone full merrily that tide,
I took my hawk, me for to play,
   My spaniel running by my side.
A pheasant hen then gan I see;
   My houndë put her soon to flight;
I let my hawk unto her flee,[1]
   To me it was a dainty sight.

My falcon flew fast unto her prey,
   My hound gan runnë with glad cheer,
And soon I spurnëd[2] in my way;
   My leg was hent[3] all in a briar.
This briar, forsooth, it did me grief;
   Iwis it made me to turn a-ye,[4]
For he bore writing in every leaf
   This Latin word, *Revertere*.[5]

I hauled and pulled this briar me fro,
   And read this word full merrily;
My heart fell down unto my toe,
   That was before full likingly.[6]
I let my hawk and pheasant fare,
   My spaniel fell down unto my knee;
It took me with a sighing sore,
   This new lesson, *Revertere*.

Liking[7] is mother of sinnës all,
   And nurse to every wicked deed;
To much mischief she maketh men fall,
   And of sorrow the dance she doth lead.
This hawk of youth is high of port,[8]

1. fly 2. stumbled 3. caught 4. again 5. turn back 6. pleasantly 7. lust
8. wide ranging

And wildness maketh him wide to flee,
And oft to fall in wicked thought,
And then is best, *Revertere.*

Anonymous
(15th century)

26 · *from* 'WHEN NETTLES IN WINTER'

When sparrows build churches and steeples high,
   And wrennës carry sacks to the mill,
And curlews carry clothes horses for to dry,
   And seamews bring butter to the market to sell,
   And wood doves wear wood knives thieves to kill,
      And griffons [1] to-goslings do obedience –
   Then put in a woman your trust and confidence.

When crabbës take woodcocks in forests and parks,
   And harës been taken with sweetness of snails,
And camels with their hair take swallows and perch,
   And mice mow corn with waving of their tails,
   When ducks of the dunghill seek the Blood of Hailes,[2]
      When shrewd[3] wives to their husbands do no offence –
   Then put in a woman your trust and confidence.

(Last 2 of 4 stanzas)

1. vultures   2. Christ's blood, which was said to be at Hailes Abbey.
3. shrewish

Anonymous
(15th century)

· 27 ·

I have a gentle[1] cock,
   Croweth me day;
He doth[2] me risen early,
   My matins for to say.

I have a gentle cock,
   Comen he is of great;[3]
His comb is of red coral,
   His tail is of jet.

I have a gentle cock,
   Comen he is of kind;[4]
His comb is of red coral,
   His tail is of inde.[5]

His leggës been of azure,
   So gentle and so small;
His spurës are of silver white
   Into the wortëwale.[6]

His eyën are of crystal,
   Locken all in amber;
And every night he percheth him
   In mine lady's chamber.

1. fine   2. makes   3. of excellent stock   4. true to his breed   5. indigo   6. root

Anonymous
(15th century)

· 28 ·

With how, fox, how! With hey, fox, hey!
Come no more unto our house to bear our geese away!

> The false fox came unto our croft,
> And so our geese full fast he sought.

> The false fox came unto our sty,
> And took our geese there by and by.

> The false fox came into our yard,
> And there he made the geese a-feared.

> The false fox came unto our gate,
> And took our geese there where they sat.

> The false fox came to our hallë door,
> And shrove our geese there in the floor.

> The false fox came into our hall,
> And assailed our geese both great and small.

> The false fox came unto our coop,
> And there he made our geese to stoop.

> He took a goose fast by the neck,
> And the goose tho[1] began to quack.

> The goodwife came out in her smock,
> And at the fox she threw her rock.[2]

> The goodman came out with his flail,
> And smote the fox upon the tail.

> He threw a goose upon his back,
> And forth he went tho with his pack.

> The goodman swore, if that he might,
> He would him slay ere it were night.

> The false fox went into his den,
> And there he was full merry then.

1. then   2. distaff

He came again yet the nextë week,
And took away both hen and chick.

The goodman said unto his wife,
'This false fox liveth a merry life!'

The false fox came upon a day,
And with our geese he made affray.

He took a goose fast by the neck,
And made her to say, 'Wheccumqueck.'

'I pray thee, fox,' said the goose tho,
'Take of my feathers but not of my toe.'

Anonymous
(15th century)

29 · *from* 'HOLLY BEARETH BERRIES'

Nay, nay, Ivy!
It may not be, iwis,
For Holly must have the mast'ry,
As the manner is.

Holly beareth berries,
Berries red enow;
The thrustle-cock, the popinjay
Dance in every bough.
Wellaway, sorry Ivy!
What fowlës hast thou,
But the sorry howlet[1]
That singeth 'How, how'?

Ivy beareth berries
As black as any sloe:
There cometh the woodë culver[2]
And feedeth her of tho.[3]
She lifteth up her tail,
And she cackës[4] ere she go:
She would not for a hundred pounds
Serve Holly so.

(Burden and first 2 of 4 stanzas)

1. owl   2. dove   3. them   4. shits

Anonymous
(15th century)

30 · *from* THE SQUIRE OF LOW DEGREE

On every branch sat birdës three,
Singing with great melody:
The laverock and the nightingale,
The ruddock and the wodëwale,
The pië and the popinjay;
The throstle sang both night and day,

The martelet and the wren alsó;
The swallow whipping to and fro;
The jayë jangled them among;

The lark began that merry song;
The sparrow spread her in the spray;
The mavis sang with notes full gay;
The nuthatch with her notës new;
The starling set her notes full true;
The goldfinch made full merry cheer,
When she was bent upon a briar,
And many other fowlës mo,[1]
The ouzel and the thrush alsó.

(ll. 43–60)

Anonymous
(late 15th century)

31 · *from* THE FLOWER AND THE LEAF

And as I stood and cast aside mine eye,
I was 'ware of the fairest medlar tree
That ever yet in all my life I see,
As full of blossomës as it might be.
Therein a goldfinch leaping prettily
Fro bough to bough, and, as him list, he eat
Here and there, of buds and flowers sweet.

And to the herber[2] sidë was joining
This fairë tree, of which I have you told;
And, at the last, the bird began to sing,
When he had eaten what he eatë would,
So passing sweetly, that, by many-fold,
It was more pleasant than I could devise;
And when his song was ended in this wise,

The nightingalë with so merry a note
Answéred him, that all the woodë rang
So suddenly, that, as it were a sot,[3]
I stood astonied; so was I with the song
Through ravishëd, that, until late and long

1. more   2. arbour   3. as if I were a fool

Ne wist I in what place I was, ne where;
And ay, me thought, she sang even by mine ear.

Wherefore about I waited¹ busily
On every side, if I her mightë see;
And, at the last, I gan full well espy
Where she sat in a fresh green laurel tree
On the further side, even right by me,
That gave so passing a delicious smell
According to² the eglantine full well.

Whereof I had so inly great pleasúre
That, as me thought, I surely ravished was
Into Paradise, where my desire
Was for to be, and no further to pass
As for that day, and on the sweetë grass
I sat me down; for, as for mine intent
The birdë's song was more convenient,

And more pleasant to me, by many-fold,
Than meat or drink, or any other thing;
Thereto the herber was so fresh and cold,
The wholesome savours eke so comforting
That, as I deemëd, sith³ the beginning
Of the world, was never seen, ere then,
So pleasant a ground of⁴ no earthly man.

(ll. 85–126)

William Dunbar
(c. 1460–c. 1520)

32 . *from* THE GOLDEN TARGE

Right⁵ as the star of day began to shine,
When gone to bed was Vesper and Lucine,
  I rose and by a rosere⁶ did me rest;
Up sprang the golden candle matutine,

1. watched   2. agreeing with   3. since   4. by   5. just   6. rose bush

With clear depurit[1] beamës crystalline,
  Gladding the merry fowlis in their nest;
  Ere Phoebus was in purple cape revest[2]
Up rose the lark, the heavens' minstrel fine
  In May, intill[3] a morrow[4] mirthfullest.

Full angel-like these birdis sang their houris
Within their curtains green, into their bow'ris
  Apparelled white and red with bloomës sweet;
Enameled was the field with all colóuris,
The pearly droppis shake in silver show'ris,
  Till all in balm did branch and leavës flete:[5]
  To part from Phoebus did Aurora grete,[6]
Her crystal tears I saw hang on the flow'ris,
  Which he for love all drank up with his heat.

For mirth of May, with skippis and with hoppis,
The birdis sang upon the tender croppis,[7]
  With curious note, as Venus' chapel clerkis:
The roses young, new spreading of their knoppis,[8]
Were powdered bright with heavenly beryl droppis
  Through beamës red burning as ruby sparkis;
  The skiës rang for shouting of the larkis,
The purple heaven, o'er scaled in silver sloppis,[9]
  O'er gilt the treës, branches, leaf and barkis.

                                              (ll. 1–27)

John Skelton
(c. 1460–1529)

33 · *from* PHILIP SPARROW

          When I remember again
          How my Philip was slain,
          Never half the pain
          Was between you twain,

---

1. purified   2. clothed   3. into   4. morning   5. float   6. weep
7. tree tops   8. buds   9. clouds

Pyramus and Thisbe,
As then befell to me.
I wept and I wailed,
The tearës down hailed,
But nothing it availed
To call Philip again,
Whom Gib, our cat, hath slain.

(ll. 17–27)

It was so pretty a fool,
It would sit on a stool,
And learnëd after my school
For to keep his cut,[1]
With 'Philip, keep your cut!'
It had a velvet cap,
And would sit upon my lap,
And seek after small worms,
And sometime white bread crumbs;
And many times and oft
Between my breastës soft
It wouldë lie and rest;
It was proper and prest.[2]
Sometime he would gasp
When he saw a wasp;
A fly or a gnat,
He would fly at that;
And prettily he would pant
When he saw an ant.
Lord, how he would pry
After the butterfly!
Lord, how he would hop
After the gressop![3]
And when I said, 'Phip, Phip!'
Then he would leap and skip,
And take me by the lip.
Alas, it will me slo
That Philip is gone me fro!

(ll. 115–42)

For it would come and go,
And fly so to and fro,

1. behave   2. neat   3. grasshopper

And on me it would leap
When I was asleep,
And his feathers shake,
Wherewith he wouldë make
Me often for to wake,
And for to take him in
Upon my naked skin.
God wot, we thought no sin:
What though he crept so low?
It was no hurt, I trow,
He did nothing, perde,
But sit upon my knee.
Philip, though he were nice,[1]
In him it was no vice.
Philip had leave to go
To pick my little toe,
Philip might be bold
And do what he would:
Philip would seek and take
All the fleäs black
That he could there espy
With his wanton eye.

(ll. 159–82)

Alas, my heart it stings,
Rememb'ring pretty things!
Alas, mine heart it sleth,
My Philip's doleful death!
When I remember it,
How prettily it would sit,
Many times and oft,
Upon my finger aloft!
I played with him tittle-tattle,
And fed him with my spittle,
With his bill between my lips,
It was my pretty Phips!
Many a pretty kiss
Had I of his sweet muss![2]
And now the cause is thus,

1. wanton   2. mouth

That he is slain me fro,
To my great pain and woe.

(ll. 349–65)

> *Kyrie, eleison,*
> *Christe, eleison,*
> *Kyrie, eleison!*

For Philip Sparrow's soul,
Set in our bead-roll,
Let us now whisper
A *Paternoster*.

> *Lauda, anima mea, Dominum!*

To weep with me look that ye come
All manner of birds in your kind;
See none be left behind.
To mourning look that ye fall
With dolorous songs funerall,
Some to sing, and some to say,
Some to weep, and some to pray,
Every birdë in his lay.
The goldfinch, the wagtail;
The jangling jay to rail,
The fleckëd pie to chatter
Of this dolorous matter;
And Robin Redbreast,
He shall be the priest
The requiem mass to sing,
Softly warbëling,
With help of the reed sparrow,
And the chatt'ring swallow,
This hearsë for to hallow;
The lark with his longë toe;
The spink, and the martinet alsó;
The shoveller with his broad beak;
The dotterel, that foolish peke,[1]
And also the mad coot,
With a bald face to toot;[2]
The fieldfare and the snite;
The crow and the kite;
The raven, called Rolfë,[3]
His plain-song to sol-fa;

1. dolt   2. peer at   3. Ralph

The partridge, the quail;
The plover with us to wail;
The woodhack, that singeth 'chur'
Hoarsely, as he had the mur;[1]
The lusty chanting nightingale;
The popinjay to tell her tale,
That toteth[2] oft in a glass,
Shall read the Gospel at mass;
The mavis with her whistle
Shall read there the Pistle.[3]
But with a large and a long
To keep just plainë-song,
Our chanters shall be the cuckoo,
The culver, the stockdowue,[4]
With Puwit the lapwing,
The Versicles shall sing.

   The bitter with his bump,
The crane with his trump,
The swan of Meander,
The goose and the gander,
The duck and the drake,
Shall watch at this wake;
The peacock so proud,
Because his voice is loud,
And hath a glorious tail,
He shall sing the Grail;
The owl, that is so foul,
Must help us to howl;
The heron so gaunt,
And the cormorant,
With the pheasánt,
And the gaggling gant,
And the churlish chough;
The rout and the ruff;
The barnacle, the buzzard,
With the wild mallard;
The divendop to sleep;
The water-hen to weep;
The puffin and the teal
Money they shall deal

1. a bad cold 2. looks 3. Epistle 4. stock dove

To poorë folk at large,
That shall be their charge;
The seamew and the titmouse;
The woodcock with the long nose;
The throstle with her warbling;
The starling with her brabling;
The rook, with the osprey
That putteth fishes to a fray;[1]
And the dainty curlew,
With the turtle most true.

　At this *Placebo*
We may not well forgo
The count'ring of the coe;
The stork alsó,
That maketh his nest
In chimneys to rest;
Within those walls
No broken galls
May there abide
Of cuckoldry side,
Or else philosophy
Maketh a great lie.

　The ostrich, that will eat
An horseshoe so great,
In the stead of meat,
Such fervent heat
His stomach doth freat;[2]
He cannot well fly,
Nor sing tunably,
Yet at a braid[3]
He hath well assayed
To sol-fa above E-la.
Fa, lorell,[4] *fa, fa!*
Ne quando
Male cantando,
The best that we can,
To make him our bell-man,
And let him ring the bells;
He can do nothing else.

---

1. fright　2. gnaw　3. whim　4. worthless person

Chanticleer, our cock,
Must tell what is of the clock
By the astrology
That he hath naturally
Conceived and caught,
And was never taught
By Albumazer
The astronomer,
Nor by Ptolomy
Prince of astronomy,
Nor yet by Häly;
And yet he croweth daily
And nightly the tides
That no man abides,
With Partlot his hen,
Whom now and then
He plucketh by the head
When he doth her tread.

The bird of Araby,
That potentially
May never die,
And yet there is none
But one alone;
A phoenix it is
This hearse that must bless
With aromatic gums
That cost great sums,
The way of thurification
To make a fumigation,
Sweetë of reflare,[1]
And redolent of air,[2]
This corsë[3] for to cense
With greatë reverence,
As patriarch or pope
In a blackë cope.
Whiles he censeth the hearse,
He shall sing the verse,
Libera me,
In *de, la, sol, re,*
Softly B moll[4]
For my sparrow's soul.

1. scent   2. smell   3. corpse   4. sing flat

Pliny showeth all
In his *Story Natural*
What he doth find
Of the phoenix kind;
Of whose incineration
There riseth a new creation
Of the same fashion
Without alteration,
Saving that oldë age
Is turnëd into corage[1]
Of freshë youth again;
This matter true and plain,
Plain matter indeed,
Whoso list to read.

  But for the eagle doth fly
Highest in the sky,
He shall be the sub-dean,
The choir to demean,[2]
As provost principal,
To teach them their Ordinal;
Also the noble falcon,
With the gyr falcon,
The tarsel[3] gentle,
They shall mourn soft and still
In their amice of grey;
The saker with them shall say
Dirige for Philip's soul;
The goshawk shall have a role
The choristers to control;
The lanners and the merlions
Shall stand in their mourning gowns;
The hobby and the musket
The censers and the cross shall fet;[4]
The kestrel in all this work
Shall be holy water clerk.

                   (ll. 379–570)

  Oremus:
Deus, cui proprium est miserere et parcere,
On Philip's soul have pity!
For he was a pretty cock,

1. vigour   2. direct   3. tercel   4. fetch

And came of a gentle stock,
And wrapt in a maiden's smock,
And cherishëd full daintily,
Till cruel fate made him to die:
Alas, for doleful destiny!
But whereto should I
Longer mourn or cry?
To Jupiter I call,
Of heaven imperial,
That Philip may fly
Above the starry sky,
To tread the pretty wren,
That is our Lady's hen:
Amen, amen, amen!

(ll. 585–602)

Anonymous
(early 16th century)

· 34 ·

By a bank as I lay,
Musing myself alone, hey ho!

A birdë's voice
Did me rejoice,
Singing before the day;
And me thought in her lay
She said, winter was past, hey ho!
Then dyry come dawn, dyry come dyry, come dyry!
Come dyry, come dyry, come dawn, hey ho!

The master of music,
The lusty nightingale, hey ho!
Full merrily
And secretly
She singeth in the thick;[1]
And under her breast a prick,
To keep her fro sleep, hey ho!
Then dyry come dawn, dyry come dyry, come dyry!
Come dyry, come dyry, come dawn, hey ho!

Awake therefore, young men,
All ye that lovers be, hey ho!
This month of May,
So fresh, so gay,
So fair be fields on fen;
Hath flourish ilka den.
Great joy it is to see, hey ho!
Then dyry come dawn, dyry come dyry, come dyry!
Come dyry, come dyry, come dawn, hey ho!

John Heywood
(c. 1497–c. 1580)

35 · OF A DAW[2]

With a crossbow, late, in hand ready bent,
To shoot at a daw in a tree I went,
Saying to one by, 'I will assay to hit
Yonder I see a daw, if she will sit.'

1. thicket   2. The word daw also meant fool.

'She is, if she sit, a daw indeed,' quoth he,
'But if she sit not, what is she then, say ye?'
'A daw also,' said I. Then said he, 'I see.
Whether a daw sit, or whether a daw flee,
Whether a daw stand, or whether a daw lie,
Whether a daw creak, or whether a daw cry,
In what case soever a daw persever,
A daw is a daw, and a daw shall be ever.'

36 · OF BIRDS AND BIRDERS

Better one bird in hand than ten in the wood:
Better for birders, but for birds not so good.

37 · THE COCK AND THE HEN

A cock and his hen perching in the night,
The cock at his hour crowed loud as he might;
The hen, heavy of sleep, prayed the cock that he
Would leave off his crowing; but it would not be.
The hen saw the cock stick to his tackling:
In her treble voice she fell so to cackling
That the cock prayed her, her cackling to cease,
And he of his crowing would hold his peace.
'Nay, churl,' quoth she, 'be sure that will I not;
And for thy learning henceforth mark this knot:
Whenever thou wouldst seem to overcrow me,
Then will I surely overcackle thee.'

38 · OF USE

Use maketh mast'ry: this hath been said alway;
But all is not alway, as all men do say:
In April the cuckoo can sing her song by rote;
In June, out of tune, she cannot sing a note:
At first, cuckoo, cuckoo, sing still can she do;
At last, cuck, cuck, cuck – six cucks to one coo.

Anonymous
(mid 16th century)

39 · THE LOVER COMPARETH HIMSELF
TO THE PAINFUL FALCONER

The soaring hawk from fist that flies,
    Her Falconer doth constrain
Sometime to range the ground unknown
    To find her out again:
And if by sight or sound of bell,
    His falcon he may see,
Wo ho ho, he cries with cheerful voice,
    The gladdest man is he.
By lure then in finest sort,
    He seeks to bring her in,
But if that she full gorgëd be,
    He can not so her win:
Although her becks and bending eyes,
    She many proffers makes,
Wo ho ho, he cries, away she flies,
    And so her leave she takes.
This woeful man with weary limbs
    Runs wand'ring round about:
At length by noise of chattering pies,
    His hawk again found out,
His heart was glad his eyes had seen
    His falcon swift of flight:
Wo ho ho, he cries, she empty gorged,
    Upon his lure doth light.
How glad was then the falconer there,
    No pen nor tongue can tell:
He swam in bliss that lately felt
    Like pains of cruel hell.
His hand sometime upon her train,
    Sometime upon her breast,
Wo ho ho, he cries with cheerful voice,
    His heart was now at rest.

My dear, likewise behold thy love,
    What pains he doth endure:
And now at length let pity move
    To stoop unto his lure.
A hood of silk and silver bells,
    New gifts I promise thee:
Wo ho ho, I cry, I come then say,
    Make me as glad as he.

Anonymous
(mid 16th century)

40 · A POEM OF A MAID FORSAKEN

As late I lay within an arbour sweet,
The air to take amongst the flowers fair,
I heard a maid to mourn and sorely weep,
That thither used to make her oft repair.[1]

Alas, poor wench, quoth she drowned in despair,
What folly fond doth breed me my unrest?
Will spiteful love increase continual care,
To work her wrath on me above the rest,

And will she still increase my sorrowing sighs,
With pinching pain of heart, with torments torn:
Are these rewards or are they Cupid's slights,
To kill the heart which is with sorrows worn?

Then witness bear, you woods and wastes about,
You craggy rocks with hills and valleys low,
Recording birds, you beasts both strong and stout,
You fishes deaf, you waves that ebb and flow.

Here have in mind that love hath slain a heart
As true as truth unto her froward friend,
Whose dying death shall show her faithful part,
Whatso my dear hath always of me deemed.

    1. That thither used often to go.

The redbreast then did seem to be the clerk,
And shrouded her under the moss so green;
He calls the birds each one to sing a part,
A sight full strange and worthy to be seen.

The lark, the thrush and nightingale,
The linnets sweet and eke the turtles true,
The chattering pie, the jay and eke the quail,
The thrustle-cock that was so black of hue,[1]

All these did sing the praise of her true heart,
And mourned her death with doleful music sound:
Each one digged earth and pliëd so their part,
Till that she was close closëd under ground.

Anonymous
(1576)

· 41 ·

Even as the raven, the crow, and greedy kite
Do swarming flock where carrion corpse doth fall,
And tiring[2] tear with beak and talons' might
Both skin and flesh to gorge their guts withal,
And never cease, but gather mo to mo,
Do all to pull the carcass to and fro,
Till barëd bones at last they leave behind,
And seek elsewhere some fatter food to find.

Even so I see where wealth doth wax at will,
And gold doth grow to heaps of great increase,
There friends resort, and proffering friendship still,
Full thick they throng, with never ceasing praise,
And slyly make a show of true intent,
When nought but guile and inward hate is meant,
For when mischance shall change such wealth to want,
They pack them thence to place of richer haunt.

1. Here thrustle-cock means blackbird.   2. pulling, tugging

Anonymous
(1578)

42 · NO PAINS COMPARABLE TO HIS ATTEMPT

Like as the doleful dove delights alone to be,
And doth refuse the bloomëd branch, choosing the leafless tree,
Whereon wailing his chance, with bitter tears besprent,
Doth with his bill his tender breast oft pierce and all to rent;
Whose grievous groanings tho,[1] whose gripes of pining pain,
Whose ghastly looks, whose bloody streams out flowing from each vein,
Whose falling from the tree, whose panting on the ground,
Examples be of mine estate, though there appear no wound.

Francis Thynne
(c. 1545–1608)

43 · INGRATITUDE

The stamm'ring cuckoo, whose lewd voice doth grieve
The dainty ears with her foul note dismayed,
In the curruca's[2] nest doth her relieve,
Sucking the eggs which that haysugge[3] hath laid,
In lieu whereof, her own egg she doth leave,
Whereby she doth the gentle bird deceive.

Which that simple haysugge finding in place
(Poor silly fool, not knowing of this guile),
Doth lovingly nourish with mother's grace,
Hatching those eggs that did her bed defile,
By daily food them fost'ring, as they were
Of her own kind, and her true form did bear.

1. then   2. the bird victimized by the cuckoo   3. hedge sparrow

But these vile bastards, as they grow in strength,
And feathered are with wings of treachery,
Their nurse and mother do assault at length,
With thankless mouth tearing her cruelly,
Till piecemeal they devour each several part,
And suck the blood of their dame's loving heart.

So wicked men, the bastards of mankind,
Whom neither love nor reason can allure,
Whom others' great rewards to them should bind,
Because their life is nourished by their cure,
Actaeon's curs and thankless men do prove,
Wounding their patrons whom they ought to love.

George Gascoigne
(c. 1542–1577)

· 44 ·

He wrote (at his friend's request) in praise of a
gentlewoman, whose name was Philip, as followeth.

Of all the birds that I do know,
Philip my sparrow hath no peer;

For sit she high or lie she low,
Be she far off or be she near,
There is no bird so fair, so fine,
Nor yet so fresh as this of mine.

Come in a morning merrily
When Philip hath been lately fed,
Or in an evening soberly
When Philip list to go to bed;
It is a heaven to hear my Phip,
How she can chirp with cherry lip.

She never wanders far abroad,
But is at hand when I do call,
If I command she lays on load[1]
With lips, with teeth, with tongue and all;
She chants, she chirps, she makes such cheer,
That I believe she hath no peer.

And yet, besides all this good sport,
My Philip can both sing and dance,
With new found toys of sundry sort
My Philip can both prick and prance;
And if you say but, Fend cut, Phip!
Lord, how the peat[2] will turn and skip!

Her feathers are so fresh of hue,
And so well preenëd every day,
She lacks none oil, I warrant you,
To trim her tail both trick and gay;
And though her mouth be somewhat wide,
Her tongue is sweet and short beside.

And for the rest I dare compare,
She is both tender, sweet and soft;
She never lacketh dainty fare,
But is well fed and feedeth oft;
For if my Phip have lust to eat,
I warrant you, Phip lacks no meat.

And then if that her meat be good,
And such as like do love alway,

1. deals heavy blows – here used playfully   2. term of endearment for a girl

She will lay lips thereon, by the rood,
And see that none be cast away;
For when she once hath felt a fit,
Philip will cry still, Yit, yit, yit!

And to tell truth, he were to blame
Which had so fine a bird as she,
To make him all this goodly game
Without suspect or jealousy;
He were a churl and knew no good,
Would see her faint for lack of food.

Wherefore I sing, and ever shall,
To praise as I have often proved,
There is no bird amongst them all
So worthy for to be beloved.
Let others praise what bird they will,
Sweet Philip shall be my bird still.

Edmund Spenser
(c. 1552–1599)

45 · SONNET LXXXIX

Like as the culver on the barëd bough
  Sits mourning for the absence of her mate,
  And in her songs sends many a wishful vow
  For his return, that seems to linger late;
So I alone, now left disconsolate,
  Mourn to myself the absence of my love,
  And wand'ring here and there all desolate,
  Seek with my plaints to match that mournful dove.
Ne joy of aught that under heaven doth hove
  Can comfort me, but her own joyous sight,
  Whose sweet aspect both God and man can move,
  In her unspotted pleasance to delight:
Dark is my day whiles her fair light I miss,
  And dead my life that wants such lively bliss.

46 · *from* PROTHALAMION

With that I saw two swans of goodly hue
Come softly swimming down along the Lee;
Two fairer birds I yet did never see;
The snow, which doth the top of Pindus strew,
Did never whiter show,
Nor Jove himself, when he a swan would be
For love of Leda, whiter did appear;
Yet Leda was, they say, as white as he,
Yet not so white as these, nor nothing near;
So purely white they were
That even the gentle stream, the which them bare,
Seemed foul to them, and bade his billows spare
To wet their silken feathers, lest they might
Soil their fair plumes with water not so fair,
And mar their beauties bright,
That shone as heaven's light,
Against their bridal day, which was not long:
   Sweet Thames! run softly, till I end my song.
                        (ll. 37–54)

John Lyly

(c. 1554–1606)

47 · SONG

What bird so sings, yet so does wail?
O 'tis the ravished nightingale.
Jug, jug, jug, jug, tereu, she cries,
And still her woes at midnight rise.
Brave prick-song! who is't now we hear?
None but the lark so shrill and clear;
Now at heaven's gates she claps her wings,
The morn not waking till she sings.

Hark, hark, with what a pretty throat
Poor Robin Redbreast tunes his note;
Hark how the jolly cuckoos sing,
Cuckoo to welcome in the spring,
Cuckoo to welcome in the spring.

Sir Philip Sidney
(1554–86)

· 48 ·

The nightingale, as soon as April bringeth
Unto her rested sense a perfect waking,
While late bare earth, proud of new clothing, springeth,
Sings out her woes, a thorn her song book making;
    And mournfully bewailing,
    Her throat in tunes expresseth
    What grief her breast oppresseth,
    For Tereus' force on her chaste will prevailing.
      O Philomela fair, O take some gladness,
      That here is juster cause of plaintful sadness:
      Thine earth now springs, mine fadeth,
      Thy thorn without, my thorn my heart invadeth.

Alas, she hath no other cause of anguish
But Tereus' love, on her by strong hand wroken,
Wherein she suff'ring all her spirits' languish,
Full womanlike complains her will was broken.
    But I, who, daily craving,
    Cannot have to content me,
    Have more cause to lament me,
    Since wanting is more woe than too much having.
      O Philomela fair, O take some gladness,
      That here is juster cause of plaintful sadness:
      Thine earth now springs, mine fadeth,
      Thy thorn without, my thorn my heart invadeth.

49 · SONNET LXXXIII

Good brother Philip,[1] I have borne you long;
   I was content you should in favour creep,
   While craftily you seemed your cut to keep,
As though that fair soft hand did you great wrong.
I bare with envy, yet I bare your song,
   When in her neck you did love ditties peep;
   Nay, more fool I, oft suffered you to sleep
In lilies' nest where Love's self lies along.
   What, doth high place ambitious thoughts augment?
Is sauciness reward of courtesy?
Cannot such grace your silly self content,
But you must needs with those lips billing be,
   And through those lips drink nectar from that tongue?
   Leave that, sir Phip, lest off your neck be wrung.

Nicholas Breton

(c. 1545–c. 1626)

· 50 ·

Upon a dainty hill sometime
   Did feed a flock of sheep,
Where Coridon would learn to climb,
   His little lambs to keep.

Where roses, with the violets sweet,
   Did grow among the briars;
Where muses and the nymphs did meet
   To talk of love's desires.

There Coridon, when corn was ripe,
   For his sweet Phillis' sake,
Would play upon his country pipe,
   And all his music make.

1. a sparrow

Now when he had but sounded out
  The Beggar and the King,
The birds would all be flockt about
  To help the shepherd sing.

And every one began to frame
  To set in tune her throat,
Till dainty Philomela came,
  Who killed them with a note.

For she, sweet mouse, had such a vein
  Within a hawthorn bush,
As made the silly shepherd swain
  Himself to be at hush.

But as thus Philomela sat,
  Recording of a ground,
And all the rest did murmur at
  The sweetness of her sound,

Came Phillis sweet out of the wood,
  And in her hand a lute,
Who when she played but *Robin Hood*,
  Struck Philomela mute.

And when she but began to sing
  Of shepherds and their sheep,
She made the little woods so ring,
  They waked me from my sleep.

Thomas Watson
(c. 1557–1592)

51 · MY LOVE IS PAST

This passion is an imitation of the first sonnet in *Seraphine*, and grounded upon
that which Aristotle writeth of the eagle, for the proof she maketh of her birds,
by setting them to behold the sun. After whom Pliny hath written as followeth:
'The sea-eagle only compels its still unfledged chicks by beating them to gaze
full at the rays of the sun, and if it notices one blinking and with its eyes watering
flings it out of the nest as a bastard and not true to stock, whereas one whose
gaze stands firm against the light it rears.' [Trans. Harris Rackham.]

The haughty eagle bird, of birds the best,
Before the feathers of her younglings grow,
She lifts them one by one from out their nest
To view the sun, thereby her own to know.
    Those that behold it not with open eye,
    She lets them fall, not able yet to fly.
Such was my case when love possessed my mind;
Each thought of mine which could not bide the light
Of her my sun, whose beams had made me blind,
I made my will suppress it with despite:
    But such a thought as could abide her best,
    I harboured still within my careful breast.
But those fond days are past and half forgot;
I practice now the quite clean contrary:
What thoughts can like of her, I like them not,
But choke them straight for fear of jeopardy;
    For though that love to some do seem a toy,
    I know by proof that love is long annoy.

Robert Greene
(c. 1558–1592)

52 · VERSES UNDER A PEACOCK
PORTRAYED IN HER LEFT HAND

The bird of Juno glories in his plumes:
Pride makes the fowl to prune his feathers so.
His spotted train, fetched from old Argus' head,
With golden rays like to the brightest sun,
Inserteth self-love in a silly bird,
Till midst his hot and glorious fumes,
He spies his feet and then lets fall his plumes.
Beauty breeds pride, pride hatcheth forth disdain,
Disdain gets hate, and hate calls for revenge,
Revenge with bitter prayers urgeth still:
Thus self-love, nursing up the pomp of pride,
Makes beauty wrack against an ebbing tide.

Anonymous
(late 16th century)

53 · *from* AN ELEGY, OR FRIEND'S PASSION,
FOR HIS ASTROPHEL[1]

WRITTEN UPON THE DEATH OF THE RIGHT HONOURABLE
SIR PHILIP SIDNEY, KNIGHT, LORD GOVERNOR OF FLUSHING

Upon the branches of those trees,
The airy wingëd people sat,
Distinguishëd in odd degrees,
One sort in this, another that.
Here Philomel, that knows full well
What force and wit in love doth dwell.

The sky bred eagle, royal bird,
Percht there upon an oak above;
The turtle by him never stirred,
Example of immortal love.
The swan that sings about to die,
Leaving Meander, stood thereby.

And that which was of wonder most,
The phoenix left sweet Araby,
And on a cedar in this coast
Built up her tomb of spicery,
As I conjecture by the same,
Prepared to take her dying flame.

(ll. 25–42)

The bending trees expressed a groan,
And sighed the sorrow of his fall,
The forest beasts made ruthful moan,
The birds did tune their mourning call,
And Philomel for Astrophel
Unto her notes annexed a Phil.[2]

---

1. Pseudonym for Sidney. 2. That is, she added a *Phil* to her notes for Philip.

The turtle dove with tunes of ruth
Showed feeling passion of his death;
Me thought she said, I tell thee truth,
Was never he that drew in breath
    Unto his love more trusty found,
    Than he for whom our griefs abound.

The swan that was in presence here
Began his funeral dirge to sing:
Good things, quoth he, may scarce appear,
But pass away with speedy wing.
    This mortal life as death is tried,
    And death gives life, and so he died.

The general sorrow that was made
Among the creätures of kind,
Fired the phoenix where she laid,
Her ashes flying with the wind,
    So as I might with reason see
    That such a phoenix ne'er should be.

Haply the cinders driven about
May breed an offspring near that kind,
But hardly a peer to that, I doubt:
It cannot sink into my mind
    That under-branches e'er can be
    Of worth and value as the tree.

The eagle markt with piercing sight
The mournful habit of the place,
And parted thence with mounting flight
To signify to Jove the case,
    What sorrow nature doth sustain
    For Astrophel by envy slain.

And while I followed with mine eye
The flight the eagle upward took,
All things did vanish by and by,
And disappearëd from my look.
    The trees, beasts, birds, and grove was gone,
    So was the friend that made this moan.
              (ll. 187–228)

William Shakespeare
(1564–1616)

· 54 ·

The woosel cock so black of hue,
  With orange-tawny bill,
The throstle with his note so true,
  The wren with little quill;

The finch, the sparrow, and the lark,
  The plain-song cuckoo grey,
Whose note full many a man doth mark,
  And dares not answer nay.

55 · *from* LOVE'S LABOUR'S LOST

ARMADO: ... Will you hear the dialogue that the two learned men have compiled in praise of the owl and the cuckoo? ...

KING: Call them forth quickly; we will do so.

ARMADO: ... This side is Hiems, Winter; this Ver, the Spring: the one maintained by the owl, th' other by the cuckoo. Ver, begin.

The Song

Spring. When daisies pied and violets blue,
    And lady-smocks all silver white,
And cuckoo-buds of yellow hue
    Do paint the meadows with delight,
The cuckoo then on every tree
Mocks married men; for thus sings he:
    'Cuckoo!
Cuckoo, cuckoo!' O word of fear,
Unpleasing to a married ear!

When shepherds pipe on oaten straws,
    And merry larks are ploughmen's clocks;
When turtles tread and rooks and daws,
    And maidens bleach their summer smocks,
The cuckoo then on every tree
Mocks married men; for thus sings he:
    'Cuckoo!
Cuckoo, cuckoo!' O word of fear,
Unpleasing to a married ear!

Winter. When icicles hang by the wall,
    And Dick the shepherd blows his nail,
And Tom bears logs into the hall,
    And milk comes frozen home in pail,
When blood is nipped, and ways be foul,
Then nightly sings the staring owl:
    'Tu who!
Tu whit, tu who!' a merry note,
While greasy Joan doth keel the pot.

When all aloud the wind doth blow,
    And coughing drowns the parson's saw,
And birds sit brooding in the snow,
    And Marion's nose looks red and raw;
When roasted crabs hiss in the bowl,
Then nightly sings the staring owl:
    'Tu who!
Tu whit, tu who!' a merry note,
While greasy Joan doth keel the pot.

              (V, ii, ll. 904–39)

56 · *from* THE RAPE OF LUCRECE

'Come, Philomele, that sing'st of ravishment,
Make thy sad grove in my dishevelled hair.
As the dank earth weeps at thy languishment,
So I at each sad strain will strain a tear,
And with deep groans the diapason bear;
   For burthen-wise I'll hum on Tarquin still,
   While thou on Tereus descants better skill;

'And whiles against a thorn thou bear'st thy part
To keep thy sharp woes waking, wretched I,
To imitate thee well, against my heart
Will fix a sharp knife to affright mine eye;
Who, if it wink, shall thereon fall and die.
   These means, as frets upon an instrument,
   Shall tune our heartstrings to true languishment.

'And for, poor bird, thou sing'st not in the day,
As shaming any eye should thee behold,
Some dark deep desert, seated from the way,
That knows not parching heat nor freezing cold,
Will we find out; and there we will unfold
   To creatures stern sad tunes, to change their kinds.
   Since men prove beasts, let beasts bear gentle minds.'

(ll. 1128–48)

Joshua Sylvester
(1563–1618)

from DU BARTAS: HIS DIVINE WEEKS
AND WORKS

57 · from *The Fifth Day of the First Week*

   The pretty lark, climbing the welkin clear,
   Chants with a cheer, here peer I near my dear;
   Then stooping thence, seeming her fall to rue,
   Adieu, she saith, adieu, dear, dear, adieu.

The spink, the linnet, and the goldfinch fill
All the fresh air with their sweet warbles shrill.
But all this's nothing to the nightingal,
Breathing so sweetly from a breast so small
So many tunes, whose harmony excels
Our voice, our viols, and all music else.
Good Lord! how oft in a green oaken grove
In the cool shadow have I stood, and strove
To marry mine immortal lays to theirs,
Rapt with delight of their delicious airs?
And yet, methinks, in a thick thorn I hear
A nightingale to warble sweetly clear:
One while she bears the base, anon the tenor,
Anon the treble, then the counter-tenor;
Then all at once, as it were challenging
The rarest voices with herself to sing:
Thence thirty steps, amid the leafy sprays,
Another nightingale repeats her lays,
Just note for note, and adds some strain at last,
That she had connëd all the winter past:
The first replies, and descants thereupon
With divine warbles of division,
Redoubling quavers; and so, turn by turn,
Alternately they sing away the morn,
So that the conquest in this curious strife
Doth often cost the one her voice and life.
Then the glad victor all the rest admire,
And after count her mistress of the choir.
At break of day, in a delicious song,
She sets the gamut to a hundred young;
And when as fit for higher tunes she sees them,
Then learnedly she harder lessons gives them,
Which strain by strain they studiously recite,
And follow all their mistress' rules aright.

(ll. 672–709)

But, gentle muse, tell me what fowls are those
That but even now from flaggy fens arose?
'Tis th'hungry hern, the greedy cormorant,
The coot and curlew, which the moors do haunt,
The nimble teal, the mallard strong in flight,
The didapper, the plover and the snite;

The silver swan, that dying singeth best,
And the king's-fisher, which so builds her nest
By the seaside in midst of winter season
That man, in whom shines the bright lamp of reason,
Cannot devise with all the wit he has,
Her little building how to raise or raze:
So long as there her quiet couch she keeps,
Sicilian sea exceeding calmly sleeps,
For Aeolus, fearing to drown her brood,
Keeps home the while, and troubles not the flood.
The pirate, dwelling always in his bark,
In's calendar her building days doth mark,
And the rich merchant resolutely venters,[1]
So soon as th'halcyon in her brood bed enters.

(ll. 770–89)

    The stork, still eying her dear Thessaly,
The pelican consorteth cheerfully:
Praiseworthy pair; which pure examples yield
Of faithful father and officious child.
Th'one quites[2] (in time) her parents' love exceeding,
From whom she had her birth and tender breeding,
Not only brooding under her warm breast
Their age-chilled bodies bed-rid in the nest;
Nor only bearing them upon her back
Through th'empty air, when their own wings they lack;
But also sparing (this let children note)
Her daintiest food from her own hungry throat,
To feed at home her feeble parents, held
From foraging, with heavy gyves[3] of eld.[4]
    The other, kindly for her tender brood,
Tears her own bowels, trilleth out her blood
To heal her young, and in a wondrous sort
Unto her children doth her life transport:
For, finding them by some fell serpent slain,
She rents her breast, and doth upon them rain
Her vital humour; whence, recovering heat,
They by her death another life do get:
A type of Christ, who, sin-thralled man to free,
Became a captive; and on shameful tree

---

1. ventures   2. requites   3. shackles, fetters   4. old age

(Self-guiltless) shed his blood, by's wounds to save us,
And salve the wounds th'old serpent firstly gave us:
And so became of mere[1] immortal, mortal,
Thereby to make frail mortal man immortal.

(ll. 810–37)

58 · from *The Seventh Day of the First Week*

There on his knee, behind a box tree shrinking,
A skilful gunner, with his left eye winking,
Levels directly at an oak hard by,
Whereon a hundred groaning culvers cry;
Down falls the cock,[2] up from the touch-pan flies
A ruddy flash that in a moment dies.
Off goes the gun, and through the forest rings
The thund'ring bullet, borne on fiery wings.

(ll. 32–9)

Thomas Campion
(1567–c. 1620)

59 · *from* 'WHAT HARVEST HALF SO SWEET IS'

The dove alone expresses
Her fervency in kisses,
    Of all most loving;
A creature as offenceless
As those things that are senseless
    And void of moving.
Let us so love and kiss,
    Though all envy us:
That which kind and harmless is,
    None can deny us.

(2nd of 2 stanzas)

1. pure, unmixed   2. a lever, or spring hammer

Sir John Davies
(1569–1626)

60 · TO THE NIGHTINGALE

Every night from even till morn,
Love's chorister amid the thorn
Is now so sweet a singer;
So sweet, as for her song I scorn
Apollo's voice and finger.

But nightingale, sith you delight
Ever to watch the starry night,
Tell all the stars of heaven,
Heaven never had a star so bright,
As now to earth is given.

Royal Astraea makes our day
Eternal with her beams, nor may
Gross darkness overcome her.
I now perceive why some do write,
No country hath so short a night,
As England hath in summer.

Thomas Dekker
(c. 1570–c. 1641)

61 · SONG

O the month of May, the merry month of May,
So frolic, so gay, and so green, so green, so green!
O and then did I unto my true love say,
Sweet Peg, thou shalt be my Summer's Queen.

Now the nightingale, the pretty nightingale,
The sweetest singer in all the forest's choir,
Entreats thee, sweet Peggy, to hear thy true love's tale:
Lo, yonder she sitteth, her breast against a briar.

But O, I spy the cuckoo, the cuckoo, the cuckoo;
See where she sitteth; come away, my joy:
Come away, I prithee, I do not like the cuckoo
Should sing where my Peggy and I kiss and toy.

O the month of May, the merry month of May,
So frolic, so gay, and so green, so green, so green!
And then did I unto my true love say,
Sweet Peg, thou shalt be my Summer's Queen.

Thomas Heywood
(c. 1575–c. 1650)

62 · *from* THE RAPE OF LUCRECE

BRUTUS: What, so early, Valerius, and your voice not up yet? thou wast
wont to be my lark, and raise me with thy early notes.
VALERIUS: I was never so hard set yet, my Lord, but I had ever a fit of mirth
for my friend.
BRUTUS: Prithee, let's hear it . . .

Pack, clouds, away, and welcome, day:
With night we banish sorrow.
Sweet air, blow soft; mount, lark, aloft
To give my love good morrow.
Wings from the wind to please her mind,
Notes from the lark I'll borrow:
Bird, prune thy wing; nightingale, sing,
To give my love good morrow.
To give my love good morrow,
Notes from them all I'll borrow.

Wake from thy nest, robin redbreast:
Sing, birds, in every furrow,

And from each bill let music shrill
Give my fair love good morrow.
Blackbird and thrush in every bush,
Stare, linnet, and cock-sparrow,
You pretty elves, amongst yourselves
Sing my fair love good morrow.
To give my love good morrow,
Sing, birds, in every furrow.
(IV, vi, ll. 11–30)

Richard Barnfield
(1574–1627)

63 · *from* THE AFFECTIONATE SHEPHERD

from *The Second Day's Lamentation*
of the Affectionate Shepherd

If thou wilt love me, thou shalt be my boy,
  My sweet delight, the comfort of my mind,
My love, my dove, my solace, and my joy;
  But if I can no grace nor mercy find,
I'll go to Caucasus to ease my smart,
And let a vulture gnaw upon my heart.

Yet if thou wilt but show me one kind look,
  A small reward for my so great affection,
I'll grave thy name in Beauty's golden book,
  And shroud thee under Helicon's protection,
Making the muses chant thy lovely praise,
For they delight in shepherds' lowly lays.

And when th'art weary of thy keeping sheep
  Upon a lovely down, to please thy mind,
I'll give thee fine ruff-footed doves to keep,
  And pretty pigeons of another kind:
A robin redbreast shall thy minstrel be,
Chirping thee sweet and pleasant melody.

Or if thou wilt go shoot at little birds
   With bow and bolt, the thrustle-cock and sparrow,
Such as our country hedges can afford,
   I have a fine bow and an ivory arrow,
And if thou miss, yet meat thou shalt not lack:
I'll hang a bag and bottle at thy back.

Wilt thou set springes in a frosty night
   To catch the long-billed woodcock and the snipe,
By the bright glimmering of the starry light,
   The partridge, pheasant, or the greedy gripe?
I'll lend thee lime-twigs and fine sparrow calls,
Wherewith the fowler silly birds enthralls.

Or in a misty morning, if thou wilt
   Make pitfalls for the lark and fieldifare,
Thy prop and sweake[1] shall be both over-gilt;
   With Cyparissus'[2] self thou shalt compare
For gins and wiles, the ouzels to beguile,
Whilst thou under a bush shalt sit and smile.

                 (ll. 25–60)

· 64 ·

As it fell upon a day
In the merry month of May,
Sitting in a pleasant shade
Which a grove of myrtles made,
Beasts did leap and birds did sing,
Trees did grow and plants did spring;
Every thing did banish moan
Save the nightingale alone.
She, poor bird, as all forlorn,
Leaned her breast against a thorn,
And there sung the dolefull'st ditty
That to hear it was great pity.
Fie, fie, fie, now would she cry;
Teru, teru, by and by:
That to hear her so complain
Scarce I could from tears refrain;
For her griefs so lively shown
Made me think upon mine own.

1. Part of a trap for catching birds.　2. Boy loved by Apollo.

Ah, thought I, thou mourn'st in vain,
None takes pity on thy pain:
Senseless trees, they cannot hear thee,
Ruthless beasts, they will not cheer thee;
King Pandion, he is dead,
All thy friends are lapped in lead:
All thy fellow birds do sing
Careless of thy sorrowing:
Even so, poor bird, like thee,
None alive will pity me.

Anonymous: Madrigals and Lute Songs

· 65 ·
(1589)

The greedy hawk with sudden sight of lure
   Doth stoop in hope to have her wishëd prey.
So many men do stoop to sights unsure,
   And courteous speech doth keep them at the bay.
Let them beware lest friendly looks be like
The lure, whereat the soaring hawk did strike.

· 66 ·
(1595)

Sweet nymph, come to thy lover.
Lo here, alone, our loves we may discover,
Where the sweet nightingale with wanton gloses,
   Hark! her love too discloses.

· 67 ·
(1600)

Lady, the birds right fairly
Are singing ever early.

The lark, the thrush, the nightingale,
The make-sport cuckoo and the quail:
These sing of love, then why sleep ye?
To love your sleep it may not be.

· 68 ·

(1600)

A sparrow hawk proud did hold in wicked jail
Music's sweet chorister, the nightingale;
To whom with sighs she said: O set me free,
And in my song I'll praise no bird but thee.
The hawk replied: I will not lose my diet
To let a thousand such enjoy their quiet.

· 69 ·

(1600)

Sweet Philomel in groves and deserts haunting
Oft glads my heart and ears with her sweet chanting.
    But then her tunes delight me best
    When perched with prick against her breast,
She sings, 'Fie, fie!' as if she suffered wrong,
Till seeming pleased, 'Sweet, sweet' concludes her song.

Sweet Jinny sings and talks and sweetly smileth,
And with her wanton mirth my griefs beguileth.
    But then methinks she pleaseth best
    When, while my hands move love's request,
She cries, 'Fie, fie!' and seeming loth gainsays,
Till better pleased, 'Sweet, sweet' content bewrays.

· 70 ·

(1606)

Surcharged with discontent,
    To Sylvane's bower I went
To ease my heavy grief-oppressëd heart,
    And try what comfort wingëd creatures
Could yield unto my inward troubled smart,
    By modulating their delightful measures
        To my ears pleasing ever.
Of strains so sweet, sweet birds deprive us never.

The thrush did pipe full clear,
And eke with very merry cheer
The linnet lifted up her pleasant voice.
The goldfinch chirped and the pie did chatter,
The blackbird whistled and bade me rejoice,
The stock dove murmured with a solemn flatter.
The little daw, ka-ka he cried;
The hic-quail[1] he beside
Tickled his part in a parti-coloured coat.
The jay did blow his hautboy gallantly.

The wren did treble many a pretty note.
The woodpecker did hammer melody.
The kite, tiw-whiw, full oft
Cried, soaring up aloft,
And down again returnëd presently.
To whom the herald of cornutos[2] all sung cuckoo
Ever, whilst poor Margery cried: Who

1. hickwall, a name for the green woodpecker   2. cuckolds

Did ring night's 'larum bell?
Withal all did do well.
O might I hear them ever.
Of strains so sweet, sweet birds deprive us never.

Then Hesperus on high
Brought cloudy night in sky,
When lo, the thicket-keeping company
Of feathered singers left their madrigals,
Sonnets and elegies, and presently
Shut them within their mossy severals,
And I came home and vowed to love them ever.
Of strains so sweet, sweet birds deprive us never.

· 71 ·
(1607)

Come, doleful owl, the messenger of woe,
Melancholy's bird, companion of despair,
Sorrow's best friend, and mirth's professëd foe,
The chief discourser that delights sad care.
O come, poor owl, and tell thy woes to me,
Which having heard, I'll do the like for thee.

· 72 ·
(1608)

The nightingale, the organ of delight,
The nimble lark, the blackbird, and the thrush,
And all the pretty choristers of flight,
That chant their music notes in every bush,
Let them no more contend who shall excel;
The cuckoo is the bird that bears the bell.

· 73 ·
(1609)

Well fare the nightingale,
Fair fall[1] the thrush-cock too;
But foul fare[2] the filthy bird that singeth cuckoo.

1. may good befall   2. may evil befall

· 74 ·
(1609)

The white hen she cackles
And lays in the puddles;
Sing hey, cock without a comb,
Cock-a-dle luddle.

· 75 ·
(1611)

Awake, mine eyes, see Phoebus bright arising,
  And lesser lights to shades obscure descending:
Glad Philomela sits, tunes of joy devising,
      Whilst in sweet notes
      From warbling throats
      The sylvan choir
      With like desire
To her are echoes sending.

· 76 ·
(1612)

The silver swan, who living had no note,
When death approached unlocked her silent throat;
Leaning her breast against the reedy shore,
Thus sung her first and last, and sung no more:
Farewell, all joys; O death, come close mine eyes;
More geese than swans now live, more fools than wise.

77 · FOR THE HERN AND DUCK
(1614)

Lure, falconers, lure! give warning to the field!
Let fly! let fly! make mounting herns to yield.
Die, fearful ducks, and climb no more so high;
The nyas-hawk[1] will kiss the azure sky.
But when our soar-hawks fly and stiff winds blow,
Then long too late we falconers cry hey lo!

---

1. eyas, meaning a young hawk

· 78 ·
(1619)

Sweet Suffolk owl, so trimly dight
With feathers like a lady bright,
Thou sing'st alone, sitting by night,
  Te whit, te whoo, te whit, te whoo
Thy note, that forth so freely rolls,
With shrill command the mouse controls,
And sings a dirge for dying souls,
  Te whit, te whoo, te whit, te whoo.

· 79 ·
(1620)

Pretty wantons, sweetly sing
In honour of the smiling spring.
Look how the light-winged chirping choir
With nimble skips the spring admire.
But O, hark how the birds sing, O mark that note,
  Jug, jug, tereu, tereu,
O prett'ly warbled from a sweet sweet throat.

Michael Drayton
(1563–1631)

80 · *from* THE MUSES' ELYSIUM

from *The Second Nymphal*

LALUS: I have two sparrows white as snow,
        Whose pretty eyes like sparks do show;
        In her bosom Venus hatcht them
        Where her little Cupid watcht them,
        Till they, too, fledge,[1] their nests forsook
        Themselves and to the fields betook,

        1. fit to fly; fledged

Where by chance a fowler caught them
Of whom I full dearly bought them;
They'll fetch you conserve from the hip,[1]
And lay it softly on your lip,
Through their nibbling bills they'll chirrup
And fluttering feed you with the syrup,
And if thence you put them by,
They to your white neck will fly,
And if you expulse them there,
They'll hang upon your braided hair;
You so long shall see them prattle,
Till at length they'll fall to battle,
And when they have fought their fill,
You will smile to see them bill.
These birds my Lirope's shall be,
So thou'llt leave him and go with me.

CLEON: His sparrows are not worth a rush:
I'll find as good in every bush.
Of doves I have a dainty pair
Which when you please to take the air,
About your head shall gently hover,
Your clear brow from the sun to cover,
And with their nimble wings shall fan you,
That neither cold nor heat shall tan you,
And like umbrellas with their feathers
Shield you in all sorts of weathers:
They be most dainty coloured things,
They have damask backs and checkered wings,
Their necks more various colours show
Than there be mixèd in the bow;
Venus saw the lesser dove
And therewith was far in love,
Offering for't her golden ball,
For her son to play withal.
These my Lirope's shall be,
So she'll leave him and go with me.

LIROPE: Then for sparrows and for doves,
I am fitted twixt my loves,
But Lalus, I take no delight
In sparrows, for they'll scratch and bite,

1. The fruit of the wild rose.

And though joined, they are ever wooing,
Always billing if not doing.
Twixt Venus' breasts if they have lyen,
I much fear they'll infect mine;
Cleon, your doves are very dainty,
Tame pigeons else you know are plenty,
These may win some of your marrows;[1]
I am not caught with doves nor sparrows.
I thank ye kindly for your cost,
Yet your labour is but lost.

(ll. 143–98)

81 · *from* POLYOLBION
(1612)

from *The Thirteenth Song*

When Phoebus lifts his head out of the winter's wave,
No sooner doth the earth her flowery bosom brave,
At such time as the year brings on the pleasant spring,
But Hunt's-up to the morn the feath'red sylvans sing:
And in the lower grove, as on the rising knoll,
Upon the highest spray of every mounting pole,
Those choristers are percht with many a speckled breast.
Then from her burnisht gate the goodly glitt'ring east
Gilds every lofty top, which late the humorous[2] night
Bespangled had with pearl, to please the morning's sight:
On which the mirthful choirs, with their clear open throats,
Unto the joyful morn so strain their warbling notes,
That hills and valleys ring, and even the echoing air
Seems all composed of sounds, about them everywhere.
The throstle, with shrill sharps, as purposely he song
T'awake the lustless sun, or chiding that so long
He was in coming forth that should the thickets thrill:
The woosel near at hand, that hath a golden bill,
As nature him had markt of purpose, t'let us see
That from all other birds his tunes should different be:
For with their vocal sounds they sing to pleasant May;
Upon his dulcet pipe the merle doth only play.*

1. companions   2. moist, humid, damp
* Of all birds, only the blackbird whistleth. – M.D.

When in the lower brake, the nightingale hard by,
In such lamenting strains the joyful hours doth ply,
As though the other birds she to her tunes would draw;
And, but that nature (by her all-constraining law)
Each bird to her own kind this season doth invite,
They else, alone to hear that charmer of the night,
The more to use their ears, their voices sure would spare,
That moduleth her tunes so admirably rare,
As man to set in parts at first had learned of her.
   To Philomel the next, the linnet we prefer;
And by that warbling bird, the wood lark place we then,
The reed sparrow, the nope, the redbreast, and the wren,
The yellow pate, which though she hurt the blooming tree,
Yet scarce hath any bird a finer pipe than she.
And of these chanting fowls, the goldfinch not behind,
That hath so many sorts descending from her kind.
The tydie for her notes as delicate as they,
The laughing hecco, then the counterfeiting jay,
The softer with the shrill (some hid among the leaves,
Some in the taller trees, some in the lower greaves)
Thus sing away the morn, until the mounting sun
Through thick exhaled fogs his golden head hath run,
And through the twisted tops of our close covert creeps
To kiss the gentle shade, this while that sweetly sleeps.

(ll. 41–86)

82 · *from* POLYOLBION
(1622)

from *The Twenty-fifth Song*

My various fleets for fowl, O who is he can tell
The species that in me for multitudes excel![1]
The duck and mallard first, the falconer's only sport
(Of river-flights the chief, so that all other sort
They only green-fowl term), in every mere abound,
That you would think they sat upon the very ground,
Their numbers be so great, the waters covering quite,
That raised, the spacious air is darkened with their flight;

---

1. The fen itself is speaking.

Yet still the dangerous dykes from shot do them secure,
Where they from flash to flash[1] like the full epicure
Waft, as they loved to change their diet every meal;
And near to them ye see the lesser dibbling teal
In bunches with the first that fly from mere to mere,
As they above the rest were lords of earth and air.
The goosander with them my goodly fens do show,
His head as ebon black, the rest as white as snow,
With whom the wigeon goes, the goldeneye, the smeath,
And in odd scatt'red pits,[2] the flags and reeds beneath,
The coot, bald, else clean black, that whiteness it doth bear
Upon the forehead starred, the water-hen doth wear
Upon her little tail in one small feather set.
The water-woosel next, all over black as jet,
With various colours, black, green, blue, red, russet, white,
Do yield the gazing eye as variable delight
As do those sundry fowls whose several plumes they be.
The diving dabchick here among the rest you see,
Now up, now down again, that hard it is to prove
Whether under water most it liveth, or above:
With which last little fowl (that water may not lack,
More than the dabchick doth, and more doth love the brack[3])
The puffin we compare, which coming to the dish
Nice palates hardly judge if it be flesh or fish.
    But wherefore should I stand upon such toys as these,
That have so goodly fowls the wand'ring eye to please.
Here in my vaster pools, as white as snow or milk
(In water black as Styx) swims the wild swan, the elk,
Of Hollanders[4] so termed, no niggard of his breath
(As poets say of swans which only sing in death)
But oft as other birds is heard his tunes to rote,[5]
Which like a trumpet comes from his long archèd throat,
And towards this wat'ry kind, about the flash's brim,
Some cloven-footed are, by nature not to swim.
There stalks the stately crane as though he marched in war,
By him that hath the hern which by the fishy carr[6]
Can fetch with their long necks out of the rush and reed,
Snigs, fry, and yellow frogs, whereon they often feed:
And under them again (that water never take,
But by some ditch's side or little shallow lake

1. pool, marshy place   2. pool, pond   3. salt water   4. This district was called
Holland.   5. to repeat   6. pool

Lie dabbling night and day) the palate-pleasing snite,
The bidcock, and like them the redshank, that delight
Together still to be in some small reedy bed,
In which these little fowls in summer's time were bred.
The buzzing bitter sits, which through his hollow bill
A sudden bellowing sends, which many times doth fill
The neighbouring marsh with noise as though a bull did roar;
But scarcely have I yet recited half my store:
And with my wondrous flocks of wild geese come I then,
Which look as though alone they peopled all the fen,
Which here in winter time when all is overflowed,
And want of solid sward enforceth them abroad,
Th'abundance then is seen that my full fens do yield,
That almost through the isle do pester¹ every field.
The barnacles with them which, wheresoe'er they breed,
On trees or rotten ships, yet to my fens for feed
Continually they come and chief abode do make,
And very hardly forced my plenty to forsake:
Who almost all this kind do challenge as mine own,
Whose like I dare aver is elsewhere hardly known.
For sure unless in me no one yet ever saw
The multitudes of fowl in mooting² time they draw:
From which to many a one much profit doth accrue.
  Now such as flying feed, next these I must pursue;
The seamew, sea-pie, gull, and curlew here do keep,
As searching every shoal and watching every deep,
To find the floating fry with their sharp-piercing sight,
Which suddenly they take by stooping from their height.
The cormorant then comes (by his devouring kind)
Which flying o'er the fen immediately doth find
The fleet best stored of fish, when from his wings at full,
As though he shot himself into the thick'ned skull,
He under water goes and so the shoal pursues,
Which into creeks do fly, when quickly he doth choose
The fin that likes him best, and rising, flying feeds.
The osprey oft here seen, though seldom here it breeds,
Which over them the fish no sooner do espy,
But (betwixt him and them, by an antipathy)
Turning their bellies up, as though their death they saw,
They at his pleasure lie to stuff his glutt'nous maw.

(ll. 51–138)

1. crowd   2. moulting

83 · *from* NOAH'S FLOOD

And as our God the beasts had given in charge
To take the ark, themselves so to imbarge,
He bids the fowl: the eagle in his flight
Cleaving the thin air, on the deck doth light;
Nor are his eyes so piercing to control
His lowly subjects, the far lesser fowl,
But the Almighty who all creatures framed,
And them by Adam in the garden named,
Had given courage, fast by him to sit,
Nor at his sharp sight are amazed one whit;
The swan by his great Maker taught this good,
T'avoid the fury of the falling flood,
His boat-like breast, his wings raised for his sail,
And oar-like feet, him nothing to avail
Against the rain which likely was to fall,
Each drop so great that like a ponderous mall
Might sink him under water and might drown
Him in the deluge, with the crane comes down,
Whose voice the trumpet is that through the air
Doth summon all the other to repair
To the new Ark: when with his moonèd train
The strutting peacock, yawling 'gainst the rain,
Flutters into the Ark, by his shrill cry
Telling the rest the tempest to be nigh;
The iron-eating ostrich, whose bare thighs
Resembling man's, fearing the low'ring skies,
Walks to the great boat; when the crownèd cock,
That to the village lately was the clock,
Comes to roost by him, with his hen, foreshowing
The shower should quickly fall, that then was brewing;
The swift-winged swallow feeding as it flies,
With the fleet martlet thrilling through the skies,
As at their pastime sportively they were,
Feeling th'unusual moisture of the air,
Their feathers flag, into the Ark they come
As to some rock or building, their own home;
The airy lark, his halleluiah sung,
Finding a slackness seize upon his tongue
By the much moisture, and the welkin dark,
Drops with his female down into the Ark;

The soaring kite there scantled[1] his large wings,
And to the Ark the hovering kestrel brings;
The raven comes, and croaking, in doth call
The carrion crow, and she again doth brall,
Foretelling rain; by these there likewise sat
The careful stork, since Adam wond'red at
For thankfulness, to those where he doth breed,
That his ag'd parents naturally doth feed,
In filial duty as instructing man;
By them there sat the loving pelican,
Whose young ones pois'ned by the serpent's sting,
With her own blood to life again doth bring;
The constant turtle up her lodging took
By these good birds; and in a little nook
The nightingale with her melodious tongue
Sadly there sits, as she had never sung;
The merle and mavis on the highest spray,
Who with their music waked the early day,
From the proud cedars to the Ark come down,
As though forewarned that God the world would drown;
The prating parrot comes to them aboard,
And is not heard to counterfeit a word;
The falcon and the dove sit there together,
And th'one of them doth prune the other's feather;
The goshawk and the pheasant there do twin,
And in the Ark are percht upon one pin;
The partridge on the sparhawk there doth tend,
Who entertains her as a loving friend;
The ravenous vulture feels the small birds sit
Upon his back, and is not moved a whit;
Amongst the thickest of these several fowl,
With open eyes still sat the broad-faced owl,
And not a small bird, as they wonted were,
Either pursued or wond'red at her there.
No wayless desert, heath, nor fen, nor moor,
But in by couples sent some of their store;
The osprey and the cormorant forbear
To fish, and thither with the rest repair;
The heron leaves watching at the river's brim,
And brings the snite and plover in with him.

1. drew in

There came the halcyon, whom the sea obeys
When she her nest upon the water lays;
The goose which doth for watchfulness excel
Came for the rest to be the sentinel.
The charitable robinet in came,
Whose nature taught the others to be tame:
All feathered things yet ever known to men,
From the huge roc unto the little wren;
From forests, fields, from rivers, and from ponds,
All that have webs, or cloven-footed ones,
To the grand Ark together friendly came,
Whose several species were too long to name.

(ll. 361–452)

William Drummond
(1585–1649)

84 · MADRIGAL

Poor turtle, thou bemoans
The loss of thy dear love,
And I for mine send forth these smoking groans:
Unhappy widowed dove!
While all about do sing,
I at the root, thou on the branch above,
Even weary with our moans the gaudy spring.
    Yet these our plaints we do not spend in vain,
    Sith sighing zephyrs answer us again.

Richard Brathwaite

(c. 1588–1673)

· 85 ·

Jug, jug! Fair fall[1] the nightingal,
    Whose tender breast
Chants out her merry madrigal,
    With hawthorn pressed:
Te'u, te'u! thus sings she even by even,
And represents the melody in heaven:
        Tis, tis,
    I am not as I wish.

Rape-defilëd Philomel
    In her sad mischance
Tells what she is forced to tell,
    While the satyrs dance:
Unhappy I, quoth she, unhappy I,
That am betrayed by Tereus' treachery;
        Tis, tis,
    I am not as I wish.

Chaste-unchaste, deflowered, yet
    Spotless in heart,
Lust was all that he could get,
    For all his art:
For I ne'er attention lent
To his suit, nor gave consent;
        Tis, tis,
    I am not as I wish.

Thus hath faithless Tereus made
    Heartless Philomele
Moan her in her forlorn shade,
    Where grief I feel –
Grief that wounds me to the heart,
Which though gone hath left her smart;
        Tis, tis,
    I am not as I wish.

1. may good befall

William Browne

(c. 1591–1643)

86 · *from* BRITANNIA'S PASTORALS

The mounting lark, day's herald, got on wing,
Bidding each bird choose out his bough and sing.
*The lofty treble sung the little wren;
Robin the mean, that best of all loves men;
The nightingale the tenor; and the thrush
The counter-tenor, sweetly in a bush:
And that the music might be full in parts,
Birds from the groves flew with right willing hearts:
But, as it seemed, they thought (as do the swains
Which tune their pipes on sacked Hibernia's plains)
There should some droning part be, therefore willed
Some bird to fly into a neighb'ring field,
In embassy unto the King of Bees,
To aid his partners on the flowers and trees;
Who, condescending, gladly flew along
To bear the base to his well-tunèd song.
The crow was willing they should be beholding
For his deep voice, but being hoarse with scolding,
He thus lends aid; upon an oak doth climb,
And nodding with his head, so keepeth time.
  O true delight, enharbouring the breasts
Of those sweet creatures with the plumy crests.
Had nature unto man such simpl'ess given,
He would like birds be far more near to heaven.

(Book I, Song 3, ll. 197–220)

*A description of a musical concert of birds. – W.B.

Patrick Hannay
(d. 1629?)

87 · *from* PHILOMELA, THE NIGHTINGALE

Upon the boughs and tops of trees,
Blithe birds did sit as thick as bees
  On blooming beans do bait:[1]
And every bird some loving note
Did warble through the swelling throat
  To woo the wanton mate.
There might be heard the throbbing thrush,
  The bullfinch blithe her by;
The blackbird in another bush,
  With thousands more her nigh.
    The ditties all,
    To great and small,
Sweet Philomel did set,
    In all the grounds
    Of music sounds,
Those darlings did direct.

With pleasure which that place did bring,
Which seemed to me perpetual spring,
  I was enforced to stay:
Leaning me lowly on the ground,
To hear the sweet celestial sound
  These sylvans did bewray.
Ravished with liking of their songs,
  I thought I understood
The several language to each 'longs,
  That lodges in the wood.
    Most Philomel
    Did me compel
To listen to her song,
    In sugared strains,
    While she complains
Of tyrant Tereus' wrong.

1. feed

Composed to sing her saddest dit,
She shrouded in a shade did sit,
   Under a budding briar;
Whose thickness so debarred the light,
It seemed an artificial night,
   Leaves linked in love so near.
It seemed she was ashamed to show
   Herself in public place,
By sight, lest seers so might know
   Her undeserved disgrace.
     Hid from the eye,
     She thought none nigh
Was for to pen her plaints;
     She 'gins relate
     Her adverse fate,
And thus her passion paints.

(ll. 49–96)

Robert Herrick
(1591–1674)

88 · UPON MRS ELIZ. WHEELER, UNDER THE NAME OF AMARILLIS

Sweet Amarillis, by a spring's
Soft and soul-melting murmurings,
Slept; and thus sleeping, thither flew
A robin redbreast; who at view,
Not seeing her at all to stir,
Brought leaves and moss to cover her:
But while he, perking, there did pry
About the arch of either eye,
The lid began to let out day,
At which poor Robin flew away,
And seeing her not dead, but all disleaved,
He chirpt for joy, to see himself deceived.

89 · COCK-CROW

Bell-man of night, if I about shall go
For to deny my Master, do thou crow.
Thou stop'st Saint Peter in the midst of sin;
Stay me, by crowing, ere I do begin.
Better it is, premonished, for to shun
A sin, then fall to weeping when 'tis done.

90 · TO ROBIN REDBREAST

Laid out for dead, let thy last kindness be
With leaves and moss-work for to cover me:
And while the wood-nymphs my cold corpse inter,
Sing thou my dirge, sweet-warbling chorister!
For epitaph, in foliage next write this:
  Here, here the tomb of Robin Herrick is.

Francis Quarles
(1592–1644)

91 · ON THE CUCKOO

The idle cuckoo, having made a feast
On sparrows' eggs, lays down her own i'th'nest;
The silly bird she owns it, hatches, feeds it,
Protects it from the weather, clocks and breeds it;
It neither wants repose nor yet repast,
And joys to see her chicken thrive so fast:
But when this gaping monster has found strength
To shift without a helper, she at length,
Nor caring for that tender care that bred her,
Forgets her parent, kills the bird that fed her:
The sin we foster in our bosom, thus,
Ere we have left to feed it, feeds on us.

Thomas Randolph
(1605–35)

92 · ON THE DEATH OF A NIGHTINGALE

Go, solitary wood, and henceforth be
Acquainted with no other harmony
Than the pies' chattering, or the shrieking note
Of boding owls, and fatal ravens' throat.
Thy sweetest chanter's dead, that warbled forth
Lays that might tempests calm and still the north,
And call down angels from their glorious sphere
To hear her songs, and learn new anthems there.
That soul is fled and to Elysium gone;
Thou a poor desert left; go then and run,
Beg there to stand a grove; and if she please
To sing again beneath thy shadowy trees,
The souls of happy lovers crowned with blisses
Shall flock about thee, and keep time with kisses.

Sir William D'Avenant
(1606–68)

93 · SONG

The lark now leaves his wat'ry nest
    And climbing, shakes his dewy wings;
He takes this window for the east,
    And to implore your light, he sings,
Awake, awake, the morn will never rise,
Till she can dress her beauty at your eyes.

The merchant bows unto the seaman's star,
    The ploughman from the sun his season takes;

But still the lover wonders what they are,
  Who look for day before his Mistress wakes.
  Awake, awake, break through your veils of lawn!
  Then draw your curtains, and begin the dawn.

John Milton
(1608–74)

94 · SONNET I

O nightingale, that on yon bloomy spray
  Warbl'st at eve, when all the woods are still,
  Thou with fresh hope the lover's heart dost fill,
  While the jolly hours lead on propitious May;
Thy liquid notes that close the eye of day,
  First heard before the shallow cuckoo's bill,
  Portend success in love: O if Jove's will
  Have linkt that amorous power to thy soft lay,
Now timely sing, ere the rude bird of hate[1]
  Foretell my hopeless doom in some grove nigh,
  As thou from year to year hast sung too late
For my relief, yet hadst no reason why:
  Whether the muse or love call thee his mate,
  Both them I serve, and of their train am I.

95 · *from* PARADISE LOST

Meanwhile the tepid caves and fens and shores
Their brood as numerous hatch from the egg that soon
Bursting with kindly rupture forth disclosed
Their callow young, but feathered soon and fledge,
They summed[2] their pens,[3] and soaring th'air sublime
With clang despised the ground, under a cloud
In prospect; there the eagle and the stork
On cliffs and cedar tops their aeries build:

---

1. the cuckoo 2. completed the growth of 3. pinions; wings

Part loosely wing the region, part more wise
In common, ranged in figure, wedge their way,[1]
Intelligent of seasons, and set forth,
Their airy caravan high over seas
Flying, and over lands with mutual wing
Easing their flight; so steers the prudent crane
Her annual voyage, borne on winds; the air
Floats as they pass, fanned with unnumbered plumes:
From branch to branch the smaller birds with song
Solaced the woods, and spread their painted wings
Till ev'n, nor then the solemn nightingale
Ceased warbling, but all night tuned her soft lays:
Others on silver lakes and rivers bathed
Their downy breast; the swan with archèd neck
Between her white wings mantling proudly, rows
Her state with oary feet: yet oft they quit
The dank, and rising on stiff pennons,[2] tower
The mid aerial sky: others on ground
Walked firm; the crested cock whose clarion sounds
The silent hours, and th'other whose gay train
Adorns him, coloured with the florid hue
Of rainbows and starry eyes. The waters thus
With fish replenisht, and the air with fowl,
Ev'ning and morn solemnized the fifth day.

(Book VII, ll. 417–48)

Richard Crashaw
(c. 1613–1649)

96 · MUSIC'S DUEL

Now westward Sol had spent the richest beams
Of noon's high glory, when hard by the streams
Of Tiber, on the scene of a green plat,
Under protection of an oak, there sat

1. fly in a wedge-shaped formation   2. wings

A sweet lute's-master, in whose gentle airs
He lost the day's heat, and his own hot cares.
   Close in the covert of the leaves there stood
A nightingale, come from the neighbouring wood
(The sweet inhabitant of each glad tree,
Their muse, their siren, harmless siren she):
There stood she list'ning, and did entertain
The music's soft report, and mould the same
In her own murmurs, that what ever mood
His curious fingers lent, her voice made good.
The man perceived his rival, and her art:
Disposed to give the light-foot lady sport,
Awakes his lute, and 'gainst the fight to come,
Informs it in a sweet *praeludium*
Of closer strains, and ere the war begin,
He lightly skirmishes on every string,
Charged with a flying touch: and straightway she
Carves out her dainty voice as readily
Into a thousand sweet distinguished tones,
And reckons up in·soft divisions
Quick volumes of wild notes, to let him know
By that shrill taste she could do something too.
   His nimble hands' instinct then taught each string
A cap'ring cheerfulness, and made them sing
To their own dance; now negligently rash,
He throws his arm, and with a long drawn dash,
Blends all together; then distinctly trips
From this to that; then, quick returning, skips
And snatches this again, and pauses there.
She measures every measure, every where
Meets art with art; sometimes as if in doubt,
Not perfect yet, and fearing to be out,
Trails her plain ditty in one long-spun note
Through the sleek passage of her open throat,
A clear unwrinkled song; then doth she point it
With tender accents, and severely joint it
By short diminutives, that being reared
In controverting warbles evenly shared,
With her sweet self she wrangles; he, amazed
That from so small a channel should be raised
The torrent of a voice whose melody
Could melt into such sweet variety,

Strains higher yet; that tickled with rare art
The tattling strings (each breathing in his part)
Most kindly do fall out; the grumbling base
In surly groans disdains the treble's grace.
The high-percht treble chirps at this, and chides
Until his finger (moderator) hides
And closes the sweet quarrel, rousing all,
Hoarse, shrill, at once, as when the trumpets call
Hot Mars to th'harvest of death's field, and woo
Men's hearts into their hands; this lesson too
She gives him back; her supple breast thrills out
Sharp airs, and staggers in a warbling doubt
Of dallying sweetness, hovers o'er her skill,
And folds in waved notes with a trembling bill,
The pliant series of her slippery song.
Then starts she suddenly into a throng
Of short thick sobs, whose thund'ring volleys float,
And roll themselves over her lubric throat
In panting murmurs, stilled[1] out of her breast,
That ever-bubbling spring, the sug'red nest
Of her delicious soul that there does lie
Bathing in streams of liquid melody,
Music's best seed-plot, whence in ripened airs
A golden-headed harvest fairly rears
His honey-dropping tops, plowed by her breath
Which there reciprocally laboureth
In that sweet soil. It seems a holy choir
Founded to th'name of great Apollo's lyre,
Whose silver-roof rings with the sprightly notes
Of sweet-lipped angel-imps, that swill their throats
In cream of morning Helicon, and then
Prefer[2] soft anthems to the ears of men
To woo them from their beds, still murmuring
That men can sleep while they their matins sing
(Most divine service): whose so early lay
Prevents[3] the eye-lids of the blushing day.
There might you hear her kindle her soft voice
In the close murmur of a sparkling noise,
And lay the ground-work of her hopeful song,
Still keeping in the forward stream, so long
Till a sweet whirl-wind (striving to get out)

1. distilled   2. present, proffer   3. precedes, comes in advance of

Heaves her soft bosom, wanders round about,
And makes a pretty earthquake in her breast,
Till the fledged notes at length forsake their nest,
Fluttering in wanton shoals, and to the sky,
Winged with their own wild echoes, prattling fly.
She opes the floodgate, and lets loose a tide
Of streaming sweetness, which in state doth ride
On the waved back of every swelling strain,
Rising and falling in a pompous train.
And while she thus discharges a shrill peal
Of flashing airs, she qualifies their zeal
With the cool epode of a graver note,
Thus high, thus low, as if her silver throat
Would reach the brazen voice of war's hoarse bird;
Her little soul is ravisht, and so poured
Into loose ecstasies, that she is placed
Above her self, music's enthusiast.

   Shame now and anger mixt a double stain
In the musician's face. Yet once again,
Mistress, I come. Now reach a strain, my lute,
Above her mock, or be forever mute.
Or tune a song of victory to me,
Or to thy self sing thine own obsequy.
So said, his hands sprightly as fire he flings,
And with a quavering coyness tastes the strings.
The sweet-lipped sisters,[1] musically frighted,
Singing their fears are fearfully delighted,
Trembling as when Apollo's golden hairs
Are fanned and frizzled in the wanton airs
Of his own breath: which married to his lyre
Doth tune the spheres, and make heaven's self look higher.
From this to that, from that to this he flies,
Feels music's pulse in all her arteries;
Caught in a net which there Apollo spreads,
His fingers struggle with the vocal threads;
Following those little rills, he sinks into
A sea of Helicon; his hand does go
Those parts of sweetness which with nectar drop,
Softer than that which pants in Hebe's cup.
The humorous[2] strings expound his learned touch
By various glosses; now they seem to grutch

     1. the strings   2. fanciful, capricious, whimsical

And murmur in a buzzing din, then jingle
In shrill tongued accents, striving to be single.
Every smooth turn, every delicious stroke
Gives life to some new grace; thus doth h'invoke
Sweetness by all her names; thus, bravely thus
(Fraught with a fury so harmonious)
The lute's light genius now does proudly rise,
Heaved on the surges of swoll'n rhapsodies,
Whose flourish (meteor-like) doth curl the air
With flash of high-born fancies: here and there
Dancing in lofty measures, and anon
Creeps on the soft touch of a tender tone,
Whose trembling murmurs, melting in wild airs,
Run to and fro, complaining his sweet cares
Because those precious mysteries that dwell
In music's ravished soul he dare not tell,
But whisper to the world; thus do they vary
Each string his note, as if they meant to carry
Their master's blest soul (snatcht out at his ears
By a strong ecstasy) through all the spheres
Of music's heaven, and seat it there on high
In th'empyreum of pure harmony.
At length (after so long, so loud a strife
Of all the strings, still breathing the best life
Of blest variety attending on
His fingers' fairest revolution
In many a sweet rise, many as sweet a fall)
A full-mouth diapason swallows all.

  This done, he lists what she would say to this,
And she, although her breath's late exercise
Had dealt too roughly with her tender throat,
Yet summons all her sweet powers for a note;
Alas! in vain! for while (sweet soul) she tries
To measure all those wild diversities
Of chatt'ring strings, by the small size of one
Poor simple voice, raised in a natural tone,
She fails, and failing, grieves, and grieving, dies.
She dies; and leaves her life the victor's prize,
Falling upon his lute; O fit to have
(That lived so sweetly), dead, so sweet a grave!

Anonymous

(17th century)

97 · THE LARK

The giddy lark reacheth the steepy air
By sweet degrees, making each note a stair.
Her voice leads softly on, the feathered strain
Follows, and leaves the last note to her train.
At the first stage she rests, seeming to tire;
Her wing mounts up her voice some eight notes higher.
At the next period in this airy hill,
Her rising voice lifts up her restive quill.
Hard tale to tell, when she her matins sings,
Whether her tongue gives, or receives her wings.
To the observing ear, attentive eye,
Her wings would seem to chant, her tongue to fly.
Brave flight of music, and a sublime song,
When wings thus sweetly fly into a tongue!
Throned on the welkin's crest, her voice the stair
Stills with her wings, and here becomes a chair:
Where seated, in a calm sweet strain she sings,
A loss to earth, without her tongue or wings.
She streams away in rapture, turnëd clear
Into a soft piece of harmonious air,
All sung into a jelly; now become
A nectar cloud, moved by a sphery tongue.
Lost to her self (poor bird!) as now to me
Who nothing but her air-strook voice might see.
But like a silver bell, that stands brim-full
Of its own sound, till the relenting pull
Shake off the pleasing trance: a broke note crossed
Put her marred wings in mind that she was lost.
Then (like the air that o'er the treble string
Trembleth its life away, soft hovering
Till by the base recalled) the liquid fowl
Strook solid, sings her body to her soul.

Lord! with what art she ruins[1] in her fall,
As he that in division[2] shuts up all:
Clad in a light held sarabrand,[3] whose pace
Merrily winds her down to her first place.
Thus, as her body biggens, still her song
Draws near our sense, we understand her tongue.
But earth (as if resolved to interrupt
And rise amongst her numbers, now abrupt)
Gives her a dampy touch, that doth benumb
Her soul, and strikes her contemplation dumb.

George Daniel
(1616–57)

98 · ODE XXIII

Poor bird,[4] I do not envy thee,
Pleased in the gentle melody
　　　Of thy own song.
Let crabbèd winter silence all
The wingèd choir; he never shall
　　　Chain up thy tongue:
　　　　　Poor innocent!
When I would please my self, I look on thee,
And guess some sparks of that felicity,
　　　　That self-content.

When the bleak face of winter spreads
The earth, and violates the meads
　　　Of all their pride;
When sapless trees and flowers are fled
Back to their causes, and lie dead
　　　To all beside;
　　　　　I see thee set,
Bidding defiance to the bitter air,
Upon a withered spray by cold made bare,
　　　　And drooping yet.

1. goes down　2. a rapid melodic passage　3. saraband　4. the robin

There, full in notes, to ravish all
My earth, I wonder what to call
    My dullness, when
I hear thee, pretty creature, bring
Thy better odes of praise, and sing
    To puzzle men:
        Poor pious elf!
I am instructed by thy harmony,
To sing away the time's uncertainty,
    Safe in my self.

Poor redbreast, carol out thy lay,
And teach us mortals what to say.
    Here cease the choir
Of airy choristers; no more
Mingle your notes; but catch a store
    From her sweet lyre;
        You are but weak,
Mere summer chanters; you have neither wing
Nor voice in winter. Pretty redbreast, sing
    What I would speak.

Martin Lluellyn
(1616–82)

99 · COCK-THROWING[1]

Cock-a-doodle-do! 'tis the bravest game,
Take a cock from his dame,
And bind him to a stake:
How he struts! How he throws!
How he swaggers! How he crows!
As if the day newly brake.
How his Mistress cackles
Thus to find him in shackles

1. On Shrove Tuesday, a cock was tied to a stake by a cord attached to its leg, and then objects were thrown at it until it was killed.

And tied to a pack-thread garter!
Oh, the bears and the bulls
Are but corpulent gulls
To the valiant Shrove-tide martyr.

Joseph Beaumont
(1616–99)

100 · THE GENTLE CHECK

MAY 19

One half of me was up and dressed,
The other still in lazy rest;
For yet my prayers I had not said;
When I close at her matins heard
A dainty-tonguëd bird,
Who little thought how she did me upbraid.

But guilt caught hold of every note,
And through my breast the anthem shot:
My breast heard more than did my ear,
For now the tune grew sharp and chode
Me into thoughts of God,
To whom most due my earlier accents were.

How shall I blush enough to see
Poor birds prevent[1] my praise to thee!
Dear Lord, my muse for pardon pants,
And every tardy guilty tone
Doth languish to a groan:
Alas, today she sings not, but recants.

Forgive, forgive my lazy rhyme,
Which in its music keeps not time;
If thy sweet patience lets me borrow
Another morn of life, I give
My promise here to strive
Before the lark to be at heav'n tomorrow.

1. anticipate (in their action)

Richard Lovelace
(1618–c. 1657)

101 · THE FALCON

Fair princess of the spacious air,
That hast vouchsafed acquaintance here,
With us are quartered below stairs,
That can reach heav'n with nought but pray'rs;
Who, when our activ'st wings we try,
Advance a foot into the sky;

Bright heir t'th' bird imperial,
From whose avenging pennons fall
Thunder and lightning twisted spun;
Brave cousin-german to the sun,
That didst forsake thy throne and sphere,
To be an humble pris'ner here;
And for a perch of her soft hand,
Resign the royal wood's command:

How often wouldst thou shoot heav'n's arc,
Then mount thy self into a lark;
And after our short faint eyes call,
When now a fly, now nought at all;
Then stoop so swift unto our sense,
As thou wert sent intelligence.

Free beauteous slave, thy happy feet
In silver fetters varvels[1] meet,
And trample on that noble wrist
The gods have kneeled in vain t'have kissed.
But gaze not, bold deceivëd spy,
Too much o'th' lustre of her eye;
The sun thou dost outstare, alas!
Winks at the glory of her face.

---

1. Metal rings – a hawk used in falconry had a strap around each leg, and the varvel
was attached to the end of the strap.

Be safe then in thy velvet helm,
Her looks are calms that do o'erwhelm,
Than the Arabian bird[1] more blest,
Chafe in the spicery of her breast,
And loose you in her breath, a wind
Sours the delicious gales of Ind.

But now a quill from thine own wing
I pluck, thy lofty fate to sing;
Whilst we behold the various fight
With mingled pleasure and affright,
The humbler hinds do fall to pray'r,
As when an army's seen i'th' air,
And the prophetic spaniels run,
And howl thy epicedium.

The heron mounted doth appear
On his own Peg'sus a lancier,
And seems on earth, when he doth hut,
A proper halberdier on foot;
Secure i'th' moor, about to sup,
The dogs have beat his quarters up.

And now he takes the open air,
Draws up his wings with tactic care,
Whilst th'expert falcon swift doth climb
In subtle mazes serpentine;
And to advantage closely twinned,
She gets the upper sky and wind,
Where she dissembles to invade,
And lies a pol'tic ambuscade.

The hedged-in heron, whom the foe
Awaits above, and dogs below,
In his fortification lies,
And makes him ready for surprise;
When rousèd with a shrill alarm,
Was shouted from beneath, they arm.

The falcon charges at first view
With her brigade of talons, through
Whose shoots the wary heron beat,
With a well counterwheeled retreat.

1. the phoenix

But the bold gen'ral, never lost,
Hath won again her airy post;
Who, wild in this affront, now fries,
Then gives a volley of her eyes.

The desp'rate heron now contracts
In one design all former facts;
Noble he is resolved to fall,
His and his en'my's funeral,
And, to be rid of her, to die
A public martyr of the sky.

When now he turns his last to wreak
The palisadoes[1] of his beak,
The raging foe impatient,
Racked with revenge, and fury rent,
Swift as the thunderbolt he strikes
Too sure upon the stand of pikes;
There she his naked breast doth hit,
And on the case of rapiers's split.

But ev'n in her expiring pangs,
The heron's pounced within her fangs,[2]
And so above she stoops to rise
A trophy and a sacrifice;
Whilst her own bells in the sad fall
Ring out the double funeral.

Ah victory unhapp'ly won!
Weeping and red is set the sun,
Whilst the whole field floats in one tear,
And all the air doth mourning wear:
Close-hooded all thy kindred come
To pay their vows upon thy tomb;
The hobby and the musket too
Do march to take their last adieu.

The lanner and the lanneret
Thy colours bear as banneret;
The goshawk and her tercel, roused,
With tears attend thee as new bowsed;[3]
All these are in their dark array
Led by the various herald-jay.

1. strong, pointed stakes   2. caught fast in her talons   3. Bowse, used of a hawk, means to drink much.

But thy eternal name shall live
Whilst quills from ashes fame reprieve,
Whilst open stands renown's wide door,
And wings are left on which to soar;
Doctor Robin, the prelate pie,
And the poetic swan shall die,
Only to sing thy elegy.

Abraham Cowley
(1618–67)

102 · THE SWALLOW

Foolish prater, what dost thou
So early at my window do
With thy tuneless serenade?
Well't had been had Tereus made
Thee as dumb as Philomel;
There his knife had done but well.
In thy undiscovered nest,
Thou dost all the winter rest,[1]
And dreamest o'er thy summer joys,
Free from the stormy season's noise,
Free from th'ill thou'st done to me:
Who disturbs, or seeks out thee?
Hadst thou all the charming notes
Of the wood's poetic throats,
All thy art could never pay
What thou'st ta'en from me away.
Cruel bird, thou'st ta'en away
A dream out of my arms today,
A dream that ne'er must equalled be
By all that waking eyes may see.

1. In the seventeenth century, it was still generally believed that swallows hibernated in the winter.

Thou this damage to repair,
Nothing half so sweet or fair,
Nothing half so good canst bring,
Though men say thou bring'st the spring.

Andrew Marvell
(1621–78)

§

103 · *from* UPON APPLETON HOUSE

When first the eye this forest sees,
It seems indeed as wood, not trees:
As if their neighbourhood[1] so old
To one great trunk them all did mould.
There the huge bulk takes place, as meant
To thrust up a fifth element,
And stretches still so closely wedged
As if the night within were hedged.

Dark all without it knits; within
It opens passable and thin;
And in as loose an order grows,
As the Corinthean porticoes.
The arching boughs unite between
The columns of the temple green;
And underneath, the wingèd choirs
Echo about their tunèd fires.

The nightingale does here make choice
To sing the trials of her voice.
Low shrubs she sits in, and adorns
With music high the squatted thorns;
But highest oaks stoop down to hear,
And list'ning elders prick the ear.
The thorn, lest it should hurt her, draws
Within the skin its shrunken claws.

1. proximity

But I have for my music found
A sadder, yet more pleasing sound:
The stock doves, whose fair necks are graced
With nuptial rings, their ensigns chaste;
Yet always, for some cause unknown,
Sad pair, unto the elms they moan.
O why should such a couple mourn,
That in so equal flames do burn!

Then as I careless on the bed
Of gelid strawberries do tread,
And through the hazels thick espy
The hatching throstle's shining eye,
The heron from the ash's top
The eldest of its young lets drop,
As if it stork-like did pretend
That tribute to its lord to send.

But most the hewel's[1] wonders are,
Who here has the holtfelster's[2] care.
He walks still upright from the root,
Meas'ring the timber with his foot;
And all the way, to keep it clean,
Doth from the bark the wood-moths glean.
He, with his beak, examines well
Which fit to stand and which to fell.

The good he numbers up, and hacks
As if he marked them with the ax.
But where he, tinkling with his beak,
Does find the hollow oak to speak,
That for his building he designs,
And through the tainted side he mines.
Who could have thought the tallest oak
Should fall by such a feeble stroke!

Nor would it, had the tree not fed
A traitor-worm, within it bred
(As first our flesh, corrupt within,
Tempts impotent and bashful sin).

1. green woodpecker 2. woodcutter's

And yet that worm triumphs not long,
But serves to feed the hewel's young,
While the oak seems to fall content,
Viewing the treason's punishment.

(ll. 497–560)

So when the shadows, laid asleep,
From underneath these banks do creep,
And on the river, as it flows,
With ebon shuts[1] begin to close,
The modest halcyon comes in sight,
Flying betwixt the day and night;
And such an horror[2] calm and dumb,
Admiring Nature does benumb.

The viscous air, wheres'e'er she fly,
Follows and sucks her azure dye;
The jellying stream compacts below,
If it might fix her shadow so;
The stupid fishes hang, as plain
As flies in crystal overta'en;
And men the silent scene assist,
Charmed with[3] the sapphire-wingëd mist.

(ll. 665–80)

Henry Vaughan
(1622–95)

104 · COCK-CROWING

Father of lights! what sunny seed,
What glance of day hast thou confined
Into this bird? To all the breed
This busy ray thou hast assigned;
      Their magnetism works all night,
      And dreams of paradise and light.

1. ebony shutters   2. a feeling of awe, of reverent fear, with no sense of terror or loathing   3. By – a meaning now obsolete. The men were not delighted with the halcyon, they were charmed by it, in the sense of being caught in its magic spell.

Their eyes watch for the morning hue,
Their little grain expelling night
So shines and sings, as if it knew
The path unto the house of light.
      It seems their candle, howe'er done,
      Was tinned and lighted at the sun.

If such a tincture, such a touch,
So firm a longing can impower,
Shall thy own image think it much
To watch for thy appearing hour?
      If a mere blast so fill the sail,
      Shall not the breath of God prevail?

O thou immortal light and heat!
Whose hand so shines through all this frame,
That by the beauty of the seat,
We plainly see who made the same.
      Seeing thy seed abides in me,
      Dwell thou in it, and I in thee.

To sleep without thee is to die;
Yea, 'tis a death partakes of hell:
For where thou dost not close the eye,
It never opens, I can tell.
      In such a dark, Egyptian border,
      The shades of death dwell and disorder.

If joys, and hopes, and earnest throes,
And hearts whose pulse beats still for light
Are given to birds, who but thee knows
A love-sick soul's exalted flight?
      Can souls be tracked by any eye
      But his, who gave them wings to fly?

Only this veil which thou hast broke,
And must be broken yet in me,
This veil, I say, is all the cloak
And cloud which shadows thee from me.
      This veil thy full-eyed love denies,
      And only gleams and fractions spies.

O take it off! make no delay,
But brush me with thy light that I

May shine unto a perfect day,
And warm me at thy glorious eye!
    O take it off! or till it flee,
    Though with no lily, stay with me!

John Bunyan
(1628–88)

105 · UPON THE LARK AND THE FOWLER

Thou simple bird, what makes thee here to play?
Look, there's the fowler, prithee come away.
Dost not behold the net? Look, there 'tis spread;
Venture a little further, thou art dead.

Is there not room enough in all the field
For thee to play in, but thou needs must yield
To the deceitful glitt'ring of a glass,
Between nets placed, to bring thy death to pass?

Bird, if thou art so much for dazzling light,
Look, there's the sun above thee: dart upright.
Thy nature is to soar up to the sky,
Why wilt thou come down to the net, and die?

Heed not the fowler's tempting flatt'ring call;
This whistle he enchanteth birds withal.
What though thou seest a live bird in his net,
She's there, because from thence she cannot get.

Look how he tempteth thee with his decoy,
That he may rob thee of thy life, thy joy.
Come, prithee, bird, I prithee come away;
Why shouldst thou to this net become a prey?

Hadst thou not wings, or were thy feathers pulled,
Or wast thou blind, or fast asleep wert lulled,
The case would somewhat alter, but for thee,
Thy eyes are ope, and thou hast wings to flee.

Remember that thy song is in thy rise,
Not in thy fall; earth's not thy paradise.
Keep up aloft then, let thy circuits be
Above, where birds from fowlers' nets are free.

Comparison

This fowler is an emblem of the devil,
His nets and whistles, figures of all evil.
His glass an emblem is of sinful pleasure,
Decoying such who reckon sin a treasure.

This simple lark's a shadow of a saint
Under allurings, ready now to faint.
What you have read, a needful warning is,
Designed to show the soul its snare and bliss,
And how it may this fowler's net escape,
And not commit upon itself this rape.

106 · OF THE CUCKOO

Thou booby, say'st thou nothing but cuckoo?
The robin and the wren can thee outdo.
They to us play thorough their little throats,
Not one, but sundry pretty tuneful notes.

But thou hast fellows, some like thee can do
Little but suck our eggs, and sing cuckoo.

Thy notes do not first welcome in our spring,
Nor dost thou its first tokens to us bring.
Birds less than thee by far, like prophets, do
Tell us 'tis coming, though not by cuckoo.

Nor dost thou summer have away with thee,
Though thou a yawling, bawling cuckoo be.
When thou dost cease among us to appear,
Then doth our harvest bravely crown our year.

But thou hast fellows, some like thee can do
Little but suck our eggs, and sing cuckoo.

Since cuckoos forward not our early spring,
Nor help with notes to bring our harvest in:

And since while here she only makes a noise,
So pleasing unto none as girls and boys,
The formalist we may compare her to,
For he doth suck our eggs, and sing cuckoo.

John Dryden
(1631–1700)

107 · *from* AN ODE ON THE DEATH OF MR HENRY PURCELL

Mark how the lark and linnet sing;
    With rival notes
They strain their warbling throats,
  To welcome in the spring.
  But in the close of night,
When Philomel begins her heav'nly lay,
  They cease their mutual spite,
Drink in her music with delight,
And list'ning and silent, and silent and list'ning,
    and list'ning and silent obey.

(1st of 3 stanzas)

Matthew Prior
(1664–1721)

108 · *from* THE TURTLE AND THE SPARROW

Behind an unfrequented glade,
Where yew and myrtle mix their shade,
A widow turtle pensive sat,
And wept her murdered lover's fate.
The sparrow chanced that way to walk
(A bird that loves to chirp and talk),
Be sure he did the turtle greet,
She answered him as she thought meet.
Sparrows and turtles, by the by,
Can think as well as you or I:
But how did they their thoughts express?
The margin shows by T and S.

T.   My hopes are lost, my joys are fled,
Alas! I weep Columbo dead:
Come, all ye wingëd Lovers, come,
Drop pinks and daisies on his tomb;
Sing, Philomel, his funeral verse;
Ye pious redbreasts, deck his hearse;
Fair swans, extend your dying throats,
Columbo's death requires your notes:
For him, my friends, for him I moan,
My dear Columbo dead and gone.

Stretched on the bier Columbo lies,
Pale are his cheeks, and closed his eyes,
Those cheeks, where beauty smiling lay,
Those eyes, where love was used to play:
Ah cruel fate, alas! how soon
That beauty and those joys are flown!

Columbo is no more: ye floods,
Bear the sad sound to distant woods;
The sound let echo's voice restore,
And say, Columbo is no more.

Ye floods, ye woods, ye echoes, moan
My dear Columbo dead and gone.

The dryads all forsook the wood,
And mournful naiads round me stood;
The tripping fauns and fairies came,
All conscious of our mutual flame;
To sigh for him, with me to moan
My dear Columbo dead and gone.

Venus disdained not to appear
To lend my grief a friendly ear;
But what avails her kindness now?
She ne'er shall hear my second vow:
The Loves that round their mother flew
Did in her face her sorrows view.
Their drooping wings they pensive hung,
Their arrows broke, their bows unstrung;
They heard attentive what I said,
And wept with me Columbo dead:
For him I sigh, for him I moan,
My dear Columbo, dead and gone.

'Tis ours to weep, great Venus said,
'Tis Jove's alone to be obeyed:
Nor birds nor goddesses can move
The just behests of fatal Jove;
I saw thy mate with sad regret,
And curst the fowler's cruel net:
Ah dear Columbo, how he fell,
Whom Turturella loved so well!
I saw him bleeding on the ground,
The sight tore up my ancient wound;
And whilst you wept, alas, I cried,
Columbo and Adonis died.

Weep, all ye streams; ye mountains, groan:
I mourn Columbo dead and gone;
Still let my tender grief complain,
Nor day nor night that grief restrain,
I said, and Venus still replied,
Columbo and Adonis died.

(ll. 1–70)

Alexander Pope
(1688–1744)

109 · *from* WINDSOR FOREST

When milder autumn summer's heat succeeds,
And in the new-shorn field the partridge feeds,
Before his lord the ready spaniel bounds,
Panting with hope, he tries the furrowed grounds;
But when the tainted gales the game betray,
Couched close he lies, and meditates the prey;
Secure they trust th'unfaithful field beset,
Till hov'ring o'er them sweeps the swelling net.
Thus (if small things we may with great compare)
When Albion sends her eager sons to war,
Some thoughtless town, with ease and plenty blest,
Near, and more near, the closing lines invest;
Sudden they seize th'amazed, defenceless prize,
And high in air Britannia's standard flies.
　See! from the brake the whirring pheasant springs,
And mounts exulting on triumphant wings:
Short is his joy; he feels the fiery wound,
Flutters in blood, and panting beats the ground.
Ah! what avail his glossy, varying dyes,
His purple crest, and scarlet-circled eyes,
The vivid green his shining plumes unfold,
His painted wings, and breast that flames with gold?
　Nor yet, when moist Arcturus clouds the sky,
The woods and fields their pleasing toils deny.
To plains with well-breathed beagles we repair,
And trace the mazes of the circling hare:
Beasts, urged by us, their fellow-beasts pursue,
And learn of man each other to undo.
With slaught'ring guns th'unwearied fowler roves,
When frosts have whitened all the naked groves;
Where doves in flocks the leafless trees o'ershade,
And lonely woodcocks haunt the wat'ry glade.
He lifts the tube, and levels with his eye;

Straight a short thunder breaks the frozen sky:
Oft, as in airy rings they skim the heath,
The clam'rous lapwings feel the leaden death:
Oft, as the mounting larks their notes prepare,
They fall, and leave their little lives in air.

(ll. 97-134)

John Gay
(1685-1732)

110 · *from* RURAL SPORTS

Nor less the spaniel, skillful to betray,
Rewards the fowler with the feathered prey.
Soon as the lab'ring horse with swelling veins,
Hath safely housed the farmer's doubtful gains,
To sweet repast th'unwary partridge flies,
With joy amid the scattered harvest lies;
Wand'ring in plenty, danger he forgets,
Nor dreads the slav'ry of entangling nets.
The subtle dog scours with sagacious nose
Along the field, and snuffs each breeze that blows;
Against the wind he takes his prudent way,
While the strong gale directs him to the prey;
Now the warm scent assures the covey[1] near,
He treads with caution, and he points with fear;
Then (lest some sentry fowl the fraud descry,
And bid his fellows from the danger fly)
Close to the ground in expectation lies,
Till in the snare the flutt'ring covey rise.
Soon as the blushing light begins to spread,
And glancing Phoebus gilds the mountain's head,
His early flight th'ill-fated partridge takes,
And quits the friendly shelter of the brakes:
Or when the sun casts a declining ray,
And drives his chariot down the western way,
Let your obsequious ranger search around,

1. a family of partridges

Where yellow stubble withers on the ground:
Nor will the roving spy direct in vain,
But numerous coveys gratify thy pain.
When the meridian sun contracts the shade,
And frisking heifers seek the cooling glade;
Or when the country floats with sudden rains,
Or driving mists deface the moist'ned plains;
In vain his toils th'unskillful fowler tries,
While in thick woods the feeding partridge lies.
    Nor must the sporting verse the gun forbear,
But what's the fowler's be the muse's care.
See how the well-taught pointer leads the way:
The scent grows warm; he stops; he springs the prey;
The flutt'ring coveys from the stubble rise,
And on swift wing divide the sounding skies;
The scatt'ring lead pursues the certain sight,
And death in thunder overtakes their flight.
Cool breathes the morning air, and winter's hand
Spreads wide her hoary mantle o'er the land;
Now to the copse thy lesser spaniel take,
Teach him to range the ditch and force the brake;
Not closest coverts can protect the game:
Hark! the dog opens; take thy certain aim;
The woodcock flutters; how he wav'ring flies![1]
The wood resounds: he wheels, he drops, he dies.

(ll. 301–50)

III · *from* THE SHEPHERD'S WEEK

from *Thursday; or, The Spell*

    When first the year, I heard the cuckoo sing,
And call with welcome note the budding spring,
I straightway set a-running with such haste,
Deb'rah, who won the smock, scarce ran so fast.
Till spent for lack of breath, quite weary grown,
Upon a rising bank I sat adown,
Then doffed my shoe, and by my troth, I swear,
Therein I spied this yellow frizzled hair,

---

1. 'Mode of flight varies . . . but when undisturbed often rather slow and wavering' (*The Handbook of British Birds*, Vol. IV, p. 185).

As like to Lubberkin's in curl and hue,
As if upon his comely pate it grew.
  With my sharp heel I three times mark the ground,
  And turn me thrice around, around, around.

(ll. 15–26)

112 · THE FARMER'S WIFE AND THE RAVEN

Why are those tears? Why droops your head?
Is then your other husband dead?
Or does a worse disgrace betide?
Hath no one since his death applied?
  Alas! you know the cause too well.
The salt is spilt, to me it fell.
Then to contribute to my loss,
My knife and fork were laid across,
On *Friday* too! the day I dread!
Would I were safe at home in bed!
Last night (I vow to heav'n 'tis true)
Bounce from the fire a coffin[1] flew.
Next post some fatal news shall tell.
God send my Cornish friends be well!
  Unhappy widow, cease thy tears,
Nor feel affliction in thy fears;
Let not thy stomach be suspended,
Eat now, and weep when dinner's ended,
And when the butler clears the table,
For thy dessert I'll read my fable.

Betwixt her swagging pannier's load,
A farmer's wife to market rode,
And, jogging on, with thoughtful care
Summed up the profits of her ware;
When, starting from her silver dream,
Thus far and wide was heard her scream.
  That raven on yon left-hand oak
(Curse on his ill-betiding croak)
Bodes me no good. No more she said,
When poor blind Ball with stumbling tread
Fell prone; o'erturned the pannier lay,
And her mashed eggs bestrowed the way.

1. a cinder shaped like a coffin

She, sprawling in the yellow road,
Railed, swore and curst. Thou croaking toad,
A murrain take thy whoreson throat!
I knew misfortune in the note.
Dame, quoth the raven, spare your oaths,
Unclench your fist, and wipe your cloaths.[1]
But why on me those curses thrown?
Goody, the fault was all your own;
For had you laid this brittle ware
On Dun, the old sure-footed mare,
Though all the ravens of the Hundred[2]
With croaking had your tongue out-thundered,
Sure-footed Dun had kept his legs,
And you, good woman, saved your eggs.

113 · THE TURKEY AND THE ANT

In other men we faults can spy,
And blame the mote that dims their eye,
Each little speck and blemish find,
To our own stronger errors blind.

A turkey, tired of common food,
Forsook the barn, and sought the wood.
Behind her ran her infant train,
Collecting here and there a grain.
Draw near, my birds, the mother cries,
This hill delicious fare supplies;
Behold, the busy Negro race,
See, millions blacken all the place!
Fear not. Like me, with freedom eat;
An ant is most delightful meat.
How blessed, how envied were our life,
Could we but 'scape the poult'rer's knife!
But man, curst man, on turkeys preys,
And Christmas shortens all our days;
Sometimes with oysters we combine,
Sometimes assist the sav'ry chine.
From the low peasant to the lord,
The turkey smokes on ev'ry board.

1. clothes   2. a subdivision of a county

Sure men for gluttony are curst,
Of the sev'n deadly sins the worst.
   An ant, who climbed beyond his reach,
Thus answered from the neighb'ring beech.
   Ere you remark another's sin,
Bid thy own conscience look within.
Control thy more voracious bill,
Nor for a breakfast nations kill.

· 114 ·

The turtle thus with plaintive crying,
   Her lover dying,
The turtle thus with plaintive crying
   Laments her dove.
Down she drops quite spent with sighing,
Paired in death, as paired in love.

· 115 ·

Before the barn door crowing,
   The cock by hens attended,
His eyes around him throwing,
   Stands for a while suspended:
Then one he singles from the crew,
   And cheers the happy hen,
With how do you do, and how do you do,
   And how do you do again.

Matthew Green
(1696–1737)

116 · THE SPARROW AND DIAMOND

I lately saw, what now I sing,
   Fair Lucia's hand displayed;
This finger graced a diamond ring,
   On that a sparrow played.

The feathered plaything she caressed,
  She stroked its head and wings;
And while it nestled on her breast,
  She lisped the dearest things.

With chiselled bill a spark ill set
  He loosened from the rest,
And swallowed down to grind his meat,
  The easier to digest.

She seized his bill with wild affright,
  Her diamond to descry:
'Twas gone! she sickened at the sight,
  Moaning her bird would die.

The tongue-tied knocker none might use,
  The curtains none undraw,
The footmen went without their shoes,
  The street was laid with straw.

The doctor used his oily art
  Of strong emetic kind,
Th'apothecary played his part,
  And engineered behind.

When physic ceased to spend its store
  To bring away the stone,
Dicky, like people given o'er,
  Picks up, when let alone.

His eyes dispelled their sickly dews,
  He pecked behind his wing;
Lucia, recovering at the news,
  Relapses for the ring.

Meanwhile within her beauteous breast
  Two different passions strove;
When av'rice ended the contest,
  And triumphed over love.

Poor little, pretty, fluttering thing,
  Thy pains the sex display,
Who, only to repair a ring,
  Could take thy life away.

Drive av'rice from your breasts, ye fair,
   Monster of foulest mien:
Ye would not let it harbour there,
   Could but its form be seen.

It made a virgin put on guile,
   Truth's image break her word,
A Lucia's face forbear to smile,
   A Venus kill her bird.

James Thomson
(1700–1748)

from THE SEASONS

117 · from *Spring*

Lend me your song, ye nightingales! oh, pour
The mazy-running soul of melody
Into my varied verse! while I deduce,
From the first note the hollow cuckoo sings,
The symphony of spring, and touch a theme
Unknown to fame – the passion of the groves.
  When first the soul of love is sent abroad
Warm through the vital air, and on the heart
Harmonious seizes, the gay troops begin
In gallant thought to plume the painted wing;
And try again the long-forgotten strain,
At first faint-warbled. But no sooner grows
The soft infusion prevalent and wide
Than all alive at once their joy o'erflows
In music unconfined. Up springs the lark,
Shrill-voiced and loud, the messenger of morn:
Ere yet the shadows fly, he mounted sings
Amid the dawning clouds, and from their haunts
Calls up the tuneful nations. Every copse
Deep-tangled, tree irregular, and bush
Bending with dewy moisture o'er the heads

Of the coy choristers that lodge within,
Are prodigal of harmony. The thrush
And wood lark, o'er the kind-contending throng
Superior heard, run through the sweetest length
Of notes, when listening Philomela deigns
To let them joy, and purposes, in thought
Elate, to make her night excel their day
The blackbird whistles from the thorny brake,
The mellow bullfinch answers from the grove;
Nor are the linnets, o'er the flowering furze
Poured out profusely, silent. Joined to these
Innumerous songsters, in the freshening shade
Of new-sprung leaves, their modulations mix
Mellifluous. The jay, the rook, the daw,
And each harsh pipe, discordant heard alone,
Aid the full concert; while the stock dove breathes
A melancholy murmur through the whole.

 'Tis love creates their melody, and all
This waste of music is the voice of love,
That even to birds and beasts the tender arts
Of pleasing teaches. Hence the glossy kind
Try every winning way inventive love
Can dictate, and in courtship to their mates
Pour forth their little souls. First, wide around,
With distant awe, in airy rings they rove,
Endeavouring by a thousand tricks to catch
The cunning, conscious, half-averted glance
Of their regardless charmer. Should she seem
Softening the least approvance to bestow,
Their colours burnish, and, by hope inspired,
They brisk advance; then, on a sudden struck,
Retire disordered; then again approach,
In fond rotation spread the spotted wing,
And shiver every feather with desire.

 Connubial leagues agreed, to the deep woods
They haste away, all as their fancy leads,
Pleasure, or food, or secret safety prompts;
That Nature's great command may be obeyed,
Nor all the sweet sensations they perceive
Indulged in vain. Some to the holly-hedge
Nestling repair, and to the thicket some;
Some to the rude protection of the thorn

Commit their feeble offspring. The cleft tree
Offers its kind concealment to a few,
Their food its insects, and its moss their nests.
Others apart far in the grassy dale,
Or roughening waste, their humble texture weave
But most in woodland solitudes delight,
In unfrequented glooms, or shaggy banks,
Steep, and divided by a babbling brook
Whose murmurs soothe them all the live-long day
When by kind duty fixed. Among the roots
Of hazel, pendent o'er the plaintive stream,
They frame the first foundation of their domes –
Dry sprigs of trees, in artful fabric laid,
And bound with clay together. Now 'tis nought
But restless hurry through the busy air,
Beat by unnumbered wings. The swallow sweeps
The slimy pool, to build his hanging house
Intent. And often, from the careless back
Of herds and flocks, a thousand tugging bills
Pluck hair and wool; and oft, when unobserved,
Steal from the barn a straw – till soft and warm,
Clean and complete, their habitation grows.
  As thus the patient dam assiduous sits,
Not to be tempted from her tender task
Or by sharp hunger or by smooth delight,
Though the whole loosened spring around her blows,
Her sympathizing lover takes his stand
High on the opponent bank, and ceaseless sings
The tedious time away; or else supplies
Her place a moment, while she sudden flits
To pick the scanty meal. The appointed time
With pious toil fulfilled, the callow young,
Warmed and expanded into perfect life,
Their brittle bondage break, and come to light,
A helpless family demanding food
With constant clamour. Oh, what passions then,
What melting sentiments of kindly care,
On the new parents seize! Away they fly
Affectionate, and undesiring bear
The most delicious morsel to their young;
Which equally distributed, again
The search begins. Even so a gentle pair,

By fortune sunk, but formed of generous mould,
And charmed with cares beyond the vulgar breast,
In some lone cot amid the distant woods,
Sustained alone by providential heaven,
Oft, as they weeping eye their infant train,
Check their own appetites, and give them all.
 Nor toil alone they scorn: exalting love,
By the great Father of the Spring inspired,
Gives instant courage to the fearful race,
And to the simple art. With stealthy wing,
Should some rude foot their woody haunts molest,
Amid a neighbouring bush they silent drop,
And whirring thence, as if alarmed, deceive
The unfeeling schoolboy. Hence, around the head
Of wandering swain, the white-winged plover wheels
Her sounding flight, and then directly on
In long excursion skims the level lawn
To tempt him from her nest. The wild duck, hence,
O'er the rough moss, and o'er the trackless waste
The heath-hen flutters, pious fraud! to lead
The hot pursuing spaniel far astray.
 Be not the muse ashamed here to bemoan
Her brothers of the grove by tyrant man
Inhuman caught, and in the narrow cage
From liberty confined, and boundless air.
Dull are the pretty slaves, their plumage dull,
Ragged, and all its brightening lustre lost;
Nor is that sprightly wildness in their notes,
Which, clear and vigorous, warbles from the beech.
Oh then, ye friends of love and love-taught song,
Spare the soft tribes, this barbarous art forbear!
If on your bosom innocence can win,
Music engage, or piety persuade.
 But let not chief the nightingale lament
Her ruined care, too delicately framed
To brook the harsh confinement of the cage.
Oft when, returning with her loaded bill,
The astonished mother finds a vacant nest,
By the hard hand of unrelenting clowns
Robbed, to the ground the vain provision falls;
Her pinions ruffle, and, low-drooping, scarce
Can bear the mourner to the poplar shade;

Where, all abandoned to despair, she sings
Her sorrows through the night, and, on the bough
Sole-sitting, still at every dying fall
Takes up again her lamentable strain
Of winding woe, till wide around the woods
Sigh to her song and with her wail resound.
   But now the feathered youth their former bounds,
Ardent, disdain; and, weighing oft their wings,
Demand the free possession of the sky.
This one glad office more, and then dissolves
Parental love at once, now needless grown:
Unlavish wisdom never works in vain.
'Tis on some evening, sunny, grateful, mild,
When nought but balm is breathing through the woods
With yellow lustre bright, that the new tribes
Visit the spacious heavens, and look abroad
On Nature's common, far as they can see
Or wing, their range and pasture. O'er the boughs
Dancing about, still at the giddy verge
Their resolution fails; their pinions still,
In loose libration stretched, to trust the void
Trembling refuse – till down before them fly
The parent-guides, and chide, exhort, command,
Or push them off. The surging air receives
The plumy burden; and their self-taught wings
Winnow the waving element. On ground
Alighted, bolder up again they lead,
Farther and farther on, the lengthening flight;
Till, vanished every fear, and every power
Roused into life and action, light in air
The acquitted parents see their soaring race,
And, once rejoicing, never know them more.
   High from the summit of a craggy cliff,
Hung o'er the deep, such as amazing frowns
On utmost Kilda's shore, whose lonely race
Resign the setting sun to Indian worlds,
The royal eagle draws his vigorous young,
Strong-pounced, and ardent with paternal fire.
Now fit to raise a kingdom of their own,
He drives them from his fort, the towering seat
For ages of his empire – which in peace
Unstained he holds, while many a league to sea

He wings his course, and preys in distant isles.
    Should I my steps turn to the rural seat
Whose lofty elms and venerable oaks
Invite the rook, who high amid the boughs
In early spring his airy city builds,
And ceaseless caws amusive; there, well-pleased,
I might the various polity survey
Of the mixed household-kind. The careful hen
Calls all her chirping family around,
Fed and defended by the fearless cock,
Whose breast with ardour flames, as on he walks
Graceful, and crows defiance. In the pond
The finely-checkered duck before her train
Rows garrulous. The stately-sailing swan
Gives out his snowy plumage to the gale,
And, arching proud his neck, with oary feet
Bears forward fierce, and guards his osier-isle,
Protective of his young. The turkey nigh,
Loud-threatening, reddens; while the peacock spreads
His every-coloured glory to the sun,
And swims in radiant majesty along.
O'er the whole homely scene the cooing dove
Flies thick in amorous chase, and wanton rolls
The glancing eye, and turns the changeful neck.
                                    (ll. 576–788)

118 · from *Autumn*

    Here the rude clamour of the sportsman's joy,
The gun fast-thundering and the winded horn,
Would tempt the Muse to sing the rural game –
How, in his mid career, the spaniel, struck
Stiff by the tainted gale, with open nose
Outstretched and finely sensible, draws full,
Fearful, and cautious on the latent prey
As in the sun the circling covey[1] bask
Their varied plumes, and, watchful every way,
Through the rough stubble turn the secret eye.
Caught in the meshy snare, in vain they beat
Their idle wings, entangled more and more:

1. partridges

Nor, on the surges of the boundless air
Though borne triumphant, are they safe; the gun,
Glanced just, and sudden, from the fowler's eye,
O'ertakes their sounding pinions, and again
Immediate brings them from the towering wing
Dead to the ground; or drives them wide-dispersed,
Wounded and wheeling various down the wind.

(ll. 360–78)

119 . from *Winter*

... The fowls of heaven,
Tamed by the cruel season, crowd around
The winnowing store, and claim the little boon
Which Providence assigns them. One alone,
The redbreast, sacred to the household gods,
Wisely regardful of the embroiling sky,
In joyless fields and thorny thickets leaves
His shivering mates, and pays to trusted man
His annual visit. Half afraid, he first
Against the window beats; then brisk alights
On the warm hearth; then, hopping o'er the floor,
Eyes all the smiling family askance,
And pecks, and starts, and wonders where he is –
Till, more familiar grown, the table crumbs
Attract his slender feet ...

(ll. 242–56)

Edward Moore
(1712–57)

120 · *from* THE GOOSE AND THE SWANS

A goose, affected, empty, vain,
The shrillest of the cackling train,
With proud and elevated crest,
Precedence claimed above the rest.
    Says she, 'I laugh at human race,
Who say geese hobble in their pace:
Look here! the sland'rous lie detect;
Not haughty man is so erect.
That peacock yonder! lord, how vain
The creature's of his gaudy train!
If both were stripped, I'd pawn my word,
A goose would be the finer bird.
Nature, to hide her own defects,
Her bungled work with finery decks;
Were geese set off with half that show,
Would men admire the peacock? No.'
    Thus vaunting, cross the mead she stalks,
The cackling breed attend her walks;
The sun shot down his noontide beams,
The swans were sporting in the streams;
Their snowy plumes and stately pride
Provoked her spleen. 'Why there,' she cried,
'Again what arrogance we see!
Those creatures! how they mimic me!
Shall every fowl the waters skim,
Because we geese are known to swim?
Humility they soon shall learn,
And their own emptiness discern.'
    So saying, with extended wings,
Lightly upon the wave she springs;
Her bosom swells, she spreads her plumes,
And the swan's stately crest assumes.
Contempt and mockery ensued,

And bursts of laughter shook the flood.
   A swan, superior to the rest,
Sprung forth, and thus the fool addressed.
   'Conceited thing, elate with pride!
Thy affectation all deride;
These airs thy awkwardness impart,
And show thee plainly as thou art.
Among thy equals of the flock,
Thou hadst escaped the public mock,
And as thy parts to good conduce,
Been deemed an honest hobbling goose.'
   Learn hence to study wisdom's rules;
Know foppery is the pride of fools;
And striving Nature to conceal,
You only her defects reveal.

                (ll. 43–90)

Richard Jago
(1715–81)

121 · THE GOLDFINCHES

AN ELEGY:
TO WILLIAM SHENSTONE

To you whose groves protect the feathered choirs,
  Who lend their artless notes a willing ear,
To you whom pity moves and taste inspires,
  The Doric strain belongs, O Shenstone, hear.

'Twas gentle spring, when all the plumy race,
  By Nature taught, in nuptial leagues combine,
A goldfinch joyed to meet the warm embrace,
  And with her mate in love's delights to join.

All in a garden, on a currant bush,
  With wondrous art they built their airy seat;
In the next orchard lived a friendly thrush,
  Nor distant far a wood lark's soft retreat.

Here blessed with ease, and in each other blessed,
    With early songs they waked the neighb'ring groves,
Till time matured their joys, and crowned their nest
    With infant pledges of their faithful loves.

And now what transport glowed in either's eye!
    What equal fondness dealt th'allotted food!
What joy each other's likeness to descry,
    And future sonnets in the chirping brood!

But ah! what earthly happiness can last?
    How does the fairest purpose often fail!
A truant schoolboy's wantonness could blast
    Their flatt'ring hopes, and leave them both to wail.

The most ungentle of his tribe was he,
    No gen'rous precept ever touched his heart,
With concord false and hideous prosody,
    He scrawled his task, and blundered o'er his part.

On mischief bent, he marked with rav'nous eyes
    Where wrapped in down the callow songsters lay,
Then rushing, rudely seized the glitt'ring prize,
    And bore it in his impious hands away!

But how shall I describe, in numbers rude,
    The pangs for poor Chrysomitris decreed,
When from her secret stand aghast she viewed
    The cruel spoiler perpetrate the deed?

'O grief of griefs!' with shrieking voice she cried,
    'What sight is this that I have lived to see!
O! that I had in youth's fair season died,
    From love's false joys and bitter sorrows free.

'Was it for this, alas! with weary bill,
    Was it for this I poised th'unwieldy straw?
For this I bore the moss from yonder hill,
    Nor shunned the pond'rous stick along to draw?

'Was it for this I picked the wool with care,
    Intent with nicer skill our work to crown?
For this, with pain, I bent the stubborn hair,
    And lined our cradle with the thistle's down?

'Was it for this my freedom I resigned,
    And ceased to rove at large from plain to plain?
For this I sat at home whole days confined
    To bear the scorching heat and pealing rain?

'Was it for this my watchful eyes grow dim?
    For this the roses on my cheek turn pale?
Pale is my golden plumage, once so trim,
    And all my wonted mirth and spirits fail.

'O plund'rer vile! O more than adders fell!
    More murd'rous than the cat with prudish face!
Fiercer than kites in whom the furies dwell,
    And thievish as the cuckoo's pilf'ring race!

'May juicy plums for thee forbear to grow,
    For thee no flow'r unveil its charming dyes;
May birch trees thrive to work thee sharper woe,
    And list'ning starlings mock thy frantic cries!'

Thus sang the mournful bird her piteous tale,
    The piteous tale her mournful mate returned,
Then side by side they sought the distant vale,
    And there in secret sadness inly mourned.

Gilbert White
(1720–93)

122 · THE NATURALIST'S
SUMMER EVENING WALK

When day declining sheds a milder gleam,
What time the mayfly haunts the pool or stream;
When the still owl skims round the grassy mead,
What time the timorous hare limps forth to feed;
Then be the time to steal adown the vale,
And listen to the vagrant* cuckoo's tale,

* Vagrant cuckoo; so called because, being tied down by no incubation or attendance
about the nutrition of its young, it wanders without control. – G.W.

To hear the clamorous curlew call his mate:
Or the soft quail his tender pain relate;
To see the swallow sweep the dark'ning plain
Belated, to support her infant train;
To mark the swift in rapid giddy ring

Dash round the steeple, unsubdued of wing:
Amusive birds! – say where your hid retreat
When the frost rages and the tempests beat;
Whence your return, by such nice instinct led,
When spring, soft season, lifts her bloomy head?
Such baffled searches mock men's prying pride,
The God of Nature is your secret guide!
   While deep'ning shades obscure the face of day,
To yonder bench, leaf-sheltered, let us stray,
Till blended objects fail the swimming sight,
And all the fading landscape sinks in night;
To hear the drowsy dor come brushing by
With buzzing wing, or the shrill cricket cry;
To see the feeding bat glance through the wood;

To catch the distant falling of the flood;
While o'er the cliff th'awakenèd churn owl hung,
Through the still gloom protracts his chattering song;
While high in air, and poised upon his wings,
Unseen, the soft enamoured wood lark* sings:
These, Nature's works, the curious mind employ,
Inspire a soothing melancholy joy:
As fancy warms, a pleasing kind of pain
Steals o'er the cheek, and thrills the creeping vein!

   Each rural sight, each sound, each smell combine;
The tinkling sheep bell, or the breath of kine;
The new-mown hay that scents the swelling breeze,
Or cottage chimney smoking through the trees.

   The chilling night dews fall: away, retire;
For see, the glowworm lights her amorous fire!
Thus, ere night's veil had half obscured the sky,
Th'impatient damsel hung her lamp on high:
True to the signal, by love's meteor led,
Leander hastened to his Hero's bed.

Joseph Warton
(1722–1800)

123 · ODE: TO THE NIGHTINGALE

O thou that to the moonlight vale
Warblest oft thy plaintive tale,
What time the village murmurs cease,
And the still eve is hushed to peace,
When now no busy sound is heard,
Contemplation's favourite bird!

Chantress of night, whose amorous song
(First heard the tufted groves among)
Warns wanton Mabba to begin

---

* In hot summer nights wood larks soar to a prodigious height, and hang singing in the air. – G.W.

Her revels on the circled green,
Whene'er by meditation led,
I nightly seek some distant mead,

A short repose of cares to find,
And soothe my love-distracted mind,
O fail not then, sweet Philomel,
Thy sadly warbled woes to tell;
In sympathetic numbers join
Thy pangs of luckless love with mine!

So may no swain's rude hand infest
Thy tender young, and rob thy nest;
Nor ruthless fowler's guileful snare
Lure thee to leave the fields of air,
No more to visit vale or shade,
Some barbarous virgin's captive made.

Mark Akenside
(1721–70)

124 · ODE XV : TO THE EVENING STAR

Tonight, retired, the queen of heaven
    With young Endymion stays:
And now to Hesper[1] is it giv'n
Awhile to rule the vacant sky,
Till she shall to her lamp supply
    A stream of brighter rays.

O Hesper, while the starry throng
    With awe thy path surrounds,
Oh listen to my suppliant song,
If haply now the vocal sphere
Can suffer thy delighted ear
    To stoop to mortal sounds.

1. the evening star

So may the bridegroom's genial strain
   Thee still invoke to shine:
So may the bride's unmarried train
To Hymen chant their flattering vow,
Still that his lucky torch may glow
   With lustre pure as thine.

Far other vows must I prefer
   To thy indulgent power.
Alas, but now I paid my tear
On fair Olympia's virgin tomb:
And lo, from thence, in quest I roam
   Of Philomela's bower.

Propitious send thy golden ray,
   Thou purest light above:
Let no false flame seduce to stray
Where gulf or steep lie hid for harm:
But lead where music's healing charm
   May soothe afflicted love.

To them, by many a grateful song
   In happier seasons vowed,
These lawns, Olympia's haunt, belong:
Oft by yon silver stream we walked,
Or fixed, while Philomela talked,
   Beneath yon copses stood.

Nor seldom, where the beechen boughs
   That roofless tow'r invade,
We came, while her enchanting Muse
The radiant moon above us held:
Till by a clam'rous owl compelled,
   She fled the solemn shade.

But hark; I hear her liquid tone.
   Now, Hesper, guide my feet
Down the red marl with moss o'ergrown,
Through yon wild thicket next the plain,
Whose hawthorns choke the winding lane
   Which leads to her retreat.

See the green space: on either hand
   Enlarged it spreads around:

See, in the midst she takes her stand,
Where one old oak his awful shade
Extends o'er half the level mead
   Enclosed in woods profound.

Hark, how through many a melting note
   She now prolongs her lays:
How sweetly down the void they float!
The breeze their magic path attends:
The stars shine out: the forest bends:
   The wakeful heifers gaze.

Whoe'er thou art whom chance may bring
   To this sequestered spot,
If then the plaintive siren sing,
Oh softly tread beneath her bower,
And think of heaven's disposing power,
   Of man's uncertain lot.

Oh think, o'er all this mortal stage,
   What mournful scenes arise:
What ruin waits on kingly rage:
How often virtue dwells with woe:
How many griefs from knowledge flow:
   How swiftly pleasure flies.

O sacred bird, let me at eve,
   Thus wand'ring all alone,
Thy tender counsel oft receive,
Bear witness to thy pensive airs,
And pity Nature's common cares
   Till I forget my own.

John Gilbert Cooper
(1723–69)

125 · *from* EPISTLES TO HIS FRIENDS
IN TOWN

from *The Temper of Aristippus*

When in the silent midnight grove,
Sweet Philomela swells her throat
With tremulous and plaintive note,
Expressive of disast'rous love,
I with the pensive pleasures dwell,
And in their calm sequestered cell
Listen with rapturous delight
To the soft songster of the night.
Here echo, in her mossy cave,
Symphonious to the love-lorn song,
Warbles the vocal rocks among,
Whilst gently trickling waters lave
The oak-fringed mountain's hoary brow,
Whose streams, united in the vale,
O'er pebbled beds loquacious flow,
Tuned to the sad melodious tale
In murmurs querulously slow.
And, whilst immersed in thought I lie,
From ages past and realms unseen,
There moves before the mental eye
The pleasing melancholy scene
Of nymphs and youths unfortunate,
Whose fame shall spread from shore to shore,
Preserved by bards from death and fate,
Till time itself shall be no more.

                    (Epistle II, ll. 25–49)

Thomas Warton
(1728–90)

126 · *from* ODE X : THE FIRST OF APRIL

The swallow, for a moment seen,
Skims in haste the village green:
From the grey moor, on feeble wing,
The screaming plovers idly spring:
The butterfly, gay-painted soon,
Explores awhile the tepid noon;
And fondly trusts its tender dyes
To fickle suns and flattering skies.

Fraught with a transient, frozen shower,
If a cloud should haply lower,
Sailing o'er the landscape dark,
Mute on a sudden is the lark;
But when gleams the sun again
O'er the pearl-besprinkled plain,
And from behind his watery veil
Looks through the thin descending hail;
She mounts, and, lessening to the sight,
Salutes the blithe return of light,
And high her tuneful track pursues
Mid the dim rainbow's scattered hues.

Where in venerable rows
Widely waving oaks enclose
The moat of yonder antique hall,
Swarm the rooks with clamorous call;
And to the toils of nature true,
Wreathe their capacious nests anew.

(ll. 35–60)

Erasmus Darwin
(1731–1802)

127 · *from* THE TEMPLE OF NATURE;
OR, THE ORIGIN OF SOCIETY

from *Reproduction of Life*

Now vows connubial chain the plighted pair,
And join paternal with maternal care;
The married birds with nice selection cull
Soft thistle-down, grey moss, and scattered wool,
Line the secluded nest with feathery rings,
Meet with fond bills, and woo with fluttering wings.
Week after week, regardless of her food,
The incumbent linnet warms her future brood;
Each spotted egg with ivory lips she turns,
Day after day with fond expectance burns,
Hears the young prisoner chirping in his cell,
And breaks in hemispheres the obdurate shell.

(Canto 2, ll. 341–52)

William Cowper

(1731–1800)

128 · ON THE DEATH
OF MRS THROCKMORTON'S BULLFINCH

Ye nymphs! if e'er your eyes were red
With tears o'er hapless fav'rites shed,
   O share Maria's grief!
Her fav'rite, even in his cage,
(What will not hunger's cruel rage?)
   Assassined by a thief.

Where Rhenus strays his vines among,
The egg was laid from which he sprung,
   And though by nature mute,
Or only with a whistle blest,
Well-taught, he all the sounds expressed
   Of flagelet or flute.

The honours of his ebon poll
Were brighter than the sleekest mole;
   His bosom of the hue
With which Aurora decks the skies
When piping winds shall soon arise
   To sweep up all the dew.

Above, below, in all the house,
Dire foe, alike to bird and mouse,
   No cat had leave to dwell;
And Bully's cage supported stood
On props of smoothest-shaven wood,
   Large-built and latticed well.

Well-latticed – but the grate, alas!
Not rough with wire of steel or brass,
   For Bully's plumage sake,
But smooth with wands from Ouse's side,
With which, when neatly peeled and dried,
   The swains their baskets make.

Night veiled the pole – all seemed secure –
When led by instinct sharp and sure,
     Subsistence to provide,
A beast forth-sallied on the scout,
Long-backed, long-tailed, with whiskered snout,
     And badger-coloured hide.

He, ent'ring at the study door,
Its ample area 'gan explore;
     And something in the wind
Conjectured, sniffing round and round,
Better than all the books he found,
     Food, chiefly, for the mind.

Just then, by adverse fate impressed,
A dream disturbed poor Bully's rest;
     In sleep he seemed to view
A rat, fast-clinging to the cage,
And, screaming at the sad presage,
     Awoke and found it true.

For, aided both by ear and scent,
Right to his mark the monster went –
     Ah, Muse! forbear to speak:
Minute the horrors that ensued;
His teeth were strong, the cage was wood –
     He left poor Bully's beak.

He left it – but he should have ta'en
That beak, whence issued many a strain
     Of such mellifluous tone,
Might have repaid him well, I wot,
For silencing so sweet a throat,
     Fast set within his own.

Maria weeps – the Muses mourn:
So when by Bacchanalians torn
     On Thracian Hebrus' side,
The tree-enchanter Orpheus fell,
His head alone remained to tell
     The cruel death he died.

129 · THE NIGHTINGALE AND THE GLOWWORM

A nightingale, that all day long
Had cheered the village with his song,
Nor yet at eve his note suspended,
Nor yet when eventide was ended,
Began to feel, as well he might,
The keen demands of appetite;
When, looking eagerly around,
He spied far off, upon the ground,
A something shining in the dark,
And knew the glowworm by his spark;
So, stooping down from hawthorn top,
He thought to put him in his crop.
The worm, aware of his intent,
Harangued him thus, right eloquent –

Did you admire my lamp, quoth he,
As much as I your minstrelsy,
You would abhor to do me wrong,
As much as I to spoil your song;
For 'twas the self-same pow'r divine
Taught you to sing, and me to shine;
That you with music, I with light,
Might beautify and cheer the night.

The songster heard his short oration,
And, warbling out his approbation,
Released him, as my story tells,
And found a supper somewhere else.

Hence jarring sectaries may learn
Their real int'rest to discern;
That brother should not war with brother,
And worry and devour each other;
But sing and shine by sweet consent,
Till life's poor transient night is spent,
Respecting in each other's case
The gifts of nature and of grace.

Those Christians best deserve the name
Who studiously make peace their aim;
Peace, both the duty and the prize
Of him that creeps and him that flies.

130 · THE JACKDAW

There is a bird who, by his coat,
And by the hoarseness of his note,
　　Might be supposed a crow;
A great frequenter of the church,
Where, bishop-like, he finds a perch,
　　And dormitory too.

Above the steeple shines a plate,
That turns and turns, to indicate
　　From what point blows the weather.
Look up – your brains begin to swim,
'Tis in the clouds – that pleases him,
　　He chooses it the rather.

Fond of the speculative height,
Thither he wings his airy flight,
　　And thence securely sees
The bustle and the raree-show
That occupy mankind below,
　　Secure and at his ease.

You think, no doubt, he sits and muses
On future broken bones and bruises,
　　If he should chance to fall.
No; not a single thought like that
Employs his philosophic pate,
　　Or troubles it at all.

He sees that this great roundabout –
The world, with all its motley rout,
　　Church, army, physic, law,
Its customs, and its bus'nesses –
Is no concern at all of his,
　　And says – what says he? – Caw.

Thrice happy bird! I too have seen
Much of the vanities of men;
　　And, sick of having seen 'em,
Would cheerfully these limbs resign
For such a pair of wings as thine,
　　And such a head between 'em.

131 · EPITAPH ON A FREE BUT TAME REDBREAST

A FAVOURITE OF MISS SALLY HURDIS

These are not dewdrops, these are tears,
  And tears by Sally shed
For absent Robin, who she fears,
  With too much cause, is dead.

One morn he came not to her hand
  As he was wont to come,
And, on her finger perched, to stand
  Picking his breakfast crumb.

Alarmed she called him, and perplext,
  She sought him, but in vain,
That day he came not, nor the next,
  Nor ever came again.

She therefore raised him here a tomb,
　　Though where he fell, or how,
None knows, so secret was his doom,
　　Nor where he moulders now.

Had half a score of coxcombs died
　　In social Robin's stead,
Poor Sally's tears had soon been dried,
　　Or haply never shed.

But Bob was neither rudely bold
　　Nor spiritlessly tame,
Nor was, like theirs, his bosom cold,
　　But always in a flame.

132 · *from* THE TASK

from *The Winter Walk at Noon*

No noise is here, or none that hinders thought.
The redbreast warbles still, but is content
With slender notes, and more than half suppressed:
Pleased with his solitude, and flitting light
From spray to spray, where'er he rests he shakes
From many a twig the pendant drops of ice,
That tinkle in the withered leaves below.
　　　　　　　　　　(Book VI, ll. 76–82)

Michael Bruce
(1746–67)

133 · ODE: TO THE CUCKOO

Hail, beauteous stranger of the wood,
　　Attendant on the spring!
Now heav'n repairs thy rural seat,
　　And woods thy welcome sing.

Soon as the daisy decks the green,
 Thy certain voice we hear:
Hast thou a star to guide thy path,
 Or mark the rolling year?

Delightful visitant! with thee
 I hail the time of flow'rs,
When heav'n is filled with music sweet
 Of birds among the bow'rs.

The schoolboy, wand'ring in the wood
 To pull the flow'rs so gay,
Starts, thy curious voice to hear,
 And imitates thy lay.

Soon as the pea puts on the bloom,
 Thou fly'st thy vocal vale,
An annual guest, in other lands,
 Another spring to hail.

Sweet bird! thy bow'r is ever green,
 Thy sky is ever clear;
Thou hast no sorrow in thy song,
 No winter in thy year!

Alas, sweet bird! not so my fate,
 Dark scowling skies I see
Fast gathering round, and fraught with woe
 And wintry years to me.

O could I fly, I'd fly with thee:
 We'd make, with social wing,
Our annual visit o'er the globe,
 Companions of the spring.

William Blake
(1757–1827)

134 · THE BLOSSOM

Merry, merry sparrow!
Under leaves so green
A happy blossom
Sees you swift as arrow
Seek your cradle narrow
Near my bosom.

Pretty, pretty robin!
Under leaves so green
A happy blossom
Hears you sobbing, sobbing,
Pretty, pretty robin,
Near my bosom.

· 135 ·

O lapwing, thou fliest around the heath,
Nor seest the net that is spread beneath.
Why dost thou not fly among the corn fields?
They cannot spread nets where a harvest yields.

136 · *from* MILTON

Thou hearest the nightingale begin the song of spring.
The lark, sitting upon his earthy bed, just as the morn
Appears, listens silent; then, springing from the waving cornfield, loud
He leads the choir of day – trill! trill! trill! trill!
Mounting upon the wings of light into the great expanse,
Re-echoing against the lovely blue and shining heavenly shell.
His little throat labours with inspiration; every feather
On throat and breast and wings vibrates with the effluence divine.
All Nature listens silent to him, and the awful sun
Stands still upon the mountain, looking on this little bird
With eyes of soft humility and wonder, love and awe.
Then loud from their green covert all the birds begin their song:
The thrush, the linnet and the goldfinch, Robin and the wren
Awake the sun from his sweet revery upon the mountain.
The nightingale again assays his song, and through the day
And through the night warbles luxuriant, every bird of song
Attending his loud harmony with admiration and love.

(Book II, Section 34, ll. 28–44)

Robert Burns
(1759–96)

137 · *from* THE HUMBLE PETITION OF BRUAR
WATER TO THE NOBLE DUKE OF ATHOLE

The sober laverock, warbling wild,
   Shall to the skies aspire;
The gowdspink, music's gayest child,
   Shall sweetly join the choir:
The blackbird strong, the lintwhite clear,
   The mavis mild and mellow;
The robin pensive autumn cheer,
   In all her locks of yellow.

(ll. 41–8)

138 · ON SCARING SOME WATERFOWL IN LOCH TURIT, A WILD SCENE AMONG THE HILLS OF OUGHTERTYRE

Why, ye tenants of the lake,
For me your wat'ry haunt forsake?
Tell me, fellow creatures, why
At my presence thus you fly?
Why disturb your social joys,
Parent, filial, kindred ties? –
Common friend to you and me,
Nature's gifts to all are free:
Peaceful keep your dimpling wave,
Busy feed, or wanton lave;
Or, beneath the sheltering rock,
Bide the surging billow's shock.

Conscious, blushing for our race,
Soon, too soon, your fears I trace:
Man, your proud usurping foe,
Would be lord of all below:
Plumes himself in freedom's pride,
Tyrant stern to all beside.

The eagle, from the cliffy brow,
Marking you his prey below,
In his breast no pity dwells,
Strong necessity compels.
But man, to whom alone is given
A ray direct from pitying heaven,
Glories in his heart humane –
And creatures for his pleasure slain.

In these savage, liquid plains,
Only known to wandering swains,
Where the mossy riv'let strays,
Far from human haunts and ways,
All on Nature you depend,
And life's poor season peaceful spend.

Or, if man's superior might
Dare invade your native right,
On the lofty ether borne,
Man with all his powers you scorn;

Swiftly seek, on clanging wings,
Other lakes and other springs;
And the foe you cannot brave,
Scorn at least to be his slave.

139 · *from* ELEGY ON CAPTAIN MATTHEW HENDERSON

Mourn, ye wee songsters o' the wood;
Ye grouse that crap[1] the heather bud;
Ye curlews calling through a clud,[2]
Ye whistling plover;
And mourn, ye whirring paitrick[3] brood;
He's gane for ever!

Mourn, sooty coots, and speckled teals;
Ye fisher herons, watching eels;
Ye duck and drake, wi' airy wheels
Circling the lake:
Ye bitterns, till the quagmire reels,
Rair[4] for his sake.

Mourn, clamouring crakes[5] at close o' day,
'Mang fields o' flowering claver[6] gay;
And when ye wing your annual way
Frae our cauld shore,
Tell thae far warlds wha lies in clay,
Wham we deplore.

Ye houlets,[7] frae your ivy bower,
In some auld tree, or eldritch tower,
What time the moon, wi' silent glowr,[8]
Sets up her horn,
Wail through the dreary midnight hour
Till waukrife[9] morn.

(ll. 37–60)

1. crop 2. cloud 3. partridge 4. roar 5. corncrakes 6. clover 7. owls 8. gleam
9. wakeful

140 · HUNTING SONG

The heather was blooming, the meadows were mawn,[1]
Our lads gaed a-hunting, ae day at the dawn,
O'er moors and o'er mosses and mony a glen,
At length they discovered a bonnie moor-hen.[2]

> I rede[3] you beware at the hunting, young men;
> I rede you beware at the hunting, young men;
> Tak some on the wing, and some as they spring,
> But cannily steal on a bonnie moor-hen.

Sweet brushing the dew from the brown heather bells,
Her colours betrayed her on yon mossy fells;
Her plumage outlustred the pride o' the spring,
And O! as she wantonëd gay on the wing.

Auld Phoebus himsel, as he peeped o'er the hill,
In spite at her plumage he triëd his skill;
He levelled his rays where she basked on the brae –
His rays were outshone, and but marked where she lay.

They hunted the valley, they hunted the hill;
The best of our lads wi' the best o' their skill;
But still as the fairest she sat in their sight,
Then, whirr! she was over, a mile at a flight.

Joanna Baillie
(1762–1851)

141 · THE BLACKCOCK

Good morrow to thy sable beak
And glossy plumage, dark and sleek,
Thy crimson moon[4] and azure eye,
Cock of the heath, so wildly shy!

1. mown   2. female of the red grouse   3. advise, warn   4. The black grouse has a red wattle above its eye.

I see thee, slyly cowering, through
That wiry web of silver dew,
That twinkles in the morning air,
Like casement of my lady fair.

A maid there is in yonder tower,
Who, peeping from her early bower,
Half shows, like thee, with simple wile,
Her braided hair and morning smile.
The rarest things with wayward will,
Beneath the covert hide them still;
The rarest things to light of day
Look shortly forth, and shrink away.

One fleeting moment of delight
I sunned me in her cheering sight;
And short, I ween, the term will be
That I shall parley hold with thee.
Through Snowdon's mist red beams the day;
The climbing herd-boy chants his lay;
The gnat-flies dance their sunny ring –
Thou art already on the wing!

Samuel Rogers
(1763–1855)

142 · AN EPITAPH ON A ROBIN REDBREAST

Tread lightly here, for here, 'tis said,
When piping winds are hushed around,
A small note wakes from underground
Where now his tiny bones are laid.
No more in lone and leafless groves,
With ruffled wing and faded breast,
His friendless, homeless spirit roves –
Gone to the world where birds are blest!
Where never cat glides o'er the green,
Or schoolboy's giant form is seen;
But love, and joy, and smiling spring
Inspire their little souls to sing!

Thomas Gisborne
(1758–1846)

143 · *from* WALKS IN A FOREST

from *Spring*

While thus the imprisoned leaves and waking flowers
Burst from their tombs, the birds that lurked unseen
Amid the hibernal shade, in busy tribes
Pour their forgotten multitudes, and catch
New life, new rapture, from the smile of spring.
The oak's dark canopy, the moss-grown thorns,
Flutter with hurried pinions, and resound
With notes that suit a forest; some, perchance,
Rude singly, yet with sweeter notes combined
In unison harmonious; notes that speak,
In language vocal to the listening wood,
The fears and hopes, the griefs and joys, that heave
The feathered breast. Proud of cerulean stains
From heaven's unsullied arch purloined, the jay
Screams hoarse. With shrill and oft-repeated cry,
Her angular course, alternate rise and fall,
The woodpecker prolongs; then to the trunk
Close clinging, with unwearied beak assails
The hollow bark; through every cell the strokes
Roll the dire echoes that from wintry sleep
Awake her insect prey; the alarmèd tribes
Start from each chink that bores the mouldering stem:
Their scattered flight with lengthening tongue the foe
Pursues; joy glistens on her verdant plumes,
And brighter scarlet sparkles on her crest.
From bough to bough the restless magpie roves,
And chatters as she flies. In sober brown
Drest, but with nature's tenderest pencil touched,
The wryneck her monotonous complaint

Continues; harbinger of her[1] who, doomed
Never the sympathetic joy to know
That warms the mother cowering o'er her young,
A stranger robs, and to that stranger's love
Her egg commits unnatural: the nurse,
Unwitting of the change, her nestling feeds
With toil augmented; its portentous throat
Wondering she views with ceaseless hunger gape,
Starts at the glare of its capacious eyes,
Its giant bulk, and wings of hues unknown.
Meanwhile the little songsters, prompt to cheer
Their mates close brooding in the brake below,
Strain their shrill throats; or, with parental care,
From twig to twig their timid offspring lead;
Teach them to seize the unwary gnat, to poise
Their pinions, in short flights their strength to prove,
And venturous, trust the bosom of the air.

(Walk I, ll. 161–206)

James Hurdis

(1763–1801)

144 · *from* THE FAVOURITE VILLAGE

But most of all subdued, or fearful least
Of man's society, with ruddy breast
Against the window beats, sagacious bird,
The robin. At the door, half open left
Or by the gale unlatched, or narrow pass
Of air-admitting casement, or (to him
Sufficient port) the splintered aperture
Of attic pane demolished, with a flirt
Enters the fledged intruder. He has left
His haunt divine, the woodhouse and the barn,

---

1. The cuckoo. Among the wryneck's folk names are cuckoo's fool, cuckoo's footman, cuckoo's messenger, cuckoo's mate, all derived from the fact that it arrives at the same time or somewhat earlier than the cuckoo.

A feathery mendicant made bold by want,
And ev'ry little action asks aloud
Alms the most indigent might well afford,
A drop of water and a crumb of bread.
Timid and sleek upon the floor he hops,
His ev'ry feather clutched, all ear, all eye,
And, springing swift at the first sound he hears,
Thumps for dismission on the healthy pane.
Sweet beggar, no. Impenetrable glass
Has closed around thee its transparent cage,
Escape denying. Satisfy thy need,
And, having fed, be free. Beneath my chair
Sit budge, a feathery bunch; upon its staves
Polish thy clatt'ring beak; with head reversed
Dress ev'ry plume that decks thy plain surtout,
And either pinion of thy slender wing;
With bridled bill thy ruddy bosom smooth,
And, all performed, delight me, if thou wilt,
With a faint sample of contented song,
Concise and sweet. Then flit around the room,
Cheerful though silent, seizing with an air
Each crumb diminutive which the last meal
Dropt unperceived, and the religious broom
Unconscious left upon the woven floor,
Or which the hand of charity lets fall
Not grudging. Banquet here, and sleep tonight,
And, when thy morning meal is finished, fly;
Nothing unwelcome if thou dare return,
And daily seek the hospitable feast,
Strewed to invite thee on the casement ledge.

(Book III, ll. 819–58)

James Grahame
(1763–1811)

145 · *from* THE BIRDS OF SCOTLAND

With earliest spring, while yet in mountain cleughs[1]
Lingers the frozen wreath, when yeanling[2] lambs,
Upon the little heath-encircled patch
Of smoothest sward, totter, the gorcock's[3] call
Is heard from out the mist, high on the hill;
But not till when the tiny heather bud
Appears are struck the spring-time leagues of love.
Remote from shepherd's hut, or trampled fold,
The new-joined pair their lowly mansion pitch,
Perhaps beneath the juniper's rough shoots;
Or castled on some plat of tuftëd heath,
Surrounded by a narrow sable moat
Of swampy moss. Within the fabric rude,
Or e'er the new moon waxes to the full,
The assiduous dam eight spotted spheroids sees,
And feels beneath her heart, fluttering with joy.
Nor long she sits, till, with redoubled joy,
Around her she beholds an active brood
Run to and fro, or through her covering wings
Their downy heads look out; and much she loves
To pluck the heather crops, not for herself,
But for their little bills. Thus by degrees,
She teaches them to find the food which God
Has spread for them amid the desert wild,
And seeming barrenness. Now they essay
Their full-plumed wings, and, whirring, spurn the ground;
But soon alight fast by yon moss-grown cairn,
Round which the berries blae[4] (a beauteous tint
Of purple, deeper dyed with darkest blue)
Lurk mid the small round leaves. Enjoy the hour,

---

1. steep gorges or ravines   2. yearling   3. red grouse   4. blue

While yet ye may, ye unoffending flock!
For not far distant now the bloody morn
When man's protection, selfishly bestowed,
Shall be withdrawn, and murder roam at will.

Low in the east, the purple tinge of dawn
Steals upward o'er the clouds that overhang
The welkin's verge. Upon the mountain side,
The wakening covey quit their mother's wing,
And spread around: lost in the mist,
They hear her call, and, quick returning, bless
A mother's eye. Meantime, the sportsman keen
Comes forth; and, heedless of the winning smile
Of infant day, pleading on mercy's side,
Anticipates, with eager joy, the sum
Of slaughter, that, ere evening hour, he'll boast
To have achieved; and many a gory wing,
Ere evening hour, exultingly he sees
Drop, fluttering, mid the heath, even mid the bush
Beneath whose blooms the brooding mother sat,
Till round her she beheld her downy young.

At last mild twilight veils the insatiate eye,
And stops the game of death. The frequent shot
Resounds no more: silence again resumes
Her lonely reign; save that the mother's call
Is heard repeated oft, a plaintive note!
Mournful she gathers in her brood, dispersed
By savage sport, and o'er the remnant spreads
Fondly her wings; close nestling 'neath her breast,
They cherished cower amid the purple blooms.

                                    (Part I, ll. 217–75)

Even in a bird, the simplest notes have charms
For me: I even love the yellowhammer's song.
When earliest buds begin to bulge, his note,
Simple, reiterated oft, is heard
On leafless brier, or half-grown hedgerow tree;
Nor does he cease his note till autumn's leaves
Fall fluttering round his golden head so bright.
Fair plumaged bird! cursed by the causeless hate
Of every schoolboy, still by me thy lot
Was pitied! never did I tear thy nest:
I loved thee, pretty bird! for 'twas thy nest

Which first, unhelped by older eyes, I found.
The very spot I think I now behold!
Forth from my low-roofed home I wandered blithe,
Down to thy side, sweet Cart, where, 'cross the stream,
A range of stones, below a shallow ford,
Stood in the place of the now spanning arch;
Up from that ford a little bank there was,
With alder-copse and willow overgrown,
Now worn away by mining winter floods;
There, at a bramble-root, sunk in the grass,
The hidden prize, of withered field-straws formed,
Well lined with many a coil of hair and moss,
And in it laid five red-veined spheres, I found.
The Syracusan's voice did not exclaim
The grand 'Eureka' with more rapturous joy,
Than at that moment fluttered round my heart.

(Part I, ll. 462–88)

When snowdrops die, and the green primrose leaves
Announce the coming flower, the merle's[1] note,
Mellifluous, rich, deep-toned, fills all the vale,
And charms the ravished ear. The hawthorn bush,
New-budded, is his perch; there the grey dawn
He hails; and there, with parting light, concludes
His melody. There, when the buds begin
To break, he lays the fibrous roots; and, see,
His jetty breast embrowned; the rounded clay
His jetty breast has soiled: but now complete,
His partner, and his helper in the work,
Happy assumes possession of her home;
While he, upon a neighbouring tree, his lay,
More richly full, melodiously renews.
When twice seven days have run, the moment snatch,
That she has flitted off her charge, to cool
Her thirsty bill, dipped in the babbling brook,
Then silently, on tiptoe raised, look in,
Admire: five cupless acorns, darkly specked,
Delight the eye, warm to the cautious touch.
In seven days more expect the fledgeless young,
Five gaping bills. With busy wing, and eye
Quick-darting, all alert, the parent pair

1. blackbird

Gather the sustenance which Heaven bestows.
But music ceases, save at dewy fall
Of eve, when, nestling o'er her brood, the dam
Has stilled them all to rest; or at the hour
Of doubtful dawning grey; then from his wing
Her partner turns his yellow bill, and chants
His solitary song of joyous praise.
From day to day, as blow the hawthorn flowers,
That canopy this little home of love,
The plumage of the younglings shoots and spreads,
Filling with joy the fond parental eye.
Alas! not long the parents' partial eye
Shall view the fledging wing; ne'er shall they see
The timorous pinion's first essay at flight.
The truant schoolboy's eager, bleeding hand,
Their house, their all, tears from the bending bush;
A shower of blossoms mourns the ruthless deed!
The piercing anguished note, the brushing wing,
The spoiler heeds not; triumphing, his way
Smiling he wends: the ruined hopeless pair,
O'er many a field follow his townward steps,
Then back return; and, perching on the bush,
Find nought of all they loved, but one small tuft
Of moss, and withered roots. Drooping they sit,
Silent: afar at last they fly, o'er hill
And lurid moor, to mourn in other groves,
And soothe, in gentler grief, their hapless lot.

                                    (Part I, ll. 582–631)

How sweet the first sound of the cuckoo's note!
Whence is the magic pleasure of the sound?
How do we long recall the very tree,
Or bush, near which we stood, when on the ear
The unexpected note, *cuckoo!* again,
And yet again, came down the budding vale?
It is the voice of spring among the trees;
It tells of lengthening days, of coming blooms;
It is the symphony of many a song.
But, there, the stranger flies close to the ground,
With hawk-like pinion, of a leaden blue.
Poor wanderer! from hedge to hedge she flies,
And trusts her offspring to another's care:

The sooty-plumed hedge sparrow frequent acts
The foster mother, warming into life
The youngling, destined to supplant her own.
Meanwhile, the cuckoo sings her idle song,
Monotonous, yet sweet, now here, now there,
Herself but rarely seen; nor does she cease
Her changeless note, until the broom, full blown,
Give warning that her time for flight is come.
Thus, ever journeying on, from land to land,
She, sole of all the innumerous feathered tribes,
Passes a stranger's life, without a home.

(Part II, ll. 1–24)

Robert Bloomfield
(1766–1823)

146 · *from* THE FARMER'S BOY

from *Summer*

He comes, the pest and terror of the yard,
His full-fledged progeny's imperious guard;
The gander: – spiteful, insolent, and bold,
At the colt's footlock takes his daring hold;
There, serpent-like, escapes a dreadful blow;
And straight attacks a poor defenceless cow:
Each booby goose th'unworthy strife enjoys,
And hails his prowess with redoubled noise.
Then back he stalks, of self-importance full,
Seizes the shaggy foretop of the bull,
Till whirled aloft he falls; a timely check,
Enough to dislocate his worthless neck:
For lo! of old, he boasts an honoured wound;
Behold that broken wing that trails the ground!
Thus fools and bravoes kindred pranks pursue;
As savage quite, and oft as fatal too.

(ll. 227–42)

James Hogg
(1770–1835)

147 · THE SKYLARK

Bird of the wilderness,
Blithesome and cumberless,
Sweet be thy matin o'er moorland and lea!
Emblem of happiness,
Blest is thy dwelling-place –
O to abide in the desert with thee!
Wild is thy lay and loud,
Far in the downy cloud,
Love gives it energy, love gave it birth.
Where, on thy dewy wing,
Where art thou journeying?
Thy lay is in heaven, thy love is on earth.

O'er fell and fountain sheen,
O'er moor and mountain green,
O'er the red streamer that heralds the day,
Over the cloudlet dim,
Over the rainbow's rim,
Musical cherub, soar, singing, away!
Then, when the gloaming comes,
Low in the heather blooms
Sweet will thy welcome and bed of love be!
Emblem of happiness,
Blest is thy dwelling-place –
O to abide in the desert with thee!

William Wordsworth
(1770–1850)

148 · TO THE CUCKOO

O blithe new-comer! I have heard,
I hear thee and rejoice.
O cuckoo! shall I call thee bird,
Or but a wandering voice?

While I am lying on the grass
Thy twofold shout I hear,
From hill to hill it seems to pass
At once far off, and near.

Though babbling only to the vale,
Of sunshine and of flowers,
Thou bringest unto me a tale
Of visionary hours.

Thrice welcome, darling of the spring!
Even yet thou art to me
No bird, but an invisible thing,
A voice, a mystery;

The same whom in my schoolboy days
I listened to; that cry
Which made me look a thousand ways
In bush, and tree, and sky.

To seek thee did I often rove
Through woods and on the green;
And thou wert still a hope, a love;
Still longed for, never seen.

And I can listen to thee yet;
Can lie upon the plain
And listen, till I do beget
That golden time again.

O blessèd bird! the earth we pace
Again appears to be
An unsubstantial, faery place;
That is fit home for thee!

149 · THE GREEN LINNET

Beneath these fruit tree boughs that shed
Their snow-white blossoms on my head,
With brightest sunshine round me spread
   Of spring's unclouded weather,
In this sequestered nook how sweet
To sit upon my orchard-seat!
And birds and flowers once more to greet,
   My last year's friends together.

One have I marked, the happiest guest
In all this covert of the blest:
Hail to thee, far above the rest
   In joy of voice and pinion!
Thou, linnet! in thy green array,
Presiding spirit here today,
Dost lead the revels of the May;
   And this is thy dominion.

While birds, and butterflies, and flowers,
Make all one band of paramours,
Thou, ranging up and down the bowers,
   Art sole in thy employment:
A life, a presence like the air,
Scattering thy gladness without care,
Too blest with any one to pair;
   Thyself thy own enjoyment.

Amid yon tuft of hazel trees,
That twinkle to the gusty breeze,
Behold him perched in ecstasies,
   Yet seeming still to hover;
There! where the flutter of his wings
Upon his back and body flings
Shadows and sunny glimmerings,
   That cover him all over.

My dazzled sight he oft deceives,
A brother of the dancing leaves;
Then flits, and from the cottage-eaves
  Pours forth his song in gushes;
As if by that exulting strain
He mocked and treated with disdain
The voiceless form he chose to feign,
  While fluttering in the bushes.

150 · *from* THE KITTEN AND FALLING
LEAVES

  Where is he, that giddy sprite,
Blue-cap, with his colours bright,
Who was blest as bird could be,
Feeding in the apple tree;
Made such wanton spoil and rout,
Turning blossoms inside out:
Hung – head pointing towards the ground –
Fluttered, perched, into a round
Bound himself, and then unbound;
Lithest, gaudiest Harlequin!
Prettiest tumbler ever seen!

Light of heart and light of limb;
What is now become of him?

(ll. 63-75)

· 151 ·

O nightingale! thou surely art
A creature of a 'fiery heart': –
These notes of thine – they pierce and pierce;
Tumultuous harmony and fierce!
Thou sing'st as if the God of wine
Had helped thee to a Valentine;
A song in mockery and despite
Of shades, and dews, and silent night;
And steady bliss, and all the loves
Now sleeping in these peaceful groves.

I heard a stock dove sing or say
His homely tale, this very day;
His voice was buried among trees,
Yet to be come-at by the breeze:
He did not cease; but cooed – and cooed;
And somewhat pensively he wooed:
He sang of love, with quiet blending,
Slow to begin, and never ending;
Of serious faith, and inward glee;
That was the song – the song for me!

152 · TO A SKYLARK

Ethereal minstrel! pilgrim of the sky!
Dost thou despise the earth where cares abound?
Or, while the wings aspire, are heart and eye
Both with thy nest upon the dewy ground?
Thy nest which thou canst drop into at will,
Those quivering wings composed, that music still!

Leave to the nightingale her shady wood;
A privacy of glorious light is thine;
Whence thou dost pour upon the world a flood
Of harmony, with instinct more divine;
Type of the wise who soar, but never roam;
True to the kindred points of heaven and home!

153 · *from* THE REDBREAST

(SUGGESTED IN A WESTMORELAND COTTAGE)

Driven in by autumn's sharpening air
From half-stripped woods and pastures bare,
Brisk Robin seeks a kindlier home:
Not like a beggar is he come,
But enters as a looked-for guest,
Confiding in his ruddy breast,
As if it were a natural shield
Charged with a blazon on the field,
Due to that good and pious deed
Of which we in the Ballad[1] read.
But pensive fancies putting by,
And wild-wood sorrows, speedily
He plays the expert ventriloquist;
And, caught by glimpses now – now missed,
Puzzles the listener with a doubt
If the soft voice he throws about
Comes from within doors or without!
Was ever such a sweet confusion,
Sustained by delicate illusion?
He's at your elbow – to your feeling
The notes are from the floor or ceiling;
And there's a riddle to be guessed,
Till you have marked his heaving chest,
And busy throat whose sink and swell
Betray the elf that loves to dwell
In Robin's bosom, as a chosen cell.

(ll. 1–26)

1. *The Children in the Wood* – ' Till Robin Redbreast piously/Did cover them with eaves.'

Sir Walter Scott
(1771–1832)

· 154 ·

It's up Glenbarchan's braes I gaed,
And o'er the bent of Killiebraid,
And mony a weary cast I made,
　　To cuittle[1] the moor-fowl's tail.

If up a bonny blackcock should spring,
To whistle him down wi' a slug in his wing,
And strap him on to my lunzie[2] string,
　　Right seldom would I fail.

· 155 ·

Proud Maisie is in the wood,
　　Walking so early;
Sweet Robin sits on the bush,
　　Singing so rarely.

'Tell me, thou bonny bird,
　　When shall I marry me?'
'When six braw gentlemen
　　Kirkward shall carry ye.'

'Who makes the bridal bed,
　　Birdie, say truly?'
'The grey-headed sexton
　　That delves the grave duly.

'The glowworm o'er grave and stone
　　Shall light thee steady.
The owl from the steeple sing,
　　"Welcome, proud lady." '

1. tickle　2. variant of lunyie, meaning loin

Samuel Taylor Coleridge
(1772–1834)

156 · THE DEATH OF THE STARLING

Pity! mourn in plaintive tone
The lovely starling dead and gone!
  Pity mourns in plaintive tone
The lovely starling dead and gone.
Weep, ye Loves! and Venus! weep
The lovely starling fall'n asleep!
Venus sees with tearful eyes –
In her lap the starling lies!
While the Loves all in a ring
Softly stroke the stiffened wing.

157 · *from* THE NIGHTINGALE

A CONVERSATION POEM, APRIL, 1798

No cloud, no relique of the sunken day
Distinguishes the west, no long thin slip
Of sullen light, no obscure trembling hues.
Come, we will rest on this old mossy bridge!
You see the glimmer of the stream beneath,
But hear no murmuring: it flows silently,
O'er its soft bed of verdure. All is still,
A balmy night! and though the stars be dim,
Yet let us think upon the vernal showers
That gladden the green earth, and we shall find
A pleasure in the dimness of the stars.
And hark! the nightingale begins its song,
'Most musical, most melancholy' bird!
A melancholy bird? Oh! idle thought!
In Nature there is nothing melancholy.
But some night-wandering man whose heart was pierced
With the remembrance of a grievous wrong,
Or slow distemper, or neglected love,
(And so, poor wretch! filled all things with himself,
And made all gentle sounds tell back the tale
Of his own sorrow) he, and such as he,
First named these notes a melancholy strain.
And many a poet echoes the conceit;
Poet who hath been building up the rhyme
When he had better far have stretched his limbs
Beside a brook in mossy forest-dell,
By sun or moonlight, to the influxes
Of shapes and sounds and shifting elements
Surrendering his whole spirit, of his song
And of his fame forgetful! so his fame
Should share in Nature's immortality,
A venerable thing! and so his song
Should make all Nature lovelier, and itself
Be loved like Nature! But 'twill not be so;
And youths and maidens most poetical,
Who lose the deepening twilights of the spring
In ball rooms and hot theatres, they still
Full of meek sympathy must heave their sighs
O'er Philomela's pity-pleading strains.

My friend, and thou, our sister! we have learnt
A different lore: we may not thus profane
Nature's sweet voices, always full of love
And joyance! 'Tis the merry nightingale
That crowds, and hurries, and precipitates
With fast thick warble his delicious notes,
As he were fearful that an April night
Would be too short for him to utter forth
His love-chant, and disburthen his full soul
Of all its music!

    And I know a grove
Of large extent, hard by a castle huge,
Which the great lord inhabits not; and so
This grove is wild with tangling underwood,
And the trim walks are broken up, and grass,
Thin grass and king-cups grow within the paths.
But never elsewhere in one place I knew
So many nightingales; and far and near,
In wood and thicket, over the wide grove,
They answer and provoke each other's song,
With skirmish and capricious passagings,
And murmurs musical and swift jug jug,
And one low piping sound more sweet than all –
Stirring the air with such a harmony,
That should you close your eyes, you might almost
Forget it was not day! On moonlight bushes,
Whose dewy leaflets are but half-disclosed,
You may perchance behold them on the twigs,
Their bright, bright eyes, their eyes both bright and full,
Glistening, while many a glowworm in the shade
Lights up her love-torch.

          (ll. 1–69)

· 158 ·

Sea-ward, white gleaming through the busy scud
With arching wings, the seamew o'er my head
Posts on, as bent on speed: now passaging,
Edges the stiffer breeze; now yielding, drifts;
Now floats upon the air, and sends from far
A wildly-wailing note.

· 159 ·

Or wren or linnet
In bush and bushet;
No tree, but in it
A cooing cushat.

· 160 ·

The spruce and limber yellowhammer
In the dawn of spring and sultry summer,
In hedge or tree the hours beguiling
With notes as of one who brass is filing.

161 · SONG

A sunny shaft did I behold,
  From sky to earth it slanted:
And poised therein a bird so bold –
  Sweet bird, thou wert enchanted!

He sank, he rose, he twinkled, he trolled
  Within that shaft of sunny mist;
His eyes of fire, his beak of gold,
  All else of amethyst!

And thus he sang: 'Adieu! adieu!
Love's dreams prove seldom true.
The blossoms they make no delay:
The sparkling dewdrops will not stay.
  Sweet month of May,
    We must away;
      Far, far away!
        Today! today!'

Percy Bysshe Shelley
(1792–1822)

162 · *from* LINES WRITTEN AMONG THE EUGANEAN HILLS

Mid the mountains Eugancan,
I stood listening to the paean
With which the legioned rooks did hail
The sun's uprise majestical;
Gathering round with wings all hoar,
Through the dewy mist they soar
Like grey shades, till the eastern heaven
Bursts, and then, as clouds of even,
Flecked with fire and azure, lie
In the unfathomable sky,
So their plumes of purple grain,
Starred with drops of golden rain,
Gleam above the sunlight woods,
As in silent multitudes
On the morning's fitful gale
Through the broken mist they sail,
And the vapours cloven and gleaming
Follow, down the dark steep streaming,
Till all is bright, and clear, and still,
Round the solitary hill.

(ll. 70 89)

from PROMETHEUS UNBOUND

163 · *Semichorus II*

There the voluptuous nightingales
    Are awake through all the broad noonday.
When one with bliss or sadness fails,
        And through the windless ivy-boughs,
    Sick with sweet love, droops dying away
On its mate's music-panting bosom,

Another from the swinging blossom,
   Watching to catch the languid close
Of the last strain, then lifts on high
The wings of the weak melody,
Till some new strain of feeling bear
   The song, and all the woods are mute;
When there is heard through the dim air
The rush of wings, and rising there
   Like many a lake-surrounded flute,
Sounds overflow the listener's brain
So sweet, that joy is almost pain.
                  (II, ii, ll. 24–40)

· 164 ·

An eagle so caught in some bursting cloud
On Caucasus, his thunder-baffled wings
Entangled in the whirlwind, and his eyes
Which gazed on the undazzling sun, now blinded
By the white lightning, while the ponderous hail
Beats on his struggling form, which sinks at length
Prone, and the aërial ice clings over it.
                  (III, ii, ll. 11–17)

165 · *from* CHARLES THE FIRST

ARCHY: I'll go live under the ivy that overgrows the terrace, and count
the tears shed on its old roots as the wind plays the song of
     'A widow bird sate mourning
     Upon a wintry bough.'

Heigho! the lark and the owl!
   One flies the morning, and one lulls the night: –
Only the nightingale, poor fond soul,
   Sings like the fool through darkness and light.

'A widow bird sate mourning for her love
   Upon a wintry bough;
The frozen wind crept on above,
   The freezing stream below.

'There was no leaf upon the forest bare,
   No flower upon the ground,
  And little motion in the air
   Except the mill-wheel's sound.'
                (v, ll. 1–17)

166 · *from* THE WITCH OF ATLAS

And whilst the outer lake beneath the lash
  Of the winds' scourge, foamed like a wounded thing,
And the incessant hail with stony clash
  Ploughed up the waters, and the flagging wing
Of the roused cormorant in the lightning flash
  Looked like the wreck of some wind-wandering
Fragment of inky thunder-smoke – . . .
              (Stanza 50, 393–9)

167 · TO A SKYLARK

Hail to thee, blithe spirit!
  Bird thou never wert,
That from heaven, or near it,
  Pourest thy full heart
In profuse strains of unpremeditated art.

    Higher still and higher
      From the earth thou springest
    Like a cloud of fire;
      The blue deep thou wingest,
And singing still dost soar, and soaring ever singest.

    In the golden lightning
      Of the sunken sun,
    O'er which clouds are bright'ning,
      Thou dost float and run,
Like an unbodied joy whose race is just begun.

    The pale purple even
      Melts around thy flight;
    Like a star of heaven,
      In the broad daylight
Thou art unseen, but yet I hear thy shrill delight,

    Keen as are the arrows
      Of that silver sphere,
    Whose intense lamp narrows
      In the white dawn clear,
Until we hardly see, we feel that it is there.

    All the earth and air
      With thy voice is loud,
    As, when night is bare,
      From one lonely cloud
The moon rains out her beams, and heaven is overflowed.

    What thou art we know not;
      What is most like thee?
    From rainbow clouds there flow not
      Drops so bright to see
As from thy presence showers a rain of melody.

    Like a poet hidden
      In the light of thought,
    Singing hymns unbidden,
      Till the world is wrought
To sympathy with hopes and fears it heeded not:

    Like a high-born maiden
      In a palace tower,
    Soothing her love-laden
      Soul in secret hour
With music sweet as love, which overflows her bower:

Like a glowworm golden
  In a dell of dew,
Scattering unbeholden
  Its aërial hue
Among the flowers and grass, which screen it from the view:

Like a rose embowered
  In its own green leaves,
By warm winds deflowered,
  Till the scent it gives
Makes faint with too much sweet those heavy-wingèd thieves:

Sound of vernal showers
  On the twinkling grass,
Rain-awakened flowers,
  All that ever was
Joyous, and clear, and fresh, thy music doth surpass.

Teach us, sprite or bird,
  What sweet thoughts are thine:
I have never heard
  Praise of love or wine
That panted forth a flood of rapture so divine.

Chorus Hymeneal,
  Or triumphal chant,
Matched with thine would be all
  But an empty vaunt,
A thing wherein we feel there is some hidden want.

What objects are the fountains
  Of thy happy strain?
What fields, or waves, or mountains?
  What shapes of sky or plain?
What love of thine own kind? what ignorance of pain?

With thy clear keen joyance
  Languor cannot be:
Shadow of annoyance
  Never came near thee:
Thou lovest; but ne'er knew love's sad satiety.

Waking or asleep,
  Thou of death must deem

Things more true and deep
    Than we mortals dream,
Or how could thy notes flow in such a crystal stream?

We look before and after,
    And pine for what is not:
Our sincerest laughter
    With some pain is fraught;
Our sweetest songs are those that tell of saddest thought.

Yet if we could scorn
    Hate, and pride, and fear;
If we were things born
    Not to shed a tear,
I know not how thy joy we ever should come near.

Better than all measures
    Of delightful sound,
Better than all treasures
    That in books are found,
Thy skill to poet were, thou scorner of the ground!

Teach me half the gladness
    That thy brain must know,
Such harmonious madness
    From my lips would flow,
The world should listen then, as I am listening now.

168 · THE AZIOLA

'Do you not hear the Aziola cry?
Methinks she must be nigh,'
    Said Mary, as we sate
In dusk, ere stars were lit, or candles brought –
    And I, who thought
This Aziola was some tedious woman,
    Asked, 'Who is Aziola?' How elate
I felt to know that it was nothing human,
    No mockery of myself to fear or hate!
    And Mary saw my soul,
And laughed and said, 'Disquiet yourself not,
    'Tis nothing but a little downy owl.'

Sad Aziola! many an eventide
   Thy music I had heard
By wood and stream, meadow and mountain-side,
And fields and marshes wide –
   Such as nor voice, nor lute, nor wind, nor bird,
    The soul ever stirred;
Unlike, and far sweeter than them all.
Sad Aziola! from that moment I
Loved thee and thy sad cry.

John Clare
(1793–1864)

169 · THE LANDRAIL

I've listened, when to school I've gone,
   That craking noise to hear,
And crept and listened on and on
   But ne'er once gotten near;

I've trampled through the meadow grass
   And dreaded to be caught,
And stood and wondered what it was,
   And very often thought

Some fairy thing had lost its way,
   Night's other worlds to find,
And hiding in the grass all day
   Mourned to be left behind;

But I've since found their eggs, forsooth,
   And so we may again,
But great the joy I missed in youth
   As not to find them then;

For when a boy a new nest meets,
   Joy gushes to his breast,
Nor would his heart so quickly beat
   Were guineas in the nest.

I've hunted till the day has been
    So vanished that I dare
Not go to school nor yet be seen
    That I was playing there;

So mid the wheat I've made a seat
    Upon an old meer-stone,[1]
And hid, and all my dinner eat,
    Till four o'clock was gone.

170 · THE LARK'S[2] NEST

From yon black clump of wheat that grows
    More rank and higher than the rest,
A lark – I marked her as she rose –
    At early morning left her nest.
Her eggs were four of dusky hue,
    Blotched brown as is the very ground,
With tinges of a purply hue
    The larger ends encircling round.

Behind a clod how snug the nest
    Is in a horse's footing fixed!
Of twitch[3] and stubbles roughly dressed,
    With roots and horsehair intermixed.
The wheat surrounds it like a bower,
    And like to thatch each bowing blade
Throws off the frequent falling shower
    – And here's an egg this morning laid!

171 · THE PETTICHAP'S NEST

Well! in my many walks I've rarely found
A place less likely for a bird to form
Its nest – close by the rut-gulled wagon-road,
And on the almost bare foot-trodden ground,
With scarce a clump of grass to keep it warm!
Where not a thistle spreads its spears abroad,
Or prickly bush, to shield it from harm's way;
And yet so snugly made, that none may spy
It out, save peradventure. You and I

1. boundary stone   2. Meadow pipit – Clare calls it lark, ground lark, and furze lark.
3. A kind of grass.

Had surely passed it in our walk today,
Had chance not led us by it! – Nay, e'en now,
Had not the old bird heard us trampling by
And fluttered out, we had not seen it lie,
Brown as the roadway side. Small bits of hay
Plucked from the old propt haystack's pleachy[1] brow,
And withered leaves, make up its outward wall,
Which from the gnarled oak-dotterel[2] yearly fall,
And in the old hedge-bottom rot away.
Built like an oven, through a little hole,
Scarcely admitting e'en two fingers in,
Hard to discern, the birds snug entrance win.
'Tis lined with feathers warm as silken stole,
Softer than seats of down for painless ease,
And full of eggs scarce bigger even than peas!
Here's one most delicate, with spots as small
As dust and of a faint and pinky red.
We'll let them be, and safety guard them well;
For fear's rude paths around are thickly spread,
And they are left to many dangerous ways.
A green grasshopper's jump might break the shells,
Yet lowing oxen pass them morn and night,
And restless sheep around them hourly stray;
And no grass springs but hungry horses bite,
That trample past them twenty times a day.
Yet, like a miracle, in safety's lap
They still abide unhurt, and out of sight.
Stop! here's the bird – that woodman at the gap
Frightened him from the hedge: 'tis olive-green.
Well! I declare it is the pettichap!
Not bigger than the wren, and seldom seen.
I've often found her nest in chance's way,
When I in pathless woods did idly roam;
But never did I dream until today
A spot like this would be her chosen home.

      1. sun-dried, bleached   2. a pollard-tree

172 · THE SAND MARTIN[1]

Thou hermit, haunter of the lonely glen
  And common wild and heath – the desolate face
Of rude, waste landscapes far away from men,
  Where frequent quarries give thee dwelling-place,
With strangest taste and labour undeterred
  Drilling small holes along the quarry's side,
More like the haunt of vermin than a bird,
  And seldom by the nesting boy descried –
I've seen thee far away from all thy tribe,
  Flirting about the unfrequented sky,
And felt a feeling that I can't describe
  Of lone seclusion, and a hermit joy
To see thee circle round nor go beyond
That lone heath and its melancholy pond.

173 · THE HAPPY BIRD

The happy whitethroat on the sweeing[2] bough,
Swayed by the impulse of the gadding wind
That ushers in the showers of April, now
Carols right joyously; and now reclined,
Crouching, she clings close to her moving seat,
To keep her hold; and till the wind for rest
Pauses, she mutters inward melodies,
That seem her heart's rich thinkings to repeat.
But when the branch is still, her little breast
Swells out in rapture's gushing symphonies;
And then, against her brown wing softly prest,
The wind comes playing, an enraptured guest,
This way and that she swees – till gusts arise
More boisterous in their play, then off she flies.

174 · EARLY NIGHTINGALE

When first we hear the shy-come nightingales,
They seem to mutter o'er their songs in fear,
And, climb we e'er so soft the spinney rails,
All stops as if no bird was anywhere.

1. This is the same species as the American bank swallow. 2. swaying, rocking

The kindled bushes with the young leaves thin
Let curious eyes to search a long way in,
Until impatience cannot see or hear
The hidden music; gets but little way
Upon the path – when up the songs begin,
Full loud a moment and then low again.
But when a day or two confirms her stay
Boldly she sings and loud for half the day;
And soon the village brings the woodman's tale
Of having heard the new-come nightingale.

175 · HEN'S NEST

Among the orchard weeds, from every search,
Snugly and sure, the old hen's nest is made,
Who cackles every morning from her perch
To tell the servant girl new eggs are laid;
Who lays her washing by, and far and near
Goes seeking all about from day to day,
And stung with nettles tramples everywhere;
But still the cackling pullet lays away.
The boy on Sundays goes the stack to pull
In hopes to find her there, but naught is seen,
And takes his hat and thinks to find it full,
She's laid so long so many might have been.
But naught is found and all is given o'er
Till the young brood come chirping to the door.

176 · AUTUMN BIRDS

The wild duck startles like a sudden thought,
And heron slow as if it might be caught;
The flopping crows on weary wing go by,
And greybeard jackdaws, noising as they fly;
The crowds of starnels whizz and hurry by
And darken like a cloud the evening sky;
The larks like thunder rise and suther[1] round,
Then drop and nestle in the stubble ground;
The wild swan hurries high and noises loud,
With white neck peering to the evening cloud.

1. make a rushing noise

The weary rooks to distant woods are gone;
With length of tail the magpie winnows on
To neighbouring tree, and leaves the distant crow,
While small birds nestle in the hedge below.

John Keats
(1795–1821)

177 · *from* 'I STOOD TIP-TOE'

Sometimes goldfinches one by one will drop
From low hung branches; little space they stop;
But sip, and twitter, and their feathers sleek;
Then off at once, as in a wanton freak:
Or perhaps, to show their black and golden wings,
Pausing upon their yellow flutterings.

(ll. 87–92)

178 · *from* TO CHARLES COWDEN CLARKE

Oft have you seen a swan superbly frowning,
And with proud breast his own white shadow crowning;
He slants his neck beneath the waters bright
So silently, it seems a beam of light

Come from the galaxy: anon he sports –
With outspread wings the naiad zephyr courts,
Or ruffles all the surface of the lake
In striving from its crystal face to take
Some diamond water drops, and them to treasure
In milky nest, and sip them off at leisure.
But not a moment can he there insure them,
Nor to such downy rest can he allure them;
For down they rush as though they would be free,
And drop like hours into eternity.
Just like that bird am I in loss of time,
Whenc'er I venture on the stream of rhyme;
With shattered boat, oar snapt, and canvas rent,
I slowly sail, scarce knowing my intent;
Still scooping up the water with my fingers,
In which a trembling diamond never lingers.

(ll. 1–20)

179 · SONG

I had a dove and the sweet dove died;
  And I have thought it died of grieving:
O, what could it grieve for? it was tied
  With a silken thread of my own hand's weaving;
Sweet little red feet! why did you die –
Why would you leave me, sweet dove! why?
You lived alone on the forest tree,
Why, pretty thing! could you not live with me?
I kissed you oft and gave you white peas;
Why not live sweetly, as in the green trees?

180 · ODE TO A NIGHTINGALE

My heart aches, and a drowsy numbness pains
  My sense, as though of hemlock I had drunk,
Or emptied some dull opiate to the drains
  One minute past, and Lethe-wards had sunk:
'Tis not through envy of thy happy lot,
  But being too happy in thine happiness –
    That thou, light-wingèd Dryad of the trees,
      In some melodious plot
Of beechen green, and shadows numberless,
  Singest of summer in full-throated ease.

O, for a draught of vintage! that hath been
  Cooled a long age in the deep-delved earth,
Tasting of Flora and the country green,
  Dance, and Provençal song, and sunburnt mirth!
O for a beaker full of the warm South,
  Full of the true, the blushful Hippocrene,
    With beaded bubbles winking at the brim,
      And purple-stainèd mouth;
    That I might drink, and leave the world unseen,
      And with thee fade away into the forest dim:

Fade far away, dissolve, and quite forget
  What thou among the leaves hast never known,
The weariness, the fever, and the fret
  Here, where men sit and hear each other groan;
Where palsy shakes a few, sad, last grey hairs,
  Where youth grows pale, and spectre-thin, and dies;
    Where but to think is to be full of sorrow
      And leaden-eyed despairs,
    Where beauty cannot keep her lustrous eyes,
      Or new love pine at them beyond tomorrow.

Away! away! for I will fly to thee,
  Not charioted by Bacchus and his pards,
But on the viewless wings of poesy,
  Though the dull brain perplexes and retards:
Already with thee! tender is the night,
  And haply the Queen-Moon is on her throne,
    Clustered around by all her starry fays;
      But here there is no light,
    Save what from heaven is with the breezes blown
      Through verdurous glooms and winding mossy ways.

I cannot see what flowers are at my feet,
  Nor what soft incense hangs upon the boughs,
But, in embalmèd darkness, guess each sweet
  Wherewith the seasonable month endows
The grass, the thicket, and the fruit tree wild;
  White hawthorn, and the pastoral eglantine;
    Fast fading violets covered up in leaves;
      And mid-May's eldest child,
    The coming musk-rose, full of dewy wine,
      The murmurous haunt of flies on summer eves.

Darkling I listen; and for many a time
  I have been half in love with easeful death,
Called him soft names in many a musëd rhyme,
  To take into the air my quiet breath;
Now more than ever seems it rich to die,
    To cease upon the midnight with no pain,
      While thou art pouring forth thy soul abroad
        In such an ecstasy!
    Still wouldst thou sing, and I have ears in vain –
      To thy high requiem become a sod.

Thou wast not born for death, immortal bird!
  No hungry generations tread thee down;
The voice I hear this passing night was heard
  In ancient days by emperor and clown:
Perhaps the self-same song that found a path
    Through the sad heart of Ruth, when, sick for home,
      She stood in tears amid the alien corn;
        The same that oft-times hath
    Charmed magic casements, opening on the foam
    Of perilous seas, in faery lands forlorn.

Forlorn! the very word is like a bell
  To toll me back from thee to my sole self!
Adieu! the fancy cannot cheat so well
  As she is famed to do, deceiving elf.
Adieu! adieu! thy plaintive anthem fades
    Past the near meadows, over the still stream,
      Up the hill-side; and now 'tis buried deep
        In the next valley-glades:
    Was it a vision, or a waking dream?
    Fled is that music: – Do I wake or sleep?

George Darley
(1795–1846)

from NEPENTHE

181 · from *Canto I*

O blest unfabled incense tree,
That burns in glorious Araby,
With red scent chalicing the air,
Till earth-life grow Elysian there!

Half buried to her flaming breast
In this bright tree, she makes her nest,
Hundred-sunned phoenix! when she must
Crumble at length to hoary dust!

Her gorgeous death-bed! her rich pyre
Burnt up with aromatic fire!
Her urn, sight high from spoiler men!
Her birthplace when self-born again!

The mountainless green wilds among,
Here ends she her unechoing song!
With amber tears and odorous sighs
Mourned by the desert where she dies!

Laid like the young fawn mossily
In sun-green vales of Araby,
I woke hard by the phoenix tree
That with shadeless boughs flamed over me,
And upward called by a dumb cry
With moonbroad orbs of wonder, I
Beheld the immortal bird on high
Glassing the great sun in her eye.
Stedfast she gazed upon his fire,
Still her destroyer and her sire!
As if to his her soul of flame
Had flown already, whence it came;
Like those that sit and glare so still,

Intense with their death struggle, till
We touch, and curdle at their chill! –
But breathing yet while she doth burn,
  The deathless daughter of the sun!
Slowly to crimson embers turn
  The beauties of the brightsome one.
O'er the broad nest her silver wings
Shook down their wasteful glitterings;
Her brinded neck high-arched in air
Like a small rainbow faded there;
But brighter glowed her plumy crown
Mouldering to golden ashes down;
With fume of sweet woods, to the skies,
Pure as a saint's adoring sighs,
Warm as a prayer in paradise,
Her life-breath rose in sacrifice!
The while with shrill triumphant tone
Sounding aloud, aloft, alone,
Ceaseless her joyful deathwail she
Sang to departing Araby!
  Deep melancholy wonder drew
Tears from my heartspring at that view.
Like cresset shedding its last flare
Upon some wistful mariner,
The bird, fast blending with the sky,
Turned on me her dead-gazing eye
Once – and as surge to shallow spray
Sank down to vapoury dust away!

  O, fast her amber blood doth flow
    From the heart-wounded incense tree,
  Fast as earth's deep-embosomed woe
    In silent rivulets to the sea!

  Beauty may weep her fair first-born,
    Perchance in as resplendent tears,
  Such golden dewdrops bow the corn
    When the stern sickleman appears.

  But oh! such perfume to a bower
    Never allured sweet-seeking bee,
  As to sip fast that nectarous shower
    A thirstier minstrel drew in me!

                              (ll. 147–215)

182 · from *Canto II*

Solitary wayfarer![1]
Minstrel winged of the green wild!
What dost thou delaying here,
Like a wood-bewildered child
Weeping to his far-flown troop,
Whoop! and plaintive whoop! and whoop!
Now from rock and now from tree,
Bird! methinks thou whoop'st to me,
Flitting before me upward still
With clear warble, as I've heard
Oft on my native Northern hill
No less wild and lone a bird,
Luring me with his sweet chee-chee
Up the mountain crags which he
Tript as lightly as a bee,
O'er steep pastures, far among
Thickets and briary lanes along,
Following still a fleeting song!
If such my errant nature, I
Vainly to curb or coop it try

1. The hoopoe. Its name is an imitation of its cry which Peterson calls a 'low, far-carrying "poo-poo-poo" '.

Now that the sundrop through my frame
Kindles another soul of flame!
Whoop on, whoop on, thou canst not wing
Too fast or far, thou well-named thing,
Hoopoe, if of that tribe which sing
Articulate in the desert ring!

(ll. 555–80)

Thomas Lovell Beddoes
(1803–49)

183 · SONG

Old Adam, the carrion crow,
  The old crow of Cairo;
He sat in the shower, and let it flow
  Under his tail and over his crest;
    And through every feather
    Leaked the wet weather;
  And the bough swung under his nest;
  For his beak it was heavy with marrow.
    Is that the wind dying? O no;
    It's only two devils, that blow
    Through a murderer's bones, to and fro,
      In the ghosts' moonshine.

Ho! Eve, my grey carrion wife,
  When we have supped on kings' marrow,
Where shall we drink and make merry our life?
  Our nest it is queen Cleopatra's skull,
    'Tis cloven and cracked,
    And battered and hacked,
  But with tears of blue eyes it is full:
  Let us drink then, my raven of Cairo.
    Is that the wind dying? O no;
    It's only two devils, that blow
    Through a murderer's bones, to and fro,
      In the ghosts' moonshine.

Alfred, Lord Tennyson
(1809–92)

184 · SONG – THE OWL

When cats run home and light is come,
    And dew is cold upon the ground,
And the far-off stream is dumb,
    And the whirring sail goes round,
    And the whirring sail goes round;
        Alone and warming his five wits,
        The white owl in the belfry sits.

When merry milkmaids click the latch,
    And rarely smells the new-mown hay,
And the cock hath sung beneath the thatch
    Twice or thrice his roundelay,
    Twice or thrice his roundelay;
        Alone and warming his five wits,
        The white owl in the belfry sits.

185 · SECOND SONG

TO THE SAME

Thy tu whits are lulled, I wot,
    Thy tu whoos of yesternight,
Which upon the dark afloat,
    So took echo with delight,
    So took echo with delight,
        That her voice untuneful grown,
        Wears all day a fainter tone.

I would mock thy chant anew;
    But I cannot mimic it;
Not a whit of thy tu whoo,
    Thee to woo to thy tu whit,
    Thee to woo to thy tu whit,
        With a lengthened loud halloo,
        Tu whoo, tu whit, tu whit, tu whoo-o-o.

186 · THE DYING SWAN

The plain was grassy, wild and bare,
Wide, wild, and open to the air,
Which had built up everywhere
  An under-roof of doleful grey.
With an inner voice the river ran,
Adown it floated a dying swan,
    And loudly did lament.
  It was the middle of the day.
Ever the weary wind went on,
    And took the reed-tops as it went.

Some blue peaks in the distance rose,
And white against the cold-white sky,
Shone out their crowning snows.
  One willow over the river wept,
And shook the wave as the wind did sigh;
Above in the wind was the swallow,
    Chasing itself at its own wild will,
    And far through the marish green and still
    The tangled water-courses slept,
Shot over with purple, and green, and yellow.

The wild swan's death-hymn took the soul
Of that waste place with joy
Hidden in sorrow: at first to the ear
The warble was low, and full and clear;
And floating about the under-sky,
Prevailing in weakness, the coronach[1] stole
Sometimes afar, and sometimes anear;
But anon her awful jubilant voice,
With a music strange and manifold,
Flowed forth on a carol free and bold;
As when a mighty people rejoice
With shawms, and with cymbals, and harps of gold,
And the tumult of their acclaim is rolled
Through the open gates of the city afar,
To the shepherd who watcheth the evening star.
And the creeping mosses and clambering weeds,
And the willow-branches hoar and dank,

1. Gaelic funeral song

And the wavy swell of the soughing reeds,
And the wave-worn horns of the echoing bank,
And the silvery marish-flowers that throng
The desolate creeks and pools among,
Were flooded over with eddying song.

187 · THE BLACKBIRD

O blackbird! sing me something well:
 While all the neighbours shoot thee round,
 I keep smooth plats of fruitful ground,
Where thou mayst warble, eat and dwell.

The espaliers and the standards[1] all
 Are thine; the range of lawn and park:
 The unnetted black-hearts[2] ripen dark,
All thine, against the garden wall.

Yet, though I spared thee all the spring,
 Thy sole delight is, sitting still,
 With that gold dagger of thy bill
To fret the summer jenneting.[3]

A golden bill! the silver tongue,
 Cold February loved, is dry:
 Plenty corrupts the melody
That made thee famous once, when young:

And in the sultry garden-squares,
 Now thy flute-notes are changed to coarse,
 I hear thee not at all, or hoarse
As when a hawker hawks his wares.

Take warning! he that will not sing
 While yon sun prospers in the blue,
 Shall sing for want, ere leaves are new,
Caught in the frozen palms of spring.

---

1. free standing trees, not dwarfed or trained against walls 2. cherries 3. a kind of early apple

188 · THE EAGLE

FRAGMENT

He clasps the crag with crookëd hands;
Close to the sun in lonely lands,
Ringed with the azure world, he stands.

The wrinkled sea beneath him crawls;
He watches from his mountain walls,
And like a thunderbolt he falls.

189 · *from* IN MEMORIAM

LXXXVIII

Wild bird,[1] whose warble, liquid sweet,
  Rings Eden through the budded quicks,[2]
  O tell me where the senses mix,
O tell me where the passions meet,

Whence radiate: fierce extremes employ
  Thy spirits in the darkening leaf,
  And in the midmost heart of grief
Thy passion clasps a secret joy:

And I – my harp would prelude woe –
  I cannot all command the strings;
  The glory of the sum of things
Will flash along the chords and go.

190 · *from* THE WINDOW

OR, THE SONG OF THE WRENS

Ay

Be merry, all birds, today,
  Be merry on earth as you never were merry before,
Be merry in heaven, O larks, and far away,
  And merry for ever and ever, and one day more.
                    Why?
    For it's easy to find a rhyme.

1. nightingale   2. quick fence or hedge

Look, look, how he flits,
  The fire-crowned king of the wrens, from out of the pine!
Look how they tumble the blossom, the mad little tits!
  'Cuck-oo! Cuck-oo!' was ever a May so fine?
                    Why?
  For it's easy to find a rhyme.

O merry the linnet and dove,
  And swallow and sparrow and throstle, and have your desire!
O merry my heart, you have gotten the wings of love,
  And flit like the king of the wrens with a crown of fire.
                    Why?
  For it's ay ay, ay ay.

191 · THE THROSTLE

'Summer is coming, summer is coming.
  I know it, I know it, I know it.
Light again, leaf again, life again, love again,'
  Yes, my wild little poet.

Sing the new year in under the blue.
  Last year you sang it as gladly.
'New, new, new, new!' Is it then *so* new
  That you should carol so madly?

'Love again, song again, nest again, young again,'
  Never a prophet so crazy!
And hardly a daisy as yet, little friend,
  See, there is hardly a daisy.

'Here again, here, here, here, happy year!'
  O warble unchidden, unbidden!
Summer is coming, is coming, my dear,
  And all the winters are hidden.

Matthew Arnold
(1822–88)

192 · PHILOMELA

Hark! ah, the nightingale –
The tawny-throated!
Hark, from that moonlit cedar what a burst!
What triumph! hark! – what pain!

O wanderer from a Grecian shore,
Still, after many years, in distant lands,
Still nourishing in thy bewildered brain
That wild, unquenched, deep-sunken, old-world pain –
Say, will it never heal?
And can this fragrant lawn
With its cool trees, and night,
And the sweet tranquil Thames,
And moonshine, and the dew,
To thy racked heart and brain
Afford no balm?

Dost thou tonight behold,
Here, through the moonlight on this English grass,
The unfriendly palace in the Thracian wild?
Dost thou again peruse
With hot cheeks and seared eyes
The too clear web, and thy dumb sister's shame?
Dost thou once more assay
Thy flight, and feel come over thee,
Poor fugitive, the feathery change
Once more, and once more seem to make resound
With love and hate, triumph and agony,
Lone Daulis, and the high Cephissian vale?
Listen, Eugenia –
How thick the bursts come crowding through the leaves!
Again – thou hearest?
Eternal passion!
Eternal pain!

William Allingham
(1824–89)

193 · ROBIN REDBREAST

(A CHILD'S SONG)

Goodbye, goodbye to summer!
  For summer's nearly done;
The garden smiling faintly,
  Cool breezes in the sun;
Our thrushes now are silent,
  Our swallows flown away –
But Robin's here, in coat of brown,
  With ruddy breast-knot gay.
Robin, Robin Redbreast,
  O Robin dear!
Robin sings so sweetly
  In the falling of the year.

Bright yellow, red, and orange,
  The leaves come down in hosts;
The trees are Indian princes,
  But soon they'll turn to ghosts;
The scanty pears and apples
  Hang russet on the bough;
It's autumn, autumn, autumn late,
  'Twill soon be winter now.
Robin, Robin Redbreast,
  O Robin dear!
And what will this poor Robin do?
  For pinching days are near.

The fireside for the cricket,
  The wheatstack for the mouse,
When trembling night-winds whistle
  And moan all round the house;
The frosty ways like iron,
  The branches plumed with snow –

Alas! in winter dead and dark
    Where can poor Robin go?
Robin, Robin Redbreast,
    O Robin dear!
And a crumb of bread for Robin,
    His little heart to cheer.

George Meredith
(1828–1909)

194 · THE LARK ASCENDING

He rises and begins to round,
He drops the silver chain of sound,
Of many links without a break,
In chirrup, whistle, slur and shake,
All intervolved and spreading wide,
Like water-dimples down a tide
Where ripple ripple overcurls
And eddy into eddy whirls;
A press of hurried notes that run
So fleet they scarce are more than one,
Yet changeingly the trills repeat
And linger ringing while they fleet,
Sweet to the quick o' the ear, and dear
To her[1] beyond the handmaid car,
Who sits beside our inner springs,
Too often dry for this he brings,
Which seems the very jet of earth
At sight of sun, her music's mirth,
As up he wings the spiral stair,
A song of light, and pierces air
With fountain ardour, fountain play,
To reach the shining tops of day,
And drink in everything discerned
An ecstasy to music turned,

1. the spirit of nature within us

Impelled by what his happy bill
Disperses; drinking, showering still,
Unthinking save that he may give
His voice the outlet, there to live
Renewed in endless notes of glee,
So thirsty of his voice is he,
For all to hear and all to know
That he is joy, awake, aglow,
The tumult of the heart to hear
Through pureness filtered crystal-clear,
And know the pleasure sprinkled bright
By simple singing of delight,
Shrill, irreflective, unrestrained,
Rapt, ringing, on the jet sustained
Without a break, without a fall,
Sweet-silvery, sheer lyrical,
Perennial, quavering up the chord
Like myriad dews of sunny sward
That trembling into fulness shine,
And sparkle dropping argentine;
Such wooing as the ear receives
From zephyr caught in choric leaves
Of aspens when their chattering net
Is flushed to white with shivers wet;
And such the water-spirit's chime
On mountain heights in morning's prime,
Too freshly sweet to seem excess,
Too animate to need a stress;
But wider over many heads
The starry voice ascending spreads,
Awakening, as it waxes thin,
The best in us to him akin;
And every face to watch him raised
Puts on the light of children praised,
So rich our human pleasure ripes
When sweetness on sincereness pipes,
Though nought be promised from the seas,
But only a soft-ruffling breeze
Sweep glittering on a still content,
Serenity in ravishment.
For singing till his heaven fills,
'Tis love of earth that he instils,

And ever winging up and up,
Our valley is his golden cup,
And he the wine which overflows
To lift us with him as he goes:
The woods and brooks, the sheep and kine,
He is, the hills, the human line,
The meadows green, the fallows brown,
The dreams of labour in the town;
He sings the sap, the quickened veins;
The wedding song of sun and rains
He is, the dance of children, thanks
Of sowers, shout of primrose-banks,
And eye of violets while they breathe;
All these the circling song will wreathe,
And you shall hear the herb and tree,
The better heart of men shall see,
Shall feel celestially, as long
As you crave nothing save the song.

Was never voice of ours could say
Our inmost in the sweetest way,
Like yonder voice aloft, and link
All hearers in the song they drink.
Our wisdom speaks from failing blood,
Our passion is too full in flood,
We want the key of his wild note
Of truthful in a tuneful throat,
The song seraphically free
Of taint of personality,
So pure that it salutes the suns,
The voice of one for millions,
In whom the millions rejoice
For giving their one spirit voice.
Yet men have we, whom we revere,
Now names, and men still housing here,
Whose lives, by many a battle-dint
Defaced, and grinding wheels on flint,
Yield substance, though they sing not, sweet
For song our highest heaven to greet:
Whom heavenly singing gives us new,
Enspheres them brilliant in our blue,
From firmest base to farthest leap,

Because their love of Earth is deep,
And they are warriors in accord
With life to serve, and pass reward,
So touching purest and so heard
In the brain's reflex of yon bird:
Wherefore their soul in me, or mine,
Through self-forgetfulness divine,
In them, that song aloft maintains,
To fill the sky and thrill the plains
With showerings drawn from human stores,
As he to silence nearer soars,
Extends the world at wings and dome,
More spacious making more our home,
Till lost on his aërial rings
In light, and then the fancy sings.

Thomas Hardy
(1840–1928)

195 · SHELLEY'S SKYLARK

(THE NEIGHBOURHOOD OF LEGHORN: MARCH 1887)

Somewhere afield here something lies
In Earth's oblivious eyeless trust
That moved a poet to prophecies –
A pinch of unseen, unguarded dust:

The dust of the lark that Shelley heard,
And made immortal through times to be –
Though it only lived like another bird,
And knew not its immortality:

Lived its meek life; then, one day, fell –
A little ball of feather and bone;
And how it perished, when piped farewell,
And where it wastes, are alike unknown.

Maybe it rests in the loam I view,
Maybe it throbs in a myrtle's green,
Maybe it sleeps in the coming hue
Of a grape on the slopes of yon inland scene.

Go find it, faeries, go and find
That tiny pinch of priceless dust,
And bring a casket silver-lined,
And framed of gold that gems encrust;

And we will lay it safe therein,
And consecrate it to endless time;
For it inspired a bard to win
Ecstatic heights in thought and rhyme.

196 · THE PUZZLED GAME BIRDS

(TRIOLET)

They are not those who used to feed us
When we were young – they cannot be –
These shapes that now bereave and bleed us?
They are not those who used to feed us,
For did we then cry, they would heed us.
– If hearts can house such treachery
They are not those who used to feed us
When we were young – they cannot be!

197 · THE DARKLING THRUSH

I leant upon a coppice gate
    When frost was spectre-grey,
And winter's dregs made desolate
    The weakening eye of day.
The tangled bine-stems scored the sky
    Like strings of broken lyres,
And all mankind that haunted nigh
    Had sought their household fires.

The land's sharp features seemed to be
    The century's corpse outleant,
His crypt the cloudy canopy,
    The wind his death-lament.

The ancient pulse of germ and birth
  Was shrunken hard and dry,
And every spirit upon earth
  Seemed fervourless as I.

At once a voice arose among
  The bleak twigs overhead
In a full-hearted evensong
  Of joy illimited;
An agëd thrush, frail, gaunt, and small,
  In blast-beruffled plume,
Had chosen thus to fling his soul
  Upon the growing gloom.

So little cause for carolings
  Of such ecstatic sound
Was written on terrestrial things
  Afar or nigh around,
That I could think there trembled through
  His happy good-night air
Some blessëd hope, whereof he knew
  And I was unaware.

198 · THE SELFSAME SONG

A bird sings the selfsame song,
With never a fault in its flow,
That we listened to here those long
    Long years ago.

A pleasing marvel is how
A strain of such rapturous rote
Should have gone on thus till now
    Unchanged in a note!

– But it's not the selfsame bird. –
No: perished to dust is he . . .
As also are those who heard
    That song with me.

Robert Bridges
(1844–1930)

199 · NIGHTINGALES

Beautiful must be the mountains whence ye come,
And bright in the fruitful valleys the streams, wherefrom
    Ye learn your song:
Where are those starry woods? O might I wander there,
   Among the flowers, which in that heavenly air
    Bloom the year long!

Nay, barren are those mountains and spent the streams:
Our song is the voice of desire, that haunts our dreams,
    A throe of the heart,
Whose pining visions dim, forbidden hopes profound,
   No dying cadence nor long sigh can sound,
    For all our art.

Alone, aloud in the raptured ear of men
We pour our dark nocturnal secret; and then,
    As night is withdrawn
From these sweet-springing meads and bursting boughs of May,
   Dream, while the innumerable choir of day
    Welcome the dawn.

200 · NOVEMBER

The lonely season in lonely lands, when fled
Are half the birds, and mists lie low, and the sun
Is rarely seen, nor strayeth far from his bed;
The short days pass unwelcomed one by one.

Out by the ricks the mantled engine stands
Crestfallen, deserted, – for now all hands
Are told to the plough, – and ere it is dawn appear
The teams following and crossing far and near,
As hour by hour they broaden the brown bands
Of the striped fields; and behind them firk and prance
The heavy rooks, and daws grey-pated dance:

As awhile, surmounting a crest, in sharp outline
(A miniature of toil, a gem's design)
They are pictured, horses and men, or now near by
Above the lane they shout lifting the share,
By the trim hedgerow bloomed with purple air;
Where, under the thorns, dead leaves in huddle lie
Packed by the gales of autumn, and in and out
The small wrens glide
With a happy note of cheer,
And yellow amorets flutter above and about,
Gay, familiar in fear.

And now, if the night shall be cold, across the sky
Linnets and twites, in small flocks helter-skelter,
All the afternoon to the gardens fly,
From thistle-pastures hurrying to gain the shelter
Of American rhododendron or cherry-laurel:
And here and there, near chilly setting of sun,
In an isolated tree a congregation
Of starlings chatter and chide,
Thickset as summer leaves, in garrulous quarrel:
Suddenly they hush as one –
The tree top springs –
And off, with a whirr of wings,
They fly by the score
To the holly-thicket, and there with myriads more
Dispute for the roosts; and from the unseen nation
A babel of tongues, like running water unceasing,
Makes live the wood, the flocking cries increasing,
Wrangling discordantly, incessantly,
While falls the night on them self-occupied;
The long dark night, that lengthens slow,
Deepening with winter to starve grass and tree,
And soon to bury in snow
The Earth, that, sleeping 'neath her frozen stole,
Shall dream a dream crept from the sunless pole
Of how her end shall be.

Gerard Manley Hopkins
(1844–89)

· 201 ·

Repeat that, repeat,
Cuckoo, bird, and open ear wells, heart-springs, delightfully sweet,
With a ballad, with a ballad, a rebound
Off trundled timber and scoops of the hillside ground, hollow hollow hollow
    ground:
The whole landscape flushes on a sudden at a sound.

202 · THE CAGED SKYLARK

As a dare-gale skylark scanted in a dull cage
    Man's mounting spirit in his bone-house, mean house, dwells –
    That bird beyond the remembering his free fells;
This in drudgery, day-labouring-out life's age.

Though aloft on turf or perch or poor low stage,
    Both sing sometímes the sweetest, sweetest spells,
    Yet both droop deadly sómetimes in their cells
Or wring their barriers in bursts of fear or rage.

Not that the sweet-fowl, song-fowl, needs no rest –
Why, hear him, hear him babble and drop down to his nest,
    But his own nest, wild nest, no prison.

Man's spirit will be flesh-bound when found at best,
But uncumbered: meadow-down is not distressed
    For a rainbow footing it nor he for his bónes rísen.

203 · THE WINDHOVER:

TO CHRIST OUR LORD

I caught this morning morning's minion, king-
   dom of daylight's dauphin, dapple-dawn-drawn falcon, in
      his riding
Of the rolling level underneath him steady air, and striding
High there, how he rung upon the rein of a wimpling wing
In his ecstasy! then off, off forth on swing,
   As a skate's heel sweeps smooth on a bow-bend: the hurl
      and gliding
Rebuffed the big wind. My heart in hiding
Stirred for a bird, – the achieve of, the mastery of the thing!

Brute beauty and valour and act, oh, air, pride, plume, here
   Buckle! AND the fire that breaks from thee then, a billion
Times told lovelier, more dangerous, O my chevalier!

   No wonder of it: shéer plód makes plough down sillion
Shine, and blue-bleak embers, ah my dear,
   Fall, gall themselves, and gash gold-vermilion.

William Ernest Henley
(1849–1903)

· 204 ·

Gulls in an aëry morrice[1]
   Gleam and vanish and gleam . . .
The full sea, sleepily basking,
   Dreams under skies of dream.

Gulls in an aëry morrice
   Circle and swoop and close . . .
Fuller and ever fuller
   The rose of the morning blows.

1. morris dance

Gulls, in an aëry morrice
   Frolicking, float and fade . . .
O, the way of a bird in the sunshine,
   The way of a man with a maid!

Arthur Symons
(1865–1945)

205 · *from* AMORIS EXSUL

In the Bay

The sea gulls whiten and dip,
Crying their lonely cry,
At noon in the blue of the bay;
And I hear the slow oars drip,
As the fisherman's boat drifts by,
And the cuckoo calls from the hillside far away.

The white birds cry for the foam,
O white birds crying to me
The cry of my heart evermore,
By perilous seas to roam
To a shore far over the sea,
And I would that my ship went down within sight of the shore!

William Butler Yeats
(1865–1939)

206 · THE WILD SWANS AT COOLE

The trees are in their autumn beauty,
The woodland paths are dry,
Under the October twilight the water
Mirrors a still sky;
Upon the brimming water among the stones
Are nine-and-fifty swans.

The nineteenth autumn has come upon me
Since I first made my count;
I saw, before I had well finished,
All suddenly mount
And scatter wheeling in great broken rings
Upon their clamorous wings.

I have looked upon those brilliant creatures,
And now my heart is sore.
All's changed since I, hearing at twilight,
The first time on this shore,
The bell-beat of their wings above my head,
Trod with a lighter tread.

Unwearied still, lover by lover,
They paddle in the cold
Companionable streams or climb the air;
Their hearts have not grown old;
Passion or conquest, wander where they will,
Attend upon them still.

But now they drift on the still water,
Mysterious, beautiful;
Among what rushes will they build,
By what lake's edge or pool
Delight men's eyes when I awake some day
To find they have flown away?

207 · LEDA AND THE SWAN

A sudden blow: the great wings beating still
Above the staggering girl, her thighs caressed
By the dark webs, her nape caught in his bill,
He holds her helpless breast upon his breast.

How can those terrified vague fingers push
The feathered glory from her loosening thighs?
And how can body, laid in that white rush,
But feel the strange heart·beating where it lies?

A shudder in the loins engenders there
The broken wall, the burning roof and tower
And Agamemnon dead.
           Being so caught up,
So mastered by the brute blood of the air,
Did she put on his knowledge with his power
Before the indifferent beak could let her drop?

Anonymous: Oral Tradition

(i) *Crow*

· 208 ·

As I was walking all alane,
I heard twa corbies making a mane;[1]
The tane unto the tother say,
'Where sall we gang and dine today?'

'In behint yon auld fail-dyke,[2]
I wot there lies a new slain knight;
And naebody kens that he lies there,
But his hawk, his hound, and lady fair.

'His hound is to the hunting gane,
His hawk to fetch the wild fowl hame,
His lady's ta'en another mate,
So we may mak our dinner sweet.

1. moan   2. wall built of sods

'Ye'll sit on his white hause-bane,[1]
And I'll pike out his bonny blue e'en;
Wi' ae lock o' his gowden hair
We'll theek[2] our nest when it grows bare.

'Mony a one for him makes mane,
But nane sall ken where he is gane;
O'er his white banes, when they are bare,
The wind sall blaw for evermair.'

· 209 ·

A hoggie dead! a hoggie dead! a hoggie dead!
O where? O where? O where?
Down i' 'e park! down i' 'e park! down i' 'e park!
Is't fat? is't fat? is't fat?
Come try! come try! come try!

· 210 ·

Crow, crow, get out of my sight,
Or I'll kill your father and mother tonight.

· 211 ·

The carrion crow sat upon an oak,
And spied a tailor cutting out a cloak;
With a heigh ho! the carrion crow!
Sing tol de rol, de riddle row!

The carrion crow he began for to rave,
And called the tailor a lousy knave;
With a heigh ho! the carrion crow!
Sing tol de rol, de riddle row!

Oh wife, fetch me my arrow and my bow,
That I may shoot this carrion crow;
With a heigh ho! the carrion crow!
Sing tol de rol, de riddle row!

The tailor he shot, and he missed his mark,
And shot the old sow through the heart;
With a heigh ho! the carrion crow!
Sing tol de rol, de riddle row!

1. neck bone   2. thatch

Oh wife, fetch me some treacle in a spoon,
For the old sow is in a terrible swoon;
    With a heigh ho! the carrion crow!
    Sing tol de rol, de riddle row!

The old sow died, and the bells they did toll,
And the little pigs prayed for the old sow's soul;
    With a heigh ho! the carrion crow!
    Sing tol de rol, de riddle row!

Zooks! quoth the tailor, I care not a louse,
For we shall have black puddings, chitterlings, and souse;
    With a heigh ho! the carrion crow!
    Sing tol de rol, de riddle row!

· 212 ·

All of a row,
Bend the bow,
Shot at a pigeon,
And killed a crow.

(ii) *Magpie*

· 213 ·

One is sorrow, two mirth,
Three a wedding, four a birth,
Five heaven, six hell,
Seven the de'il's ain sell.[1]

· 214 ·

One is a sign of mischief,
Two is a sign of mirth,
Three is a sign of a wedding,
Four is a sign of a death,
Five is a sign of rain,
Six is the sign of a bastard bairn.

1. the devil's own self

· 215 ·

One for sorrow, two for mirth,
Three for a wedding, four for a birth,
Five for rich, six for poor,
Seven for a bitch, eight for a whore,
Nine for a burying, ten for a dance,
Eleven for England, twelve for France.

· 216 ·

I crossed the pynot,[1]
  And the pynot crossed me,
The devil take the pynot,
  And God save me.

· 217 ·

A pie sat on a pear tree,
A pie sat on a pear tree,
A pie sat on a pear tree,
  Heigh O, heigh O, heigh O!

Once so merrily hopped she,
Twice so merrily hopped she,
Thrice so merrily hopped she,
  Heigh O, heigh O, heigh O!

· 218 ·

Round about, round about,
  Maggoty pie;
My father loves good ale,
  And so do I.

1. magpie

(iii) *Cuckoo*

· 219 ·

Cuckoo, cuckoo,
What do you do?
In April,
I open my bill;
In May,
I sing night and day;
In June,
I change my tune;
In July,
Away I fly;
In August,
Go I must.

· 220 ·

The cuckoo is a merry bird,
  She sings as she flies;
She brings us good tidings,
  And tells us no lies.

She sucks little birds' eggs
  To make her voice clear,
That she may sing Cuckoo!
  Three months in the year.

· 221 ·

Cuckoo, cherry tree,
Lay an egg, give it me,
Lay another,
Give it my brother.

· 222 ·

Cuckoo, scabbëd[1] gowk,
Mickle said, little wrought.

1. scurvy, contemptible

(iv) *Owl*

· 223 ·

Of all the gay birds that e'er I did see,
The owl is the fairest by far to me,
For all day long she sits on a tree,
And when the night comes away flies she.

· 224 ·

Once I was a monarch's daughter,
   And sat on a lady's knee;
But am now a nightly rover,
   Banished to the ivy tree.

Crying hoo, hoo, hoo, hoo, hoo, hoo,
   Hoo, hoo, hoo, my feet are cold.
Pity me, for here you see me
   Persecuted, poor, and old.

(v) *Dove*

· 225 ·

Take two-o coo, Taffy!
Take two-o coo, Taffy![1]

· 226 ·

I had two pigeons bright and gay,
They flew from me the other day;
What was the reason they did go?
I cannot tell for I do not know.

· 227 ·

The dove says, Coo, coo,
What shall I do?
I can scarce maintain two.
Pooh, pooh, says the wren,
I have got ten,
And keep them all like gentlemen.

1. This is an imitation of the notes of the wood pigeon (also called ring dove).

· 228 ·

Coo-pe-coo,
Me and my poor two;
Two sticks across,
And a little piece of moss,
And it will do, do, do.

(vi)   *Blackbird*

· 229 ·

As I went over the water,
   The water went over me.
I saw two little blackbirds
   Sitting on a tree:
The one called me a rascal,
   The other called me a thief;
I took up my little black stick,
   And knocked out all their teeth.

(vii)   *Lark*

· 230 ·

Larikie, larikie, lee!
Wha'll gang up to heaven wi' me?
No the lout that lies in his bed,
No the doolfu' that dreeps his head.

· 231 ·

Up in the lift go we,
Te-hee, te-hee, te-hee, te-hee!
There's not a shoemaker on the earth
Can make a shoe to me, to me!
Why so, why so, why so?
Because my heel is as long as my toe!

(viii) *Cock and Hen*

· 232 ·

The cock crows in the morn
    To tell us to rise,
And he that lies late
    Will never be wise:
For early to bed,
    And early to rise,
Makes a man healthy
    And wealthy and wise.

· 233 ·

Higgledy, piggledy, my black hen,
She lays eggs for gentlemen;
Gentlemen come every day
To see what my black hen doth lay.

· 234 ·

COCK: Lock the dairy door,
          Lock the dairy door!
HEN: Chickle, chackle, chee,
          I haven't got the key!

· 235 ·

HEN: Cock, cock, cock, cock,
          I've laid an egg,
          Am I to go ba-are foot?

COCK: Hen, hen, hen, hen,
          I've been up and down,
          To every shop in town,
          And cannot find a shoe
          To fit your foot,
          If I'd crow my hea-art out.

· 236 ·

HEN: The cock gaed to Rome, seeking shoon, seeking shoon,
The cock gaed to Rome, seeking shoon,
And yet I aye gang barefit, barefit!

· 237 ·

EN: Buy tobacco, buy tobacco;
I'll pay a'!

(ix) *Goose*

· 238 ·

I went to the sea,
And saw twentee
Geese all in a row:
My glove I would give
Full of gold, if my wife
Was as white as those.

· 239 ·

Grey goose and gander,
Waft your wings together,
And carry the good king's daughter
Over the one-strand river.

· 240 ·

Here's a string o' wild geese,
How mony for a penny?
Ane to my lord,
And ane to my lady;
Up the gate and down the gate,
They're a' flown frae me!

· 241 ·

Three grey geese in a green field grazing,
Grey were the geese and green was the grazing.

· 242 ·

A fox jumped up one winter's night,
And begged the moon to give him light,
For he'd many miles to trot that night
Before he reached his den O!
    Den O! Den O!
For he'd many miles to trot that night
Before he reached his den O!

The first place he came to was a farmer's yard,
Where the ducks and the geese declared it hard
That their nerves should be shaken and their rest so marred
By a visit from Mr Fox O!
    Fox O! Fox O!
That their nerves should be shaken and their rest so marred
By a visit from Mr Fox O!

He took the grey goose by the neck,
And swung him right across his back;
The grey goose cried out, Quack, quack, quack,
With his legs hanging dangling down O!
    Down O! Down O!
The grey goose cried out, Quack, quack, quack,
With his legs hanging dangling down O!

Old Mother Slipper Slopper jumped out of bed,
And out of the window she popped her head:
Oh! John, John, John, the grey goose is gone,
And the fox is off to his den O!
    Den O! Den O!
Oh! John, John, John, the grey goose is gone,
And the fox is off to his den O!

John ran up to the top of the hill,
And blew his whistle loud and shrill;
Said the fox, That is very pretty music – still,
I'd rather be in my den O!
    Den O! Den O!
Said the fox, That is very pretty music – still,
I'd rather be in my den O!

The fox went back to his hungry den,
And his dear little foxes, eight, nine, ten;
Quoth they, Good daddy, you must go there again,
If you bring such good cheer from the farm O!
    Farm O! Farm O!
Quoth they, Good daddy, you must go there again,
If you bring such good cheer from the farm O!

The fox and his wife, without any strife,
Said they never ate a better goose in all their life:
They did very well without fork or knife,
And the little ones picked the bones O!
    Bones O! Bones O!
They did very well without fork or knife,
And the little ones picked the bones O!

· 243 ·

Goosey, goosey, gander,
   Where shall I wander?
Upstairs, downstairs,
   And in my lady's chamber.
There I met an old man
   Who would not say his prayers;
I took him by the left leg
   And threw him down the stairs.

· 244 ·

Old Mother Goose
   When she wanted to wander,
Would ride through the air
   On a very fine gander.

· 245 ·

Cackle, cackle, Mother Goose,
Have you any feathers loose?
Truly have I, pretty fellow,
Half enough to fill a pillow.
Here are quills, take one or two,
And down to make a bed for you.

· 246 ·

Snow, snow faster,
Ally-ally-blaster;
The old woman's plucking her geese,
Selling the feathers a penny a piece.

(x)   *Bird Scaring Songs*

· 247 ·

O all you little blackey-tops,
Pray don't you eat my father's crops,
While I lie down to take a nap,
   Shu-a-O! Shu-a-O!

If father he by chance should come
With his cocked hat and his long gun,
Then you must fly and I must run,
   Shu-a-O! Shu-a-O!

· 248 ·

Shoo over!
Out of the wheat,
Into the clover!
Powder and shot
Shall be thy lot,
And I'll cry out,
Shoo over!

(xi)   *Weather Rhymes*

· 249 ·

If the robin sings in the bush,
Then the weather will be coarse,
But if the robin sings on the barn,
Then the weather will be warm.

· 250 ·

Crow on the fence,
Rain will go hence;
Crow on the ground,
Rain will come down.

· 251 ·

Wild geese, wild geese, ganging to the sea,
Good weather it will be.
Wild geese, wild geese, ganging to the hill,
The weather it will spill.

(xii)   *Robin and Wren*

· 252 ·

I'm called by the name of a man,[1]
    Yet am as little as a mouse;
When winter comes I love to be
    With my red target near the house.

1. Robin, a nickname for Robert

· 253 ·

Little Robin Redbreast,
  Sitting on a pole,
Niddle noddle went his head,
  And poop went his hole.

· 254 ·

Little Cock Robin
Peeped out of his cabin
  To see the cold winter come in:
Tit for tat,
What matter for that,
  He'll hide his head under his wing.

· 255 ·

My dear, do you know
How a long time ago,
  Two poor little children,
Whose names I don't know,
Were stolen away
On a fine summer's day,
  And left in a wood,
As I've heard people say.

And when it was night,
So sad was their plight,
  The sun it went down,
And the moon gave no light.
They sobbed and they sighed,
And they bitterly cried,
  And the poor little things,
They lay down and died.

And when they were dead,
The robins so red
  Brought strawberry leaves,
And over them spread;
And all the day long,
They sung them this song –

Poor babes in the wood!
Poor babes in the wood!
And don't you remember
The babes in the wood?

· 256 ·

The north wind doth blow,
And we shall have snow,
And what will poor Robin do then,
  Poor thing.
He'll sit in a barn
And keep himself warm,
And hide his head under his wing,
  Poor thing.

· 257 ·

Cock Robin got up early
  At the break of day,
And went to Jenny's window
  To sing a roundelay.
He sang Cock Robin's love
  To little Jenny Wren,
And when he got unto the end,
  Then he began again.

· 258 ·

The wren she lies in care's bed,
  In care's bed, in care's bed,
The wren she lies in care's bed,
  In mickle dule and pyne,[1] O,
When in came Robin Redbreast,
  Redbreast, Redbreast,
When in came Robin Redbreast,
  Wi' succar-saps[2] and wine, O.

Now, maiden, will ye taste o' this,
  Taste o' this, taste o' this,
Now, maiden, will ye taste o' this?
  It's succar-saps and wine, O.

1. much dole and pain   2. sugar sops

Na, ne'er a drap, Robin,
   Robin, Robin,
Na, ne'er a drap, Robin,
   Gin it was ne'er so fine, O.

And where's the ring that I gied ye,
   That I gied ye, that I gied ye,
And where's the ring that I gied ye,
   Ye little cutty quyne,[1] O?
I gied it till[2] a soger,[3]
   A soger, a soger,
I gied it till a soger,
   A kind sweetheart o' mine, O.

· 259 ·

The robin and the wren,
They fought upon the porridge pan;
But ere the robin got a spoon,
The wren had eat the porridge down.

· 260 ·

Says Robin to Jenny, 'If you will be mine,
We'll have cherry tart, and drink currant wine.'
So Jenny consented – the day was named,
The joyful news the cock proclaimed.
Together came the rook and lark,
One was parson, the other clerk:
The goldfinch gave the bride away,
Who promised always to obey:
The feathered tenants of the air
Towards the feast gave each a share.
Some brought grain, and some brought meat,
Some brought savours, some brought sweet,
And as it was most pleasant weather,
The jovial party dined together;
And long did Robin and his mate
Live in the happy married state,
Till, doleful to relate! one day
A hawk with Jenny flew away;
And Robin, by the cruel sparrow
Was shot quite dead with bow and arrow.

1. cutty quean, a folk name for the wren   2. to   3. soldier

· 261 ·

Who killed Cock Robin?
I, said the sparrow,
With my bow and arrow,
I killed Cock Robin.

Who saw him die?
I, said the fly,
With my little eye,
I saw him die.

Who caught his blood?
I, said the fish,
With my little dish,
I caught his blood.

Who'll make the shroud?
I, said the beetle,
With my thread and needle,
I'll make the shroud.

Who'll dig his grave?
I, said the owl,
With my pick and shovel,
I'll dig his grave.

Who'll be the parson?
I, said the rook,
With my little book,
I'll be the parson.

Who'll be the clerk?
I, said the lark,
If it's not in the dark,
I'll be the clerk.

Who'll carry the link?[1]
I, said the linnet,
I'll fetch it in a minute,
I'll carry the link.

Who'll be chief mourner?
I, said the dove,
I'll mourn for my love,
I'll be chief mourner.

1. torch

Who'll carry the coffin?
I, said the kite,
If it's not through the night,
I'll carry the coffin.

Who'll bear the pall?
We, said the wren,
Both the cock and the hen,
We'll bear the pall.

Who'll sing a psalm?
I, said the thrush,
As she sat on a bush,
I'll sing a psalm.

Who'll toll the bell?
I, said the bull,[1]
Because I can pull,
I'll toll the bell.

All the birds of the air
Fell a-sighing and a-sobbing,
When they heard the bell toll
For poor Cock Robin.

· 262 ·

Kill a robin or a wren,
Never prosper, boy or man.

· 263 ·

Malisons, malisons, more than ten,
That harry the Lady of Heaven's hen.[2]

· 264 ·

The robin and the redbreast,
The robin and the wren,
If ye take out o' their nest,
Ye'll never thrive again.

1. Abbreviated form of bullfinch, as Cowper's 'Bully'.   2. One of the wren's folk names was Our Lady's hen.

The robin and the redbreast,
The martin and the swallow,
If ye touch one o' their eggs,
Bad luck will sure to follow.

· 265 ·

The robin and the wren
Are God's cock and hen.

Sir John Collings Squire
(1884–1958)

266 · *from* THE BIRDS

O let your strong imagination turn
The great wheel backward, until Troy unburn,
And then unbuild, and seven Troys below
Rise out of death, and dwindle, and outflow,
Till all have passed, and none has yet been there:
Back, ever back. Our birds still crossed the air;
Beyond our myriad changing generations
Still built, unchanged, their known inhabitations.
A million years before Atlantis was
Our lark sprang from some hollow in the grass,
Some old soft hoof-print in a tussock's shade;
And the wood pigeon's smooth snow-white eggs were laid.
High amid green pines' sunset-coloured shafts,
And rooks their villages of twiggy rafts
Set on the tops of elms, where elms grew then,
And still the thumbling tit and perky wren
Popped through the tiny doors of cosy balls
And the blackbird lined with moss his high-built walls;
A round mud cottage held the thrush's young,
And straws from the untidy sparrow's hung.
And, skimming forktailed in the evening air,
When man first was were not the martins there?

Did not those birds some human shelter crave,
And stow beneath the cornice of his cave
Their dry tight cups of clay? And from each door
Peeped on a morning wiseheads three or four.
Yes, daw and owl, curlew and crested hern,
Kingfisher, mallard, water rail and tern,
Chaffinch and greenfinch, wagtail, stonechat, ruff,
Pied warbler, robin, flycatcher and chough,
Mistle thrush, magpie, sparrow hawk and jay,
Built, those far ages gone, in this year's way.

And the first man who walked the cliffs of Rome,
As I this year, looked down and saw the same
Blotches of rusty red on ledge and cleft
With grey-green spots on them, while right and left
A dizzying tangle of gulls were floating and flying,
Wheeling and crossing and darting, crying and crying,
Circling and crying, over and over and over,
Crying with swoop and hover and fall and recover.
And below on a rock against the grey sea fretted,
Pipe-necked and stationary and silhouetted,

Cormorants stood in a wise, black, equal row
Above the nests and long blue eggs we know.
O delicate chain over all the ages stretched,
O dumb tradition from what far darkness fetched:
Each little architect with its one design
Perpetual, fixed and right in stuff and line,
Each little ministrant who knows one thing,
One learnèd rite to celebrate the spring.
Whatever alters else on sea and shore,
These are unchanging: man must still explore.

(ll. 37–88)

Selected Bibliography

Field Guides

Peterson, Roger Tory, *et al.*, *A Field Guide to the Birds of Britain and Europe* (Boston: Houghton Mifflin, n.d.).

Witherby, Harry Forbes, *et al.*, *The Handbook of British Birds*, 5 vols. (London: H. F. & G. Witherby, 1938–41).

Natural History

Aristotle, *Historia Animalium*, trans. D'Arcy Wentworth Thompson, Vol. IV of *The Works of Aristotle*, eds. John Alexander Smith and William David Ross (Oxford: Clarendon Press, 1910).

Bewick, Thomas, *1800 Woodcuts by Thomas Bewick and his School*, ed. Blanche Cirker, introd. by Robert Hutchinson (New York: Dover, 1962).

Browne, Sir Thomas, 'Notes on the Natural History of Norfolk', Vol. III in *The Works of Sir Thomas Browne*, ed. Geoffrey Keynes (Chicago: University of Chicago Press, 1964).

Browne, Sir Thomas, *Pseudodoxia Epidemica*, Vol. II in *The Works of Sir Thomas Browne* (*see above*). Commonly known as *Vulgar Errors*. See especially Book III, Chs. 10 and 27, and Book V, Ch. 1.

Hudson, William Henry, *Birds in Town and Village* (London: J. M. Dent; New York: E. P. Dutton, 1919).

Pliny, Book X in *Pliny: Natural History*, Vol. III, trans. Harris Rackham (The Loeb Classical Library, Cambridge: Harvard University Press; London: William Heinemann, 1940).

Raven, Charles Earle, *John Ray, Naturalist, his Life and Works*, 2nd edn (Cambridge: Cambridge University Press, 1950).

Richmond, Kenneth, *Birds in Britain* (London: Odhams Press, 1962).

Teale, Edwin Way, *Springtime in Britain* (New York: Dodd, Mead, 1970).

White, Gilbert, *Gilbert White's Journals*, ed. Walter Johnson (London: George Routledge, 1931).

White, Gilbert, *The Natural History and Antiquities of Selborne*, ed. Thomas Bell, 2 vols. (London: John Van Voorst, 1877).

Literary Background

Durling, Dwight Leonard, *Georgic Tradition in English Poetry* (New York: Columbia University Press, 1935).

Sampson, George, *The Concise Cambridge History of English Literature* (Cambridge: Cambridge University Press; New York: Macmillan, 1941).

Birds in Literature

Chandler, Albert Richard, *Larks, Nightingales and Poets* (Columbus: The Author, Ohio State University, 1937).

Christian, Garth (ed.), *Wings of Light* (London: Newnes, 1965).

Harrison, Thomas Perrin, *They Tell of Birds* (Austin: University of Texas Press, 1956).

Harting, James Edmund, *The Ornithology of Shakespeare* (London: John Van Voorst, 1871). Reissued as *The Birds of Shakespeare* (Chicago: Argonaut, 1965).

Folklore and Legend

Armstrong, Edward Allworthy, *The Folklore of Birds* (London: Collins, 1958). Reissued in paperback with corrections and new appendix (New York: Dover, 1970).

Ingersoll, Ernest, *Birds in Legend, Fable and Folklore* (New York: Longmans, Green, 1923).

Physiologus, trans. & introd. by James Carlill in *The Epic of the Beast*, introd. by William Rose (London: George Routledge; New York: E. P. Dutton, n.d. [1924?]).

Randall, Richard H., Jr., *A Cloisters Bestiary* (New York: Metropolitan Museum of Art, 1960).

Swainson, Charles, *The Folk Lore and Provincial Names of British Birds* (London: published for the Folk Lore Society by Elliot Stock, 1886).

Thiselton Dyer, Thomas F., 'Birds', Ch. III in *English Folk-Lore* (London: W. H. Allen, 1884).

White, Terence Hanbury (ed. & trans.), *The Book of Beasts* (London: Jonathan Cape; New York: G. P. Putnam's, 1954). Reissued in paperback as *The Bestiary, A Book of Beasts* (New York: Capricorn Books, G. P. Putnam's, 1960).

Oral Tradition

Chambers, Robert (ed.), *Popular Rhymes of Scotland*, rev. & enlarg. (London and Edinburgh: W. & R. Chambers, 1870).

Halliwell, James Orchard (ed.), *Popular Rhymes and Nursery Tales* (London: J. R. Smith, 1849).

Northall, G. F. (ed.), *English Folk-Rhymes* (London: K. Paul, Trench, Trübner, 1892).

Opie, Iona and Peter (eds.), *The Oxford Dictionary of Nursery Rhymes* (Oxford: Clarendon Press, 1952).

Texts for Translations

Atkins, John William Hey (ed. and trans.), *The Owl and the Nightingale* (Cambridge: Cambridge University Press, 1922).

Bennett, Jack Arthur Walter and Geoffrey Victor Smithers (eds.), 'The Bestiary', Ch. XII in *Early Middle English Verse and Prose* (Oxford: Clarendon Press, 1966).

Blake, Norton Francis (ed.), *The Phoenix* (Manchester: Manchester University Press, 1964).

Campbell, Alistair (ed.), *The Battle of Brunanburh* (London: Heinemann, 1938).

Gordon, I. L. (ed.), *The Seafarer* (London: Methuen, 1960).

Krapp, George Philip and Elliott Van Kirk Dobbie (eds.), Vols. I, III, and VI of *The Anglo-Saxon Poetic Records* (New York: Columbia University Press, 1931, 1936, and 1942).

Morris, Richard (ed.), 'A Bestiary' in *An Old English Miscellany* (London: Early English Text Society, Original Series No. 49, 1872).

Offord, M. Y. (ed.), *The Parlement of the Thre Ages* (London: Early English Text Society, Original Series No. 246, 1959).

Skeat, Walter William (ed.), *The Vision of William concerning Piers the Plowman* (London: Oxford University Press, 1954).

Stanley, Eric Gerald (ed.), *The Owl and the Nightingale* (London: Thomas Nelson, 1960).

Tupper, Frederick, Jr., *The Riddles of the Exeter Book* (Boston: Ginn, 1910).

Glossary of Bird Names

(American names are in italics)

Alp: BULLFINCH

Barnacle: BARNACLE GOOSE

Bidcock: see WATER RAIL

Bitter: BITTERN – same genus as the *American bittern*. The two are very similar, except that the American lacks the extraordinary voice of the European, a deep booming which can sometimes be heard for a mile.

Blackbird: not related to the American blackbirds. Famous for its song, the European BLACKBIRD is really a thrush, all black with a yellow bill. It belongs to the same genus as the American *robin*.

Blackcock: BLACK GROUSE

Blue-cap: BLUE TIT. See TITS

Chalaundre: CALANDRA LARK

Churn owl: see NIGHTJAR

Clodhopper: WHEATEAR

Coe: JACKDAW

Corbie: RAVEN, CROW

Corncrake: a European rail which looks something like the American *sora*

Crake: see CORNCRAKE

Culver: DOVE

Cushat: WOOD PIGEON

Cutty quean: see WREN (cutty means bobtailed; a quean is a hussy)

Dabchick: LITTLE GREBE

Daw: JACKDAW

Didapper: LITTLE GREBE

Divendop: LITTLE GREBE

Elk: WHOOPER SWAN

Ern: EAGLE

Gant: usually GANNET, but it can also mean WILD GOOSE

Gentle falcon: FALCON GENTLE, the female of the PEREGRINE. See PEREGRINE

Goldcrest: closely related and very similar to the *golden-crowned kinglet*

Goldfinch: same family as the *American goldfinch* but a different species. Unlike the American, which is all yellow with a black cap and black wings, the European is a brownish bird with a bright red face. Its yellow is limited to a band of yellow on its black wings.

Goosander: *American merganser*

Gorcock: RED GROUSE

Gowdspink: see GOLDFINCH

Gowk: CUCKOO

Green linnet: GREENFINCH

Griffon: VULTURE

Gripe: VULTURE

Halcyon: see KINGFISHER

Haysugge, heysoge: HEDGE SPARROW

Heath-cock, heath-hen: BLACK GROUSE

Hecco: GREEN WOODPECKER

Hern: HERON

Hewel: GREEN WOODPECKER

Hic-quail: GREEN WOODPECKER
Hobby: a kind of hawk
Hoolet: OWL
Howlet: OWL

Jay: same family as the American jays but a different species. The Old World JAY is a pinkish-brown bird with a black tail, a black moustache, and a patch of blue on its wings.

Kingfisher: same family as the *belted kingfisher* but a different species. A sparrow-sized bird with bright red feet, it is iridescent blue-green above and orangey-chestnut below.

Lanner, lanneret: a kind of hawk
Laverock: SKYLARK
Lintwhite: LINNET

Martinet: MARTIN
Martlet, martelet: MARTIN
Mavis: see SONG THRUSH
Merle: see BLACKBIRD
Merlion, merlioun: MERLIN – *pigeon hawk*
Moorhen: *common* or *Florida gallinule*
Moor-hen, moor-fowl: old names for the RED GROUSE
Musket: male SPARROW HAWK. See SPARROW HAWK

Nightjar: same genus as the *whip-poor-will*. The two are generally similar except for the voice, the European having a vibrant churring note which can last for minutes at a time. The British call the family NIGHTJARS, the Americans *goatsuckers*.
Nope: BULLFINCH

Our Lady's hen: see WREN
Ouzel: see BLACKBIRD

Peregrine: *duck hawk* or *peregrine falcon*
Pertelote, Partlot: HEN
Pettichap: WILLOW WARBLER. See WARBLERS
Philip: see SPARROW
Philomela: NIGHTINGALE
Pie: MAGPIE
Popinjay: usually PARROT, but it was also a name for the GREEN WOODPECKER
Puwit, pewit: LAPWING
Pynot: MAGPIE

Ralph: a folk name for the RAVEN
Redbreast: see ROBIN
Redshank: a shore-bird which looks something like the *lesser yellow-legs*
Reed sparrow: REED BUNTING
Robin: not related to the American *robin*. About the size of a sparrow, the Old World ROBIN is a plump brown bird with an orange-red face and breast.
Rout: some kind of wild goose, probably the BRENT GOOSE since it has similar folk names, such as rott goose and rat goose
Ruddock: see ROBIN

Saker: a kind of hawk
Sand martin: *bank swallow*
Seamew: GULL
Sea-pie: OYSTERCATCHER
Shoveller: SPOONBILL
Smeath: some kind of wild duck, possibly the SMEW since one of its folk names is smee
Snite: SNIPE – *Wilson's snipe*

Song thrush and mistle thrush:
related and similar in appearance
to the American *wood* and *hermit
thrushes*

Sparhawk: see SPARROW HAWK

Sparrow: *house* or *English sparrow*

Sparrow hawk: not the same as the
American. The New World
sparrow hawk is really a falcon
(long, pointed wings), while the
European is a true hawk (short,
rounded wings).

Spink: FINCH

Stare: STARLING

Starnel: STARLING

Swallow: *barn swallow*

Tarsel: a male hawk

Tercel, tercelet: a male hawk

Terin: SISKIN

Titmouse: see TITS

Tits: small acrobatic birds which
are closely related to the
American chickadees. (Among the
older names for the *black-capped
chickadee* are the *black-capped
titmouse* and the *black-cap tit*.)

Turtle: TURTLE DOVE

Tydie: a small bird, species unknown

Warblers: not related to the
American *wood warblers*, which
belong to a New World family

Water-hen: see MOORHEN

Water rail: similar to the *clapper
rail*, only smaller

Water-woosel: DIPPER

Willow-biter: WILLOW WARBLER.
See WARBLERS

Windhover: KESTREL

Wodewale: GREEN WOODPECKER

Woodhack: WOODPECKER

Woosel: see BLACKBIRD

Wren: *winter wren*

Wren 'with a crown of fire': see
GOLDCREST

Yellowhammer: a kind of bunting.
In America, yellowhammer is one
of the *flicker's* names, but in
Britain, it is the name of a
sparrow-like bird with a yellow
head and yellow underparts.

Yellow pate: see YELLOWHAMMER

Index of Birds

(The numbers refer to the poem numbers. Numbers in italics indicate that an illustration of that bird appears in the text.)

Bittern, bitter, butter-bump: 33, 82, 139
Blackbird: see THRUSHES

Cock, Chauntecleer, Chanticleer: 20, *21,* 27, 33, 37, 83, 89, 95, 99, 104, 115, 117, 184, **232,** 234, 235, 236, 260
    Chick: 28
    Hen, Pertelote, Partlot, pullet: 10, *21,* 28, 33, 37, 74, 83, 115, 117, 175, **233,** 234, 235, 236, 237
Coot: 33, 57, 82, 139
Cormorant: 20, 33, 57, 82, 83, **166,** 266
Corncrake, crake, landrail: 139, **169**
Crane: 20, 33, 82, 83, 95
CROW FAMILY
    Carrion Crow, crow, corbie: 20, 33, 41, 83, 86, 176, 183, *208,* **209, 210, 211, 212, 250**
    Chough: 20, 33, 266
    Jackdaw, daw, coe: 33, **35,** 55, 70, 117, **130,** 176, 200, 266
    Jay: 7, 20, 30, 33, 40, 70, 81, 101, 117, 143, 266
    Magpie, pie, pynot, maggoty pie: 15, 20, 30, 33, 39, 40, 70, 92, 101, 143, 176, **213, 214, 215, 216, 217, 218,** 266
    Raven, corbie, Ralph: 2, 3, 8, 20, 33, 41, 83, 92, **112, 208**
    Rook: 33, 55, 117, 126, *162,* 176, 200, 260, 261, 266
Cuckoo, gowk: 6, 11, 20, **22,** 33, **38,** 43, 47, 54, **55,** 61, 67, 70, 72, 73, 91, 94, **106,** 111, 117, 122, **133,** 143, 145, 148, 190, **201,** 205, **219, 220, 221, 222**
Curlew: 1, 26, 33, 57, 82, 122, 139, 266

Dipper, water-woosel: 82
Dotterel: 33
DOVES
    Dove, culver, pigeon: 8, 20, **23,** 26, 29, 33, **42, 45,** 58, **59,** 63, 80, 83, 84, 109, 117, 179, 190, 212, **225, 226, 227, 228,** 261
        Stock Dove: 33, 70, **103,** 117, **151**
        Turtle Dove, turtle: **14,** 18, 20, 33, 40, 53, 55, 83, 84, **108, 114**
        Wood Pigeon or *Ring Dove,* cushat, queest: 159, 266
DUCKS
    Duck, drake: 17, 20, 26, 33, 77, 82, 117, 139, 242
    Goldeneye: 82
    Goosander: 82
    Mallard, wild duck: 17, 33, 57, 82, 117, 176, 266
    Smew, smeath: 82
    Teal: 17, 33, 57, 82, 139
    Wigeon: 82

Eagle, ern: 1, 3, 7, 9, 13, 20, 33, 51, 53, 83, 95, 117, 138, 164, 188

Falcon: see HAWKS
FINCHES
   Finch, spink: 18, 33, 54, 57
     Bullfinch, alp, nope: 18, 81, 87, 117, 128, 261
     Chaffinch, pink: 266
     Goldfinch, gowdspink, redcap: 30, 31, 33, 57, 70, 81, 121, 136, 137, 177, 260
     Greenfinch, green linnet: 149, 266
     Linnet, lintwhite: 40, 57, 62, 70, 81, 107, 117, 127, 136, 137, 159, 190, 200, 261
     Siskin, terin: 18
     Twite: 200
Flycatcher: 266

Game Bird, game fowl: 17, 196
Gannet: 1
GEESE
   Goose, gander, gosling: 7, 20, 26, 28, 33, 76, 83, 120, 146, 238, 239, 241, 242, 243,
   244, 245, 246
     Barnacle Goose, barnacle: 33, 82
     Brent Goose, rout: 33
     Wild Goose, gant: 33, 82, 240, 251
Goldcrest: wren 'with a crown of fire': 190
Goldfinch: see FINCHES
GROUSE
   Grouse: 139
     Black Grouse, blackcock, heath-cock, heath-hen: 117, 141, 154
     Red Grouse, gorcock, moor-hen, moor-fowl: 140, 145, 154
Gull: sea gull, seamew: 1, 7, 26, 33, 82, 158, 204, 205, 266

HAWKS (Hawk is the generic term. Up to the eighteenth century, falcon was used to
mean a female hawk, the name for the male being tercel.)
   Buzzard, puddock, puttock: 33
   Falcon: 2, 20, 25, 33, 39, 83, 101, 203
   Goshawk: 20, 33, 83, 101
   Gyr falcon: 33
   Hawk: 2, 7, 17, 25, 39, 65, 68, 77, 208, 260
   Hobby: 33, 101
   Kestrel, staniel, windhover: 33, 83, 203
   Kite, puddock, puttock, glede: 7, 20, 33, 41, 70, 83, 261
   Lanner, lanneret: 17, 33, 101
   Merlin, merlion, merlioun: 20, 33
   Peregrine, gentle falcon: 20
   Saker: 33
   Sparrow Hawk, sparhawk, musket: 20, 24, 33, 68, 83, 101, 266
   Tercel, tercelet, tarsel: 17, 33, 101
Hedge Sparrow, haysugge, heysoge: 10, 43, 91, 145

Heron, hern: **17**, 20, 33, 57, 77, **82**, 83, **101**, 103, 139, 176, 266
Hoopoe: 182

Jackdaw: see CROW FAMILY
Jay: see CROW FAMILY

Kingfisher, halcyon: **57**, 83, **103**, 266
Kite: see HAWKS

Lapwing, puwit, pewit: 20, 33, 109, **135**
LARKS
  Calandra Lark, chalaundre: 18
  Skylark, lark, laverock: 16, 18, 20, **23**, 30, 32, 33, 40, 47, 54, 55, 57, 62, 63, 67, 72, 83, 86, **93**, **97**, **100**, **101**, **105**, 107, 109, 117, 126, **136**, 137, **147**, **152**, 165, *167*, 176, 190, **194**, **195**, **202**, **230**, **231**, 260, 261, 266
  Wood Lark: 81, 117, 121, 122
Linnet: see FINCHES
Little Grebe, dabchick, didapper, divendop: 33, 57, **82**

Magpie: see CROW FAMILY
Martin, martinet, martlet, martelet: 30, 33, 83, 264, 266
  *Sand Martin: **172***
*Meadow Pipit: **170***
Moorhen, water-hen: 33, **82**

Nightingale, Philomela, Philomel, Philomele: 5, **10**, 12, 20, **22**, **23**, 30, **31**, 33, *34*, 40, 47, **48**, **50**, 53, 56, **57**, **60**, **61**, 62, **64**, 66, 67, **68**, **69**, 72, 73, 75, 79, 81, 83, **85**, 86, **87**, **92**, **94**, 95, **96**, **103**, 107, 108, 117, **123**, **124**, **125**, **129**, 136, **151**, 152, **157**, **163**, 165, 174, **180**, **189**, **192**, **199**
Nightjar, churn owl, dor-hawk, eve-jar, fern owl, nighthawk: 122
Nuthatch: 30

Osprey: 33, **82**, 83
Ostrich: 33, 83
Owl, hoolet, howlet, Madge: **10**, 20, 29, 33, **55**, 71, 78, 83, **92**, 122, 124, 139, 155, 165, **168**, 184, **185**, **223**, **224**, 261, 266
Oystercatcher, sea-pie: 82

Parrot, popinjay: 20, 30, 33, 83
Partridge: 33, 63, 83, **109**, **110**, 118, 139
Peacock, peahen, pavone: 9, 15, **16**, 20, 33, **52**, 83, 95, 117, 120
*Pelican: **23**, **57**, 83*
Pheasant: 20, 25, 33, 63, 83, **109**
*Phoenix: **9**, 33, 53, 101, **181***
Plover: 33, 57, 83, 117, 126, 139
Puffin: 33, 82

Quail: 20, 33, 40, 67, 122

Raven: see CROW FAMILY
Redshank: 82
Reed Bunting, reed sparrow: 33, 81
Robin, ruddock, redbreast, Robin Redbreast, robinet, Cock Robin, Bob: 20, 30, 33, 40, 47, 62, 63, 81, 83, 86, 88, **90**, 98, 101, 106, 108, **119**, *131*, **132**, **134**, 136, 137, **142**, **144**, **153**, **155**, **193**, 249, *252*, 253, 254, **255**, **256**, **257**, **258**, **259**, **260**, **261**, **262**, **264**, **265**, 266
Roc: 83
Rook: see CROW FAMILY
Ruff: 33, 266

Snipe, snite: 33, 57, 63, 82, 83
Sparrow, Philip Sparrow, Philip: 20, 26, 30, **33**, *44*, 49, 54, 62, 63, 80, 108, **116**, 134, 190, 260, 261, 266
Spoonbill, shoveller: 33
Starling, stare, starnel: 20, 30, 33, 62, *156*, 176, **200**
Stonechat: 266
Stork: 20, 33, 57, 83, 95
Swallow: 20, 26, 30, 33, 83, **102**, 117, 122, 126, 190, 193, 264
SWANS
   Mute Swan, swan: 4, 9, 20, 33, **46**, 53, 57, **76**, 83, 95, 101, 108, 117, **120**, **178**
   Whooper Swan, swan, wild swan, elk, ilke: 1, 82, 176, **186**, **206**, **207**
Swift: *122*

Tern: 1, 266
THRUSHES (Throstle usually means song thrush, but in early poems it is sometimes used for the mistle thrush.)
   Blackbird, merle, ouzel, woosel: 30, 40, 54, 62, 63, 70, 72, 81, 83, 87, 117, 137, **145**, **187**, **229**, 266
   Fieldfare: 20, 33, 63
   Mistle Thrush, thrush, throstle: 18, *30*, 33, 266
   Song Thrush, thrush, throstle, thrustle-cock, mavis: 12, 18, 20, 29, 30, 33, 40, 54, 62, 63, 67, 70, 72, 73, 81, 83, 86, 103, 117, 136, 137, 190, **191**, 193, **197**, 261, 266
TITS
   Tit, titmouse: 10, 33, 190, *266*
     Blue Tit, blue-cap: *150*
     Long-tailed Tit, bumbarrel
Turkey: **113**, 117

Vulture, griffon, gripe: 26, 63, 83

Wagtail, little washdish: 33, 266
WARBLERS
   Pied Warbler: 266
   Whitethroat: **173**
   Willow Warbler, pettichap, willow-biter: **171**

Waterfowl: 17, 138

Water Rail, bidcock: 82, 266

Woodcock: 26, 33, 63, 109, 110

WOODPECKERS

   Woodpecker, woodhack: 33, 70, 143

      Green Woodpecker, hecco, hewel, hic-quail, popinjay, wodewale: 18, 23, 29, 30, 70, 81, 103, 143

      Wryneck: 143

Wren, Jenny Wren, Jenny, cutty quean, Our Lady's hen: 26, 30, 33, 54, 70, 81, 83, 86, 106, 136, 159, 200, 227, 257, 258, 259, 260, 261, 262, 263, 264, 265, 266

Yellowhammer, yellow pate, yellow yorling: 81, 145, 160

Index of Poets

(The numbers refer to the poem numbers.)

Akenside, Mark, 124
Allingham, William, 193
Anonymous, 1–14, 17, 18, 24–31, 34, 39–42, 53, 65–79, 97, 208–265
Arnold, Matthew, 192

Baillie, Joanna, 141
Barnfield, Richard, 63, 64
Beaumont, Joseph, 100
Beddoes, Thomas Lovell, 183
Blake, William, 134–136
Bloomfield, Robert, 146
Brathwaite, Richard, 85
Breton, Nicholas, 50
Bridges, Robert, 199, 200
Browne, William, 86
Bruce, Michael, 133
Bunyan, John, 105, 106
Burns, Robert, 137–140

Campion, Thomas, 59
Chaucer, Geoffrey, 19–21
Clanvowe, Sir Thomas, 22
Clare, John, 169–176
Coleridge, Samuel Taylor, 156 161
Cooper, John Gilbert, 125
Cowley, Abraham, 102
Cowper, William, 128–132
Crashaw, Richard, 96

Daniel, George, 98
Darley, George, 181, 182
Darwin, Erasmus, 127
D'Avenant, Sir William, 93
Davies, Sir John, 60
Dekker, Thomas, 61
Drayton, Michael, 80–83
Drummond, William, 84
Dryden, John, 107
Dunbar, William, 32

Gascoigne, George, 44
Gay, John, 110–115

Gisborne, Thomas, 143
Grahame, James, 145
Green, Matthew, 116
Greene, Robert, 52

Hannay, Patrick, 87
Hardy, Thomas, 195–198
Henley, William Ernest, 204
Herrick, Robert, 88–90
Heywood, John 35–38
Heywood, Thomas, 62
Hogg, James, 147
Hopkins, Gerard Manley, 201–203
Hurdis, James, 144

Jago, Richard, 121

Keats, John, 177–180

Langland, William, 15, 16
Lluellyn, Martin, 99
Lovelace, Richard, 101
Lydgate, John, 23
Lyly, John, 47

Marvell, Andrew, 103
Meredith, George, 194
Milton, John, 94, 95
Moore, Edward, 120

Pope, Alexander, 109
Prior, Matthew, 108

Quarles, Francis, 91

Randolph, Thomas, 92
Rogers, Samuel, 142

Scott, Sir Walter, 154, 155
Shakespeare, William, 54–56
Shelley, Percy Bysshe, 162–168
Sidney, Sir Philip, 48, 49
Skelton, John, 33
Spenser, Edmund, 45, 46
Squire, Sir John Collings, 266

Sylvester, Joshua, 57, 58
Symons, Arthur, 205

Tennyson, Alfred, Lord, 184–191
Thomson, James, 117–119
Thynne, Francis, 43

Vaughan, Henry, 104

Warton, Joseph, 123
Warton, Thomas, 126
Watson, Thomas, 51
White, Gilbert, 122
Wordsworth, William, 148–153

Yeats, William Butler, 206, 207

Index of First Lines

(The numbers refer to the page numbers.
Italics are used for extracts.)

A bird sings the selfsame song	310
A cock and his hen perching in the night	153
A fox jumped up one winter's night	327
A goose, affected, empty, vain	235
A hoggie dead! a hoggie dead! a hoggie dead!	319
A nightingale, that all day long	249
A pie sat on a pear tree	321
A sparrow hawk proud did hold in wicked jail	179
A sudden blow: the great wings beating still	317
A sunny shaft did I behold	278
All of a row	320
Among the orchard weeds, from every search	289
An eagle so caught in some bursting cloud	280
And as I stood and cast aside mine eye	141
And as our God the beasts had given in charge	189
And whilst the outer lake beneath the lash	281
Another shall hang from the gallows' height	103
As a dare-gale skylark scanted in a dull cage	313
As for the birds and the beasts, the men in bygone times	122
As I me walkèd one morning	134
As I was walking all alane	318
As I went over the water	324
As it fell upon a day	177
As late I lay within an arbour sweet	155
Awake, mine eyes, see Phoebus bright arising	182
Be merry, all birds, today	301
Beautiful must be the mountains whence ye come	311
Before the barn door crowing	226
Behind an unfrequented glade	219
Bell-man of night, if I about shall go	196
Beneath these fruit tree boughs that shed	270
Better one bird in hand than ten in the wood	153
Bird of the wilderness	268
Birds I beheld building nests in the bushes	121
But as I lay this other night waking	130
But most of all subdued, or fearful least	261
Buy tobacco, buy tobacco	326
By a bank as I lay	151
Cackle, cackle, Mother Goose	328
Cock-a-doodle-do! 'tis the bravest game	206
Cock, cock, cock, cock	325

Cock Robin got up early   332
Come, doleful owl, the messenger of woe   181
'*Come, Philomele, that sing'st of ravishment*   170
Coo-pe-coo   324
Crow, crow, get out of my sight   319
Crow on the fence   329
Cuckoo, cherry tree   322
Cuckoo, cuckoo   322
Cuckoo, scabbëd gowk   322

'Do you not hear the Aziola cry?   284
Driven in by autumn's sharpening air   273

Ethereal minstrel! pilgrim of the sky!   272
Even as the raven, the crow, and greedy kite   156
Every night from even till morn   174

Fair princess of the spacious air   208
Father of lights! what sunny seed   214
Foolish prater, what dost thou   211
From yon black clump of wheat that grows   286

Go, solitary wood, and henceforth be   197
Good brother Philip, I have borne you long   163
Goodbye, goodbye to summer!   304
Good morrow to thy sable beak   258
Goosey, goosey, gander   328
Grey goose and gander   326
Gulls in an aëry morrice   314

Hail, beauteous stranger of the wood   252
Hail to thee, blithe spirit!   281
Hark! ah, the nightingale   303
He clasps the crag with crookëd hands   301
He comes, the pest and terror of the yard   267
He rises and begins to round   305
Heigho! the lark and the owl!   280
Here the rude clamour of the sportsman's joy   233
Here's a string o' wild geese   326
Higgledy, piggledy, my black hen   325
His comb was redder than the fine corál   128
Holly beareth berries   139

I am a wonder. I vary my voice   105
I caught this morning morning's minion, king-   314
I crossed the pynot   321
I had a dove and the sweet dove died   291
I had two pigeons bright and gay   323

I have a gentle cock   137
I have two sparrows white as snow   183
I lately saw, what now I sing   226
I leant upon a coppice gate   309
I talk through my mouth with many tongues   105
I went to the sea   326
I will make known the eagle's nature   118
If the robin sings in the bush   329
If thou wilt love me, thou shalt be my boy   176
I'm called by the name of a man   330
In a book the life of the turtle dove   120
In a time of a summer's day   135
In other men we faults can spy   225
It's up Glenbarchan's braes I gaed   274
I've listened, when to school I've gone   285

Jug, jug! Fair fall the nightingal   192

Kill a robin or a wren   335

Lady, the birds right fairly   178
Laid out for dead, let thy last kindness be   196
Larikie, larikie, lee!   324
Lend me your song, ye nightingales! oh, pour   228
Lenten is come with love to town   118
Like as the culver on the barèd bough   160
Like as the doleful dove delights alone to be   157
Little Cock Robin   331
Little Robin Redbreast   331
Lock the dairy door   325
Lure, falconers, lure! give warning to the field!   182

Malisons, malisons, more than ten   335
Mark how the lark and linnet sing   218
Me thoughtë thus: that it was May   125
Meanwhile the tepid caves and fens and shores   198
Merry, merry sparrow!   254
Mid the mountains Euganean   279
Mourn, ye wee songsters o' the wood   257
My clothes are silent when I walk on the earth   104
My dear, do you know   331
My heart aches, and a drowsy numbness pains   291
My various fleets for fowl, O who is he can tell   186

No cloud, no relique of the sunken day   276
No noise is here, or none that hinders thought   252
Nor less the spaniel, skilful to betray   222

Now vows connubial chain the plighted pair   246
Now westward Sol had spent the richest beams   199

O all you little blackey-tops   329
O blackbird! sing me something well   300
O blest unfabled incense tree   294
O blithe new-comer! I have heard   269
O lapwing, thou fliest around the heath   254
O let your strong imagination turn   336
O nightingale, that on yon bloomy spray   198
O nightingale! thou surely art   272
O the month of May, the merry month of May   174
O thou that to the moonlight vale   240
Of all the birds that I do know   158
Of all the gay birds that e'er I did see   323
Oft have you seen a swan superbly frowning   290
Old Adam, the carrion crow   297
Old Mother Goose   328
On every branch sat birdës three   140
Once I was a monarch's daughter   323
One for sorrow, two for mirth   321
One half of me was up and dressed   207
One is a sign of mischief   320
One is sorrow, two mirth   320
Or wren or linnet   278

Pack, clouds, away, and welcome, day   175
Pity! mourn in plaintive tone   275
Poor bird, I do not envy thee   205
Poor turtle, thou bemoans   191
Pretty wantons, sweetly sing   183
Proud Maisie is in the wood   274

Repeat that, repeat   313
Right as the star of day began to shine   142
Round about, round about   321

Says Robin to Jenny, 'If you will be mine   333
Sea-ward, white gleaming through the busy scud   277
Shoo over!   329
Snow, snow faster   329
Solitary wayfarer!   296
Sometimes goldfinches one by one will drop   290
Somewhere afield here something lies   308
'Summer is coming, summer is coming   302
Summer is y-comen in   117
Surcharged with discontent   179
Sweet Amarillis, by a spring's   195

Sweet nymph, come to thy lover 178
Sweet Philomel in groves and deserts haunting 179
Sweet Suffolk owl, so trimly dight 183

Take two-o coo, Taffy 323
That man cannot know 103
The bird of Juno glories in his plumes 165
The carrion crow sat upon an oak 319
The cock crows in the morn 325
The cock gaed to Rome, seeking shoon, seeking shoon 326
The cuckoo is a merry bird 322
The dove alone expresses 173
The dove says, Coo, coo 323
The false fox came unto our croft 138
The fowls of heaven 234
The giddy lark reacheth the steepy air 204
The greedy hawk with sudden sight of lure 178
The happy whitethroat on the sweeing bough 288
The haughty eagle bird, of birds the best 165
The heather was blooming, the meadows were mawn 258
The idle cuckoo, having made a feast 196
The lark now leaves his wat'ry nest 197
The lonely season in lonely lands, when fled 311
The mounting lark, day's herald, got on wing 193
The nightingale, as soon as April bringeth 162
The nightingale, the organ of delight 181
The north wind doth blow 332
The plain was grassy, wild and bare 299
The pretty lark, climbing the welkin clear 170
The robin and the redbreast 335
The robin and the wren 336
The robin and the wren,/They fought 333
The sea gulls whiten and dip 315
The silver swan, who living had no note 182
The soaring hawk from fist that flies 154
The sober laverock, warbling wild 255
The son of Lamech let a black raven 106
The spruce and limber yellowhammer 278
The stamm'ring cuckoo, whose lewd voice doth grieve 157
The swallow, for a moment seen 245
The trees are in their autumn beauty 316
The turtle thus with plaintive crying 226
The white hen she cackles 182
The wild duck startles like a sudden thought 289
The woosel cock so black of hue 168
The wren she lies in care's bed 332

Then I heard a voice celestial 132
Then the Northmen fled in their nailed ships 104
There is a bird who, by his coat 250
There is no place in paradise 124
There mightë men the royal eagle find 126
There on his knee, behind a box tree shrinking 173
There the voluptuous nightingales 279
These are not dewdrops, these are tears 251
They are not those who used to feed us 309
Thou booby, say'st thou nothing but cuckoo? 217
Thou hearest the nightingale begin the song of spring 255
Thou hermit, haunter of the lonely glen' 288
Thou simple bird, what makes thee here to play? 216
Three grey geese in a green field grazing 326
Thy tu whits are lulled, I wot 298
To you whose groves protect the feathered choirs 236
Tonight, retired, the queen of heaven 241
Tread lightly here, for here, 'tis said 259

Up in the lift go we 324
Upon a dainty hill sometime 163
Upon the boughs and tops of trees 194
Upon the branches of those trees 166
Use maketh mast'ry: this hath been said alway 153

Well fare the nightingale 181
Well! in my many walks I've rarely found 286
What bird so sings, yet so does wail? 161
When cats run home and light is come 298
When daisies pied and violets blue 169
When day declining sheds a milder gleam 238
When first the eye this forest sees 212
When first the year, I heard the cuckoo sing 223
When first we hear the shy-come nightingales 288
When I remember again 143
When I was born, my mother and father 105
When I was in a summer valley 110
When icicles hang by the wall 169
When in the silent midnight grove 244
When milder autumn summer's heat succeeds 221
When Phoebus lifts his head out of the winter's wave 185
When sparrows build churches and steeples high 136
When the sun comes up from the salt sea 107
When the water fowl are found, the falconers hasten 123
Where is he, that giddy sprite 271
While thus the imprisoned leaves and waking flowers 260
Who killed Cock Robin? 334

Why are those tears? Why droops your head? 224

Why, ye tenants of the lake 256

Wild bird, whose warble, liquid sweet 301

Wild geese, wild geese, ganging to the sea 330

With a crossbow, late, in hand ready bent 152

With earliest spring, while yet in mountain cleughs 263

With that I saw two swans of goodly hue 161

Ye nymphs! if e'er your eyes were red 247